JOSHUA, JUDGES, AND RUTH

A. GRAEME AULD

THE WESTMINSTER PRESS
PHILADELPHIA

Published by
The Saint Andrew Press
Edinburgh, Scotland
and
The Westminster Press®
Philadelphia, Pennsylvania

Printed in the United States of America
4 6 8 9 7 5 3

Library of Congress Cataloging in Publication Data

Auld, A. Graeme.
  Joshua, Judges, and Ruth.

  (The Daily study Bible series)
  Bibliography: p.
  1. Bible. O.T. Joshua—Commentaries. 2. Bible. O.T.
Judges—Commentaries. 3. Bible. O.T. Ruth—Commentaries.
I. Title. II. Series: Daily study Bible series
(Westminster Press)
BS1295.3.A94 1984   222'.207   84-22076
ISBN 0-664-21809-1
ISBN 0-664-24576-5 (pbk.)

GENERAL PREFACE

This series of commentaries on the Old Testament, to which Dr. Auld's volume on *Joshua, Judges, and Ruth* belongs, has been planned as a companion series to the much-acclaimed New Testament series of the late Professor William Barclay. As with that series, each volume is arranged in successive headed portions suitable for daily study. The Biblical text followed is that of the Revised Standard Version or Common Bible. Eleven contributors share the work, each being responsible for from one to three volumes. The series is issued in the hope that it will do for the Old Testament what Professor Barclay's series succeeded so splendidly in doing for the New Testament—make it come alive for the Christian believer in the twentieth century.

Its two-fold aim is the same as his. Firstly, it is intended to introduce the reader to some of the more important results and fascinating insights of modern Old Testament scholarship. Most of the contributors are already established experts in the field with many publications to their credit. Some are younger scholars who have yet to make their names but who in my judgment as General Editor are now ready to be tested. I can assure those who use these commentaries that they are in the hands of competent teachers who know what is of real consequence in their subject and are able to present it in a form that will appeal to the general public.

The primary purpose of the series, however, is *not* an academic one. Professor Barclay summed it up for his New Testament series in the words of Richard of Chichester's prayer—to enable men and women "to know Jesus Christ more clearly, to love Him more dearly, and to follow Him more nearly." In the case of the Old Testament we have to be a little more circumspect than that. The Old Testament was completed long before the time of Our Lord, and it was (as it still is) the sole Bible of the Jews, God's first people, before it became part of the Christian Bible. We must take this fact seriously.

Yet in its strangely compelling way, sometimes dimly and sometimes directly, sometimes charmingly and sometimes embarrassingly, it holds up before us the things of Christ. It should not be forgotten that Jesus Himself was raised on this Book, that He based His whole ministry on what it says, and that He approached His death with its words on His lips. Christian men and women have in this ancient collection of Jewish writings a uniquely illuminating avenue not only into the will and purposes of God the Father, but into the mind and heart of Him who is named God's Son, who was Himself born a Jew but went on through the Cross and Resurrection to become the Saviour of the world. Read reverently and imaginatively the Old Testament can become a living and relevant force in their everyday lives.

It is the prayer of myself and my colleagues that this series may be used by its readers and blessed by God to that end.

New College   JOHN C. L. GIBSON
Edinburgh   General Editor

CONTENTS

INTRODUCTION

(i)

The three books studied in this volume are the Bible's prime witness to Israel's early history in her land. They tell the story of how under Joshua the land was first taken by Israel and then apportioned to her various tribes. They tell how after Joshua there was a long period of ups and downs: of religious apostasy within the community and repeated harassment from abroad answered by a series of divinely impelled "Judges" or "Deliverers". They offer some samples of life in Israel, "in the days when the Judges ruled" or "when there was not yet a king in Israel".

These books are handled together here because they appear together in our English Bibles. They have been listed together in Christian tradition at least since the great Greek Biblical manuscripts of the fourth and fifth centuries A.D. These great codices like our modern Bibles group together at the beginning all the Bible's narrative books: they belong in the *past*. Next come the poetical books, mainly of praise and wisdom: perennially relevant in the *present*. And the final grouping is of the "prophetic" books which tended to be read, especially by Christians, because of their hints and anticipations of the Christian *future* still to come.

However, we have learned a different tradition from the Jews. In the Hebrew Bible the five Books of Moses also come first, but are regarded as "teaching" (*Torah*) rather than narrative about the remotest past. "Prophecy" comes next in the Jewish Bible and we have to notice two important differences. (1) The prophetic books are read not so much because of their intimations of the future but because of the way in which they illustrate the Mosaic Torah in everyday life. (2) The prophetic books are held to include not just Isaiah, Jeremiah, Ezekiel and the Book of the

Twelve—these are termed the Latter Prophets; the Former Prophets in Jewish tradition are also in four books—Joshua, Judges, Samuel and Kings. The third and final section in this arrangement of the Bible is a miscellaneous one called simply "Writings". It starts with Psalms and the great wisdom books of Job and Proverbs. It ends with Daniel and the late narrative books of Ezra, Nehemiah and Chronicles. And in the middle it has a sub-collection of five "scrolls" (Ruth, Song of Solomon, Ecclesiastes, Lamentations, Esther), each of these being the appropriate synagogue reading for a major annual Jewish Festival.

Each of the two great religious traditions that have inherited the Hebrew Scriptures view these Scriptures from a different perspective and this is important for our study of Joshua, Judges and Ruth. We should try to look at these books from both vantage points, treating them like the red and green lenses which we sometimes have to wear to give us a richer, more lively, stereoscopic image from a cinema or television screen. Christian tradition is predisposed to see Joshua, Judges and Ruth as telling that part of Israel's story which belongs between Moses and the arrival of the Kings. Jewish tradition sees Ruth as part of the lectionary for Harvest Festival and as a stranger among the Former Prophets. Joshua and Judges on the other hand portray Israel's struggle with the Moses inheritance.

(ii)

We shall leave further introductory comment on Ruth until the final part of this volume. However, it is appropriate to say something more at this stage about Joshua and Judges together, and as part of a larger context. Modern critical investigation is almost unanimous in concluding that the Jewish arrangement of the Hebrew Scriptures is prior to the Christian one at least as far as our three books are concerned. Ruth interrupts the transition from Judges to Samuel. Moreover, Ruth shows no trace of the recurring editorial activity of writers whose language and ideas are closely akin to the Book of Deuteronomy—that "Deuteronomic" editorial activity which gives a relative unity to the four books of the Former Prophets. Deuteronomic influence on Joshua, Judges, Samuel and Kings has long been noticed by scholars, but it was only some forty years ago that Martin Noth propounded the thesis which has held sway in scholarship ever since. Noth argued against his predecessors (1) that there had been no prior draft of the whole story from Joshua to the fall of Jerusalem to the Babylonians for such an editorial group simply to touch up; rather this whole connected story was the creation of a writer or a number of writers to whom he gave the useful collective title "the Deuteronomist"; and (2) that this Deuteronomistic history began originally not at Joshua 1 but at Deuteronomy 1. He observed that the source materials used in Joshua, Judges, Samuel and Kings are very diverse and that it is *only* the freshly written Deuteronomic material which gives the books their unity. Of great importance in the whole structure are the Deuteronomist's own summarizing passages, principally Joshua 12, Judges 2, and 2 Kings 17—and even more strikingly the great speeches put into the mouths of the main characters, Joshua 23 or 24, 1 Samuel 12 and 1 Kings 8. However, the longest of these Deuteronomic speeches takes up almost the whole of Deuteronomy itself: the great farewell speech of Moses. It is because that speech so powerfully anticipates the significant speeches of Joshua, Samuel and Solomon and because the surrounding narrative in Deuteronomy 1–3 and 31–34 anticipates so neatly the beginning of Joshua that Noth became convinced that Deuteronomy itself was originally the first in a five-book series. Only subsequently in the history of the making of the Canon was it detached and added to the other Moses traditions in Exodus to Numbers.

Details of Martin Noth's views on the Deuteronomic history have been much disputed but his main thesis has remained intact. We shall look at some of the evidence in Joshua 1, 13, 23–24 and Judges 2 that a second Deuteronomist revised his master's work from a rather different point of view. We shall also notice how some parts of both books have been contributed after the main Deuteronomistic effort: most notably Judges 1 and 17–21.

One last word before we turn to the texts themselves. Joshua and Judges are about the past; but if the main thrust of Noth's arguments is valid then it is a past viewed from a great distance. The Israelite and Judean monarchy lasted for a little over four hundred years. If Deuteronomy or Joshua through to Kings is a unit then it was written after the last king had fallen. And the first chapters of the story were more distant from its writer or writers than Elizabeth I and Shakespeare and the founding fathers of the new world across the Atlantic are from us. Memory of the past they may be—but historical record hardly.

JOSHUA

MOSES IS DEAD: LONG LIVE JOSHUA

Joshua 1:1–6

> [1]After the death of Moses the servant of the Lord, the Lord said to
> Joshua the son of Nun, Moses' minister, [2]"Moses my servant is dead;
> now therefore arise, go over this Jordan, you and all this people, into
> the land which I am giving to them, to the people of Israel. [3]Every
> place that the sole of your foot will tread upon I have given to you, as I
> promised to Moses. [4]From the wilderness and this Lebanon as far as
> the great river, the river Euphrates, all the land of the Hittites to the
> Great Sea toward the going down of the sun shall be your territory.
> [5]No man shall be able to stand before you all the days of your life; as I
> was with Moses, so I will be with you; I will not fail you or forsake you.
> [6]Be strong and of good courage; for you shall cause this people to
> inherit the land which I swore to their fathers to give them."

Continuity is the keynote of this opening passage of Joshua and
this continuity has two main aspects. It reports a smooth succession from Moses to Joshua. And it is easy to demonstrate how
smoothly the Book of Joshua itself picks up and follows on from
the Book of Deuteronomy.

(i)
It is not the whole story, but in this opening section the equality of
Joshua and Moses before God is stressed. Note verse five: "As I
was with Moses, so I will be with you". A new era is dawning, a
new stage in the people's pilgrimage is being inaugurated. Moses
belongs to the time outside the land, before the land was taken.
Joshua is his counterpart for the taking and dividing of the land.
"As I was with Moses, so I will be with you". Joshua is leader
now, no less than Moses was then. No less, but also no greater:
there is no dwelling on Moses' failings. Moses died outside the

land because of breaking faith but he is still simply, honourably, "the servant of the Lord".

The succession of Joshua is here described as the promotion of a "minister" to the place once occupied by his master. "Minister", in Hebrew *sharet*, is used in the Bible of service in two different sorts of settings. (a) It is used often in texts concerning the priests about their "service" in the sanctuary and especially at the altar. (b) Then in a small but important set of passages *sharet* is used of a particularly personal and even intimate type of ministry or service. In a palace context it is Amnon's minister who throws Tamar out after his royal master has raped her (2 Sam. 13); and it is to minister to the aged David that the beautiful young Abishag, the Shunammite, is engaged (1 Kings 1). Perhaps rather closer to our situation in Joshua 1, Joseph was minister to Potiphar, and then to his butcher and baker, long before he became Viceroy of all Egypt; and Elisha was personal minister to Elijah before succeeding him.

In passing we might note how the twin aspects of *sharet*— priestly ministry in the sanctuary and intimate personal service— are beautifully linked in the story of the boy Samuel who "was ministering to the Lord under Eli" (1 Sam. 3:1), who had been promised to the Lord by his still barren mother, and whose very sleeping place was the sanctuary beside the Ark. Perhaps the "ministry" of the priests to God was regarded as both mundane and intimate.

With this short quest behind us we can now look briefly at the three places in the Pentateuch where we can glimpse some sight of the nature of Joshua's ministry "to Moses". (a) In Numbers 11:28–29 he has a special role in a chosen team; but just like the disciples of Jesus this does not save him from his master's displeasure. He has tried to protect his master from something to which Moses would rather be exposed—the contagion of prophetic experience. (b) Then twice in Exodus Joshua is in attendance on Moses during Moses' closest encounters with God. In 33:7–11 we see him present in the tent of meeting, at whose door Moses communes with God in a pillar of cloud. (c) In Exod. 24:12–14 Joshua is clearly only one step behind Moses as he goes up the holy mountain to receive the tables of stone.

Like Joseph and Elisha, menial service to a great man would stand Joshua in good stead. It is perennially true that quiet, unobtrusive, observant apprenticeship to a great leader is a perfect preparation for a good succession.

(ii)

The very smoothness of the transfer of the responsibility from Moses to Joshua—I don't say power, because power and authority rest with God—corresponds to and is in part a result of the easy transition from the Book of Deuteronomy to the Book of Joshua. Indeed, although in our familiar Bible Deuteronomy now ends the Books of Moses while Joshua begins the next section of the Bible, it is natural to read Deuteronomy and Joshua as the first and second sections of a connected work.

The links are many and suggestive. (a) Moses has already been (posthumously) designated "the servant of the Lord" in Deut. 34:5. (b) Deut. 3:21–29 explains the background fully: Joshua will do to all the kingdoms across the Jordan what he has seen done under Moses to two Transjordanian kingdoms. Moses has pled to see more of the outworking of God's greatness but has been refused. He must be content with viewing the land from outside. It is Joshua who will take what Moses will only see. (c) After the massive presentation of divine teaching which is the main purpose of Deuteronomy, this theme is resumed in 31:1–8, 14–15, 23 and then again in chapter 34. Moses was only to *see* the land from *outside*, Joshua would tread on it with his own feet (Josh. 1:3). (Personal inspection of a property from one edge to the other may well have been an ancient symbol involved in the transfer of ownership. Deut. 11:24–25 has already promised Israel corporately what is now repeated to Joshua personally, that what he walks on he will own.) (d) And then finally it is precisely in Deut. 1–3 and 31 that we find most often outside Josh. 1 the instruction to "be strong and of good courage".

The same encouragement concludes two psalms which complain of conflict and opposition:

> I believe that I shall see the goodness of the Lord
>   in the land of the living!
> Wait for the Lord;
>   be strong, and let your heart take courage;
> Yea, wait for the Lord!
>
> (Ps. 27:13–14; cf. 31:24)

On the darker side, "mighty and strong" (the translation is different but the Hebrew is the same as in Josh. 1) is how God's violent destroyer of Ephraim is described in Isa. 28:2. For the people of Canaan, Joshua was just such an agent of destruction.

MOSES LIVES ON—IN HIS WORD

Joshua 1:7–9

> 7"Only be strong and very courageous, being careful to do according to all the law which Moses my servant commanded you; turn not from it to the right hand or to the left, that you may have good success wherever you go. 8This book of the law shall not depart out of your mouth, but you shall meditate on it day and night, that you may be careful to do according to all that is written in it; for then you shall make your way prosperous, and then you shall have good success. 9Have I not commanded you? Be strong and of good courage; be not frightened, neither be dismayed; for the Lord your God is with you wherever you go."

"Be strong and of good courage". At the end of our first section we drew attention to these words of God to Joshua: (a) they are used to encourage a military commander and even to describe a divine destructive agent; (b) they are used in psalms of confidence in times of trouble. Military and religious resolve are both hinted at.

(1) In verses 1–6 the military aspect has been uppermost. The Lord repeats to Joshua practical advice already given by Moses. Beginning to take his farewell in Deut. 31:1–6, Moses had said to all Israel that the Lord their God himself would go over before them and would destroy the nations before them so that they would dispossess them; and he concluded:

"And the Lord will give them over to you, and you shall do to them according to all the commandment which I have commanded you. Be strong and of good courage, do not fear or be in dread of them: for it is the Lord your God who goes with you; he will not fail you or forsake you."

These instructions had been practical, military, and administrative; and with this said to all Israel, Moses turned to Joshua his designated successor as commander-in-chief, and said:

"Be strong and of good courage; for you shall go with this people into the land which the Lord has sworn to their fathers to give them; and you shall put them in possession of it. It is the Lord who goes before you; he will be with you, he will not fail you or forsake you; do not fear or be dismayed."

(31:7–8)

The outgoing commander speaks at a final parade of his troops and briefs his successor; and the Lord reinforces Moses' words to Joshua at the beginning of our book (1:1–6).

(2) But in this new short section what a change comes over these repeated words from Deuteronomy! Military resolve and practical instructions have become transposed into resolute adherence to the whole Mosaic teaching or "law". There can be no doubt about what "all the law which Moses my servant commanded you" means. Verse 8 says it shortly and simply: "This book of the law". Moses' words are no longer simply instructions to be followed, but teaching to be meditated on and a constant topic of discussion. There is no question now of an equal relationship between Moses and Joshua, each the leader of successive stages in their people's campaign. Moses is not just first but foremost. Moses has become more of a message than a man. Indeed Moses lives on in his word.

(3) It may help us to understand this redefinition of resolve if we look at the small number of passages in the Bible in which similar notes are struck to those in our passage. Two of these concern the commissioning of prophets. The Lord encourages Ezekiel to be resolute whatever response he meets:

"... be not afraid of their words, nor be dismayed at their looks, for they are a rebellious house. And you shall speak my words to them whether they hear or refuse to hear; for they are a rebellious house."

(Ezek. 2:6–7)

This encouragement is repeated in Ezekiel 3:9.

The report of Jeremiah's call ends in even more explicitly military terms:

"But you, gird up your loins; arise, and say to them everything that I command you. Do not be dismayed by them, lest I dismay you before them. And I, behold, I make you this day a fortified city, an iron pillar, and bronze walls, against the whole land, against the kings of Judah, its princes, its priests, and the people of the land. They will fight against you; but they shall not prevail against you, for I am with you, says the Lord, to deliver you."

(Jer. 1:17–19)

In the traditional Jewish arrangement of these same Hebrew Scriptures it is not only Jeremiah and Ezekiel and their like who are numbered among the prophets. In fact the books from Joshua to Kings are understood as the "Former Prophets". Hardly surprising then that this final version of the commissioning of Joshua should take a turn similar to the commissioning of Ezekiel and Jeremiah.

The other striking parallel to our passage is the opening of the *first* psalm.

Blessed is the man
  who walks not in the council of the wicked,
nor stands in the way of sinners,
  nor sits in the seat of scoffers;
but his delight is in the law of the Lord,
  and on his law he meditates day and night.
He is like a tree
  planted by streams of water,
that yields its fruit in its season,
  and its leaf does not wither.
In all that he does, he prospers.

Within the Book of Psalms this devotion to God's *Law* is most obvious and most memorable in the first psalm and in the longest psalm (Psalm 119). These are amongst the latest of the psalms and it is almost certain that the "law" they celebrate is the "law" we know as the Books of Moses.

And so the charge given to Joshua has a tinge of the prophetic. And he is ordered to fulfil the developed ideal of the psalter. Were it our business to make deductions and draw conclusions about the stages in which the Book of Joshua was drafted, we might well conclude that verses 7–9 are a later development of the ideas in Joshua 1:1–6. Practical encouragement seems to have been redirected into spiritual exhortation. Yet something important would be lost if we stopped there.

What I have in mind can perhaps best be illustrated by a heated discussion which is always current in today's Israel. There is always a scrupulous minority of Israelis who are not happy to rest their claim to their ancient land on either ancient promises or the power of arms. For them Israel is only vindicated if it is a freer, more open society than those around, if the ancient traditions are still making a qualitative difference. It is not for an outsider to take sides in that discussion, but I see in it something of the flavour of Joshua 1:7–9 after verses 1–6. Memories of Chinese groups confronting Soviet guards by waving Chairman Mao's "little red book" may seem alien to us. And stories of young Iranian fundamentalists with Khomeini's name on their lips and passion for the Islamic revolution in their breasts hurling themselves against Iraqi tanks may seem unrealistic. Or are they?

Israel's struggle in Canaan begun under Joshua was to be moral and religious and not just military.

LAND PROMISED: LAND TAKEN

Joshua 1:10–18

[10]Then Joshua commanded the officers of the people, [11]"Pass through the camp, and command the people, 'Prepare your provisions; for within three days you are to pass over this Jordan, to go in to take possession of the land which the Lord your God gives you to possess.'"

¹²And to the Reubenites, the Gadites, and the half-tribe of Manasseh Joshua said, ¹³"Remember the word which Moses the servant of the Lord commanded you, saying, 'The Lord your God is providing you a place of rest, and will give you this land.' ¹⁴Your wives, your little ones, and your cattle shall remain in the land which Moses gave you beyond the Jordan; but all the men of valour among you shall pass over armed before your brethren and shall help them, ¹⁵until the Lord gives rest to your brethren as well as to you, and they also take possession of the land which the Lord your God is giving them; then you shall return to the land of your possession, and shall possess it, the land which Moses the servant of the Lord gave you beyond the Jordan toward the sunrise." ¹⁶And they answered Joshua, "All that you have commanded us we will do, and wherever you send us we will go. ¹⁷Just as we obeyed Moses in all things, so we will obey you; only may the Lord your God be with you, as he was with Moses! ¹⁸Whoever rebels against your commandment and disobeys your words, whatever you command him, shall be put to death. Only be strong and of good courage."

(i)

After the interlude about meditating on Mosaic teaching we return here to Joshua the practical commander. He calls the officers, and has them warn the people that the campaign is imminent. Then, anticipating Napoleon's immortal remark about an army marching on its stomach, he gives instructions about provisions for his force.

Within three days they are to pass over the Jordan to take possession of the land which the Lord their God gives them to possess. To reach the promised land the people have to cross the Jordan westwards. This land is not just *promised* by God, it will also be *given* by him. Despite the practical measures Joshua is taking, this divine grant will not just be of the religious title deeds to the land. Several narratives of the book of Joshua portray God as very actively involved in the struggle to evict the present tenants. The people will *take* possession. Yes, but only of what the Lord their God *gives* them to possess.

(ii)

Everything so far in this introductory chapter to the Book of Joshua has been written from a Transjordanian point of view. The promised land is still ahead, the Jordan is still to be crossed, the people are still in the east. Indeed the people are thought of as one and undivided—verse 2 talks of Joshua "and all this people" crossing the Jordan. But Moses himself had already made an exception. Deuteronomy 3:12–20 reports his grant to two and a half tribes of Israel of land "east of the Jordan", land stretching roughly from east of the Dead Sea northwards to east of the Sea of Galilee. The southern portions of this territory had already been taken under his own direction. The northern portions were apparently added after a successful initiative by Jair of the clan of Manasseh. In our portion of Joshua 1 the new commander reminds Reuben, Gad and half-Manasseh of the bargain Moses had struck with them. They *could* settle in the east; but for the moment it would be a matter only of women, children and herds. Their men folk would not just swell the main Israelite attacking force but in fact would pass over the Jordan at their head.

There seems an air of unreality about the scheme of removing fighting men from an area just taken. The unreality of the situation is reinforced by a sudden change in geographical orientation: there is a clash between two different senses of "cross the Jordan". The matter-of-fact one comes first. Joshua and his people still have to cross the river before they achieve their goal. However, the two banks of the Jordan river are not equivalent to each other. Many who have fought in an army or swum as refugees for their freedom, and many more for whom homecoming means returning to their town across a river, will easily understand crossing the Jordan as no neutral thing—but a matter of entering and leaving. The other sense presumably only developed once that people had long been in their promised land. Then the two and a half tribes were the people "beyond" or "across the Jordan", on the *other* side.

(iii)

Despite the paragraphing of many translations of the Bible into

English, it seems to me that verses 16 to 18 are best understood as the loyal response of the officers whom Joshua had despatched in verses 10 and 11. Some sort of response from them is certainly in order. The intervening verses 12–15 may then well be an editorial afterthought, drafted as an "aside" by Joshua to the Transjordanians. If an afterthought, it is easier to understand the lack of geographical consistency. On the other hand, these four verses are a skilful addition—a pledge of loyalty to the new commander is appropriate from *everyone* to whom he speaks.

Editorial insertion or not, this section about Transjordan allows an important note to be sounded for which we would otherwise wait until the end of the book. The theme of the promised land as God's "place of rest" is of course given classical expression at the end of Psalm 95.

> For forty years I loathed that generation
>   and said, "They are a people who err in heart,
>   and they do not regard my ways."
> Therefore I swore in my anger
>   that they should not enter my rest.

Two other texts may help us to bring out the flavour of this idea. The beginning of Lamentations talks of Judah in exile:

> She dwells now among the nations,
>   but finds no resting place.

> (Lam. 1:3)

And the curses at the end of Deuteronomic Law talk of exactly the same situation:

> "And the Lord will scatter you among all peoples, from one end of the earth to the other; and there you shall serve other gods, of wood and stone, which neither you nor your fathers have known. And among these nations you shall find no ease, and there shall be no rest for the sole of your foot."

> (Deut. 28:64, 65)

It is in the *promised* land that God offers rest to his people. Only on the authority of Moses do the two and a half tribes find rest *elsewhere*.

(iv)

A last word about Joshua 1 as a whole. In a sense this introduction to the Book of Joshua is like a reflection of the Book of Deuteronomy in a small mirror. It works from back to front. We start with the death of Moses and the succession of Joshua which Deuteronomy relates in its concluding chapters. We are then urged to meditate on the Book of the Law which is the teaching at the core of that great book; and we conclude with the implications of some victories in Transjordan which are the material of Deuteronomy chapters 1 to 3. Deuteronomy so resumed, the action proceeds.

A WOMAN OF EASY VIRTUE?

Joshua 2:1–11

¹And Joshua the son of Nun sent two men secretly from Shittim as spies, saying, "Go, view the land, especially Jericho." And they went, and came into the house of a harlot whose name was Rahab, and lodged there. ²And it was told the king of Jericho, "Behold, certain men of Israel have come here tonight to search out the land." ³Then the king of Jericho sent to Rahab, saying, "Bring forth the men that have come to you, who entered your house; for they have come to search out all the land." ⁴But the woman had taken the two men and hidden them; and she said, "True, men came to me, but I did not know where they came from; ⁵and when the gate was to be closed, at dark, the men went out; where the men went I do not know; pursue them quickly, for you will overtake them." ⁶But she had brought them up to the roof, and hid them with the stalks of flax which she had laid in order on the roof. ⁷So the men pursued after them on the way to the Jordan as far as the fords; and as soon as the pursuers had gone out, the gate was shut.

⁸Before they lay down, she came up to them on the roof, ⁹and said to the men, "I know that the Lord has given you the land, and that the fear of you has fallen upon us, and that all the inhabitants of the land melt away before you. ¹⁰For we have heard how the Lord dried up the water of the Red Sea before you when you came out of Egypt, and what you did to the two kings of the Amorites that were beyond the Jordan, to Sihon and Og, whom you utterly destroyed. ¹¹And as soon as we heard it, our hearts melted, and there was no courage left in any

man, because of you; for the Lord your God is he who is God in heaven above and on earth beneath."

(i)

General Joshua, having dealt with the provisions for his force, now turns to reconnaissance. We suppose that his two spies were doing their work in the same period as the force was being prepared. (The "three days" we read about in 1:11, 2:22 and 3:2 will be a round number for the same brief period.) The king of Jericho also gathers intelligence and the evening entry of the two Israelite spies is promptly reported to him.

There is more ribald humour here than many readers might expect to find in the pages of "holy writ". (That may say more about their expectations than it does about the Scriptures!) To be fair to the general reader the English versions tend to play down some of the innuendoes of the Hebrew. "Lodged" is not nearly so appropriate at the end of verse 1 as it is at the end of the first verse of chapter 3. There it translates quite a neutral word for an overnight stop—a word that has produced the modern Hebrew word for hotel. But here at the beginning of chapter 2 the Hebrew verb means "lay" or "slept"—and that has very different overtones in the house of a prostitute. Again, when the king of Jericho himself stops outside Rahab's house and shouts in about the men who have "come to her", his words surely suggest more than a polite visit. Indeed the king seems to go on to tease her for "professional" one-track mindedness. She had thought their interest was in her. He knows it is the whole *land* they have come to view.

(ii)

What we make of this story will probably tell a lot about our prejudices. A few translators and commentators have sought to rescue Rahab's reputation by a discreet change of terms. For them she is a hotel-keeper or, if that is too grand and formal, the landlady of a bed and breakfast establishment. Given the suggestiveness of the story, that will suffer the fate of many well-meaning but ill-thought-out schemes. Men and women of the world will quickly point out what they have heard about the goings on in seedy hotels and lodging houses.

Many of us who enjoy the twilight world of the intelligence services in novel or in film will shrug our shoulders and admit it is a dirty business, but necessarily so. All the best secrets are learned in bed. One favour deserves another. And where, after all, would a stranger expect to meet the riff-raff prepared to sell their country?

Other readers with some knowledge of how society works may suggest to us that Rahab was a widow. In some societies part of the curse of widowhood and the attendant loss of status, income and protection is that a woman has to offer the only thing that many men want from a woman. They will also wonder if she was a foreigner owing little loyalty to the citizens who allowed her residence and employment only at their own convenience.

(iii)

With so much to speculate on it is wise to stay close to the text. It is quite explicit about *where* the two spies spent their night in Jericho. It does not make clear what passed between Rahab and the two men before the king of Jericho's visit. The king's ribald but not unfriendly conversation with Rahab may have given her her first inkling of the identity of her two clients; and it may say something for her reputation in Jericho that her word was accepted and her house not searched. No official harassment here with police heavies shouldering in the door! She was quick to hide the spies perhaps because of the laws of eastern hospitality; perhaps because the ethics of her profession demand confidentiality. The king's words made her take a quick decision about what might be in her own long-term interest. The men stayed hidden.

Artfully, when the coast is clear and she visits them on the roof, she addresses them very much in their own terms. "The Lord"— and in Hebrew that is a proper name, "Yahweh"—has given them the land, and fear of them and of him has knocked all the stuffing out of the land's inhabitants. She knows what Yahweh had done to the waters of the sea as they left Egypt and what they had done to two kings across in Transjordan. However, in the climax of the declaration Rahab goes beyond simply repeating Israel's own traditions of what her God had done and still would do for her. Yahweh, their God, "is he who is God in heaven above and on earth beneath." In other words Yahweh was both God of gods and also God of mankind and all else in the world.

(iv)

We shall return in the next section to further consideration of Rahab's declaration. We should conclude this section with two more general comments. Even if we are persuaded that Rahab, by the very fact of being a prostitute, is one of the doubtful characters of the Bible, she is still in good company—a company that includes deceitful Jacob and adulterous David, and father Abraham himself prepared to trade wife for life, and many others in Scripture. From them we may draw some comfort about God's ways with the most wayward of us.

Rahab too may remind readers of the women of the New Testament with whom Jesus dealt. His acceptance of them gave the wagging tongues of detractors much play. One of them was the woman who interrupted him at a polite meal (Mark 14:3–9) to kiss his feet and anoint his head. He compared her action to preparing his body for burial and promised her that as long as he was remembered and proclaimed she would not be forgotten. So it is with Rahab.

FAITHFUL RAHAB

Joshua 2:12–24

12"Now then, swear to me by the Lord that as I have dealt kindly with you, you also will deal kindly with my father's house, and give me a sure sign, 13and save alive my father and mother, my brothers and sisters, and all who belong to them, and deliver our lives from death." 14And the men said to her, "Our life for yours! If you do not tell this business of ours, then we will deal kindly and faithfully with you when the Lord gives us the land."

[15]Then she let them down by a rope through the window, for her house was built into the city wall, so that she dwelt in the wall. [16]And she said to them, "Go into the hills, lest the pursuers meet you; and hide yourselves there three days, until the pursuers have returned; then afterward you may go your way." [17]The men said to her, "We will be guiltless with respect to this oath of yours which you have made us swear. [18]Behold, when we come into the land, you shall bind this scarlet cord in the window through which you let us down; and you shall gather into your house your father and mother, your brothers, and all your father's household. [19]If any one goes out of the doors of your house into the street, his blood shall be upon his head, and we shall be guiltless; but if a hand is laid upon any one who is with you in the house, his blood shall be on our head. [20]But if you tell this business of ours, then we shall be guiltless with respect to your oath which you have made us swear." [21]And she said, "According to your words, so be it." Then she sent them away, and they departed; and she bound the scarlet cord in the window.

[22]They departed, and went into the hills, and remained there three days, until the pursuers returned; for the pursuers had made search all along the way and found nothing. [23]Then the two men came down again from the hills, and passed over and came to Joshua the son of Nun; and they told him all that had befallen them. [24]And they said to Joshua, "Truly the Lord has given all the land into our hands; and moreover all the inhabitants of the land are fainthearted because of us."

(i)

The first section of the Rahab story culminated in her solemn declaration that Israel's God was God of all. She had entertained Israel's representatives. She had shown perception of their business. Indeed to this point she had done all the giving. Now she asks her price. At one level the proposed exchange of life for silence, of safe conduct for secrecy, is a typical trade-off between disreputable parties. Both Rahab and her guests are now compromised in Jericho. Yet though their vulnerability cannot be denied, two aspects of their bargaining deserve a more sympathetic consideration.

Firstly, Rahab is not just saving her own skin. It is almost idle to speculate about Rahab's connections with her family. Were they ordinarily dependent on her? Was she the sole breadwinner for a whole family at the margin of Jericho's society? Or does her concern with her father's house echo part of the Joseph story? She has—however briefly—the opportunity in her hands to influence events. Will she, like Joseph, grasp this chance and use it for the benefit of a family who do not deserve it of her? Whether her day-to-day relationships with her family were cordial or non-existent, it was *their* responsibility to look after *her*, not the other way round. An unmarried woman, whether before marriage or after divorce, was the responsibility of her father.

Then beyond her concern for family Rahab goes on to demonstrate her intuitive grasp of what is important to Israel. She is not just able to voice Israel's traditions about what God did for them in the exodus from Egypt and in the desert thereafter. No. Her bargain with the spies is expressed in terms that echo through several Biblical books and enshrine a vital element in the character of God, and of any true servant of his. Again unhappily the translators of this passage have done the key word less than justice. What they translate as "kindness" is the Hebrew word *hesed*. This is a rich term in the Bible, whose principal components are loyalty and steadfastness. Kindness in this and many other Old Testament passages is hallowed by the Authorised Version, and it may have been more appropriate four centuries ago. But in more modern English, kindness seems hardly resolute enough to describe the one who stands by you and stands by what has been promised against all the odds. And when coupled with faithfulness the word almost demands a stronger translation. In most parts of the Bible the Revised Standard Version prefers the rendering "steadfast love" for *hesed*.

(ii)

Several psalms sum up God's character as manifested in steadfast love and faithfulness. Psalm 89 expects the same of the king in Jerusalem. Proverbs 3:3 urges all of us:

> Let not loyalty and faithfulness forsake you;
>> bind them about your neck,
>> write them on the tablet of your heart.

And Exodus 34:6 (reminiscent of Psalm 86:15) describes God as "merciful and gracious, slow to anger, and abounding in steadfast love and faithfulness". No one familiar with this characteristic of God, or who loves his standards, could mistake the terms of Rahab's pact with her clients for that honour we scorn to find among thieves. Against this background it may be less of a surprise that, when the writer of the Letter to the Hebrews comes to illustrate that faith which "is the assurance of things hoped for, the conviction of things not seen", he sketches just two scenes from the Book of Joshua:

> By faith the walls of Jericho fell down after they had been encircled for seven days. By faith Rahab the harlot did not perish with those who were disobedient, because she had given friendly welcome to the spies.
> (Heb. 11:30–31)

Rahab is mentioned when even Joshua himself is passed over in silence. And when James in his general letter comes to develop his insight that "faith by itself, if it has no works, is dead" (2:17), he illustrates his point by just two characters from the whole Old Testament. First, Abraham and then Rahab:

> And in the same way was not also Rahab the harlot justified by works when she received the messengers and sent them out another way?
> (Jas. 2:25)

Note how both these New Testament writers emphasize not Rahab's *words* to the spies but her *actions* on their behalf.

After it was arranged how the invaders would recognize her house and spare it, she let them down over the wall with the practical advice that they should make for the hills because their pursuers from the city were bound to be searching the roads to the Jordan fords. In due time our two worthies crossed back to Joshua. The terms of their report offer a last attractive twist to a well-told story. Their debriefing ends with them quoting Rahab's own declaration. But this is introduced seemingly inconsequentially by the phrase "and they told him all that had befallen them". Literally translated the Hebrew phrase is a much more delightful part of a story of two spies: "and they told him everything *that had found them*"!

CROSSING THE JORDAN

Joshua 3:1–17

¹Early in the morning Joshua rose and set out from Shittim, with all the people of Israel; and they came to the Jordan, and lodged there before they passed over. ²At the end of three days the officers went through the camp ³and commanded the people, "When you see the ark of the covenant of the Lord your God being carried by the Levitical priests, then you shall set out from your place and follow it, ⁴that you may know the way you shall go, for you have not passed this way before. Yet there shall be a space between you and it, a distance of about two thousand cubits; do not come near it." ⁵And Joshua said to the people, "Sanctify yourselves; for tomorrow the Lord will do wonders among you." ⁶And Joshua said to the priests, "Take up the ark of the covenant, and pass on before the people." And they took up the ark of the covenant, and went before the people.

⁷And the Lord said to Joshua, "This day I will begin to exalt you in the sight of all Israel, that they may know that, as I was with Moses, so I will be with you. ⁸And you shall command the priests who bear the ark of the covenant, 'When you come to the brink of the waters of the Jordan, you shall stand still in the Jordan.'" ⁹And Joshua said to the people of Israel, "Come hither, and hear the words of the Lord your God." ¹⁰And Joshua said, "Hereby you shall know that the living God is among you, and that he will without fail drive out from before you the Canaanites, the Hittites, the Hivites, the Perizzites, the Girgashites, the Amorites, and the Jebusites. ¹¹Behold, the ark of the covenant of the Lord of all the earth is to pass over before you into the Jordan. ¹²Now therefore take twelve men from the tribes of Israel, from each tribe a man. ¹³And when the soles of the feet of the priests who bear the ark of the Lord, the Lord of all the earth, shall rest in the waters of the Jordan, the waters of the Jordan shall be stopped from flowing, and the waters coming down from above shall stand in one heap."

¹⁴So, when the people set out from their tents, to pass over the Jordan with the priests bearing the ark of the covenant before the people, ¹⁵and when those who bore the ark had come to the Jordan,

and the feet of the priests bearing the ark were dipped in the brink of the water (the Jordan overflows all its banks throughout the time of harvest), [16]the waters coming down from above stood and rose up in a heap far off, at Adam, the city that is beside Zarethan, and those flowing down toward the sea of the Arabah, the Salt Sea, were wholly cut off; and the people passed over opposite Jericho. [17]And while all Israel were passing over on dry ground, the priests who bore the ark of the covenant of the Lord stood on dry ground in the midst of the Jordan, until all the nation finished passing over the Jordan.

Two main aspects of Israel's wonderful passage across the Jordan require our attention. The first of these is its meaning for Joshua. The second is the role of the Ark of the Covenant.

But first a word about the "wonder" itself. The Bible tells two other similar stories. One concerns Moses and the other Elijah. As they escape from Egypt Moses leads Israel dry-shod across a sea or lake (Exod. 14). Then Elijah before being caught up into heaven takes Elisha with him across the Jordan in the opposite direction (2 Kings 2). Scholars are much divided over what body of water is meant by the Red or Reed Sea—whether great or small, wide or open. But we do know more about the Jordan. The greatness of that river is not in proportion to its size. It has often been a border, a frontier; but only in a very limited sense is it a barrier. It is readily fordable at several points and the first bridge was constructed only after the Arab invasion in the seventh century A.D. Our chapter (v. 15) dates the crossing in harvest period, and that means roughly between Easter and Pentecost. At that time the waters are swollen after winter rain and with the melting of Mount Hermon's snows. But even high waters in the Jordan only increase discomfort at the fords. They do not make passage impossible. A divine interruption of the natural sequence of events was not *required*.

(1) But it was *important* for Joshua. When the waters of the Jordan parted as Elijah struck them with his rolled up mantle, his authority was strengthened in the sight of Elisha who accompanied him and the prophetic bands who watched at a distance. And when Elisha returned dry-shod after using Elijah's mantle in the name of Elijah's God, the watching prophets de-

duced that "the spirit of Elijah rests on Elisha" (2 Kings 2:15). And they prostrated themselves before him. So it is with Joshua. He calls on the people to sanctify themselves "for tomorrow the Lord will do wonders among you" (v. 5). He also goes on to explain (vv. 10–13) that what Israel will witness will convince them that the Living God is among them. In so speaking to the people Joshua gives *God* the glory. But God has told *him* (v. 7) that he is about to begin keeping the promise he made at the beginning of the book (1:5): "this day I will begin to exalt you in the sight of all Israel, that they may know that, as I was with Moses, so I will be with you". The interruption of the Jordan's waters some fifteen miles to the north is not a requirement of Israel's crossing the border; but it does raise the stock of both Joshua and God himself.

(2) The Ark of the Covenant of the Lord does not make many appearances in the pages of the Scriptures; but it is an extraordinarily potent presence when it is there. It has some of the characteristics of a military palladium. At some times it seems to embody the very power and presence of God himself. Israel carries it in the battle when the going is rough against the Philistines (1 Sam. 4:2–4). Captured by the Philistines it topples their god from his very pedestal (1 Sam. 5:1–5). And on its ascent to Jerusalem the wretched Uzzah, who sought only to support it when the oxen stumbled, was struck down dead (2 Sam. 6:6–8). Little wonder that Joshua should specify a good half mile should separate the Ark and its priestly bearers from the main force!

Then the Ark goes in front, so that Israel may know the way— they have not passed this way before. This reminds us of their earlier departure from Sinai:

> So they set out from the mount of the Lord three days' journey; and the ark of the covenant of the Lord went before them three days' journey, to seek out a resting place for them.　　　　　　(Numbers 10:33)

This same passage goes on to underscore the intimate association of God and Ark:

> And whenever the ark set out, Moses said, "Arise, O Lord, and let thy

enemies be scattered; and let them that hate thee flee before thee."
And when it rested, he said, "Return, O Lord, to the ten thousand
thousands of Israel." (10:35–36)

When the Ark was lifted Moses asked God to rise; when it was
put down again he asked his Lord to return to the hosts of Israel.
In Joshua chapter 3 also there is a real sense in which the Living
God (v. 10), that Lord of all the earth (v. 13) who is giving Israel a
new *land*, is also crossing Jordan before them.

Not only was the Ark an important symbol of the presence of
God: it also actually contained his will, his teaching. God had
Moses deposit the stone copy of the Ten Commandments within
the Ark (Deut. 10:1–5). And it was further arranged that a copy
of the whole teaching of Deuteronomy be placed alongside the
Ark (Deut. 31:24–26). It is in the light of these arrangements that
the Ark is often called the Ark of the Covenant. "Covenant" is a
complicated word, and it means rather different things in different parts of the Bible. But in Deuteronomy and related literature like the Book of Joshua, God's "Covenant" is fundamentally
his demand, his law, his teaching, his instruction. The Ark is the
"Ark of the Covenant" because it physically holds the essence of
his will. This teaching was given through Moses *before* Israel
entered her land so that she would know how to behave in the
land. The Covenant was given because Israel had not lived life
this way before. The Ark contained her vade-mecum.

The Ark is no more. Its disappearance probably coincided with
the sack of Jerusalem by the Babylonians. The Book of Jeremiah
(3:16) even counsels us not to mourn its loss. And a Christian will
naturally turn to Jesus for the properties we have seen in the Ark.
He is the perfect embodiment of God's presence, and the living
vehicle of his teaching; and he too leads his people from the front.

WHAT MEAN THESE STONES?

Joshua 4:1–5:1

[1]When all the nation had finished passing over the Jordan, the Lord
said to Joshua, [2]"Take twelve men from the people, from each tribe a

man, ³and command them, 'Take twelve stones from here out of the midst of the Jordan, from the very place where the priests' feet stood, and carry them over with you, and lay them down in the place where you lodge tonight.'" ⁴Then Joshua called the twelve men from the people of Israel, whom he had appointed, a man from each tribe; ⁵and Joshua said to them, "Pass on before the ark of the Lord your God into the midst of the Jordan, and take up each of you a stone upon his shoulder, according to the number of the tribes of the people of Israel, ⁶that this may be a sign among you, when your children ask in time to come, 'What do those stones mean to you?' ⁷Then you shall tell them that the waters of the Jordan were cut off before the ark of the covenant of the Lord; when it passed over the Jordan, the waters of the Jordan were cut off. So these stones shall be to the people of Israel a memorial for ever."

⁸And the men of Israel did as Joshua commanded, and took up twelve stones out of the midst of the Jordan, according to the number of the tribes of the people of Israel, as the Lord told Joshua; and they carried them over with them to the place where they lodged, and laid them down there. ⁹And Joshua set up twelve stones in the midst of the Jordan, in the place where the feet of the priests bearing the ark of the covenant had stood; and they are there to this day. ¹⁰For the priests who bore the ark stood in the midst of the Jordan, until everything was finished that the Lord commanded Joshua to tell the people, according to all that Moses had commanded Joshua.

The people passed over in haste; ¹¹and when all the people had finished passing over, the ark of the Lord and the priests passed over before the people. ¹²The sons of Reuben and the sons of Gad and the half-tribe of Manasseh passed over armed before the people of Israel, as Moses had bidden them; ¹³about forty thousand ready armed for war passed over before the Lord for battle, to the plains of Jericho. ¹⁴On that day the Lord exalted Joshua in the sight of all Israel; and they stood in awe of him, as they had stood in awe of Moses, all the days of his life.

¹⁵And the Lord said to Joshua, ¹⁶"Command the priests who bear the ark of the testimony to come up out of the Jordan." ¹⁷Joshua therefore commanded the priests, "Come up out of the Jordan." ¹⁸And when the priests bearing the ark of the covenant of the Lord came up from the midst of the Jordan, and the soles of the priests' feet were lifted up on dry ground, the waters of the Jordan returned to their place and overflowed all its banks, as before.

¹⁹The people came up out of the Jordan on the tenth day of the first month, and they encamped in Gilgal on the east border of Jericho. ²⁰And those twelve stones, which they took out of the Jordan, Joshua set up in Gilgal. ²¹And he said to the people of Israel, "When your children ask their fathers in time to come, 'What do these stones mean?' ²²then you shall let your children know, 'Israel passed over this Jordan on dry ground.' ²³For the Lord your God dried up the waters of the Jordan for you until you passed over, as the Lord your God did to the Red Sea, which he dried up for us until we passed over, ²⁴so that all the peoples of the earth may know that the hand of the Lord is mighty; that you may fear the Lord your God for ever."

¹When all the kings of the Amorites that were beyond the Jordan to the west, and all the kings of the Canaanites that were by the sea, heard that the Lord had dried up the waters of the Jordan for the people of Israel until they had crossed over, their heart melted, and there was no longer any spirit in them, because of the people of Israel.

We did not pause to consider any tensions in the first part of the record of the crossing of the Jordan, but in this second chapter there is no escaping them. Twelve memorial stones are a constant theme, and they are carried by twelve men, each representing a tribe of Israel. But at one point they are taken from the east bank and set up in the Jordan bed; at another they are collected from that Jordan bed and set up in the west. Then for each part-account an official explanation is given. Some readers might find it attractive to harmonize both versions and suppose that the memorial stones were taken in two stages from east to west, resting in the middle of the river for a period. However, this proposal is clearly precluded by "they are there to this day", said in verse 9 of the twelve stones in the river bed, and by "those twelve stones, which they took out of the Jordan, Joshua set up in Gilgal" reported in verse 20. Gilgal's very name probably means "stone circle".

All of us, whether religious believers or not, vary considerably in our tolerance of diversity. Some of us are happily tolerant of pluralism. Others have a strong hunch that if truth exists it is likely to be fairly straightforward. The second group certainly have their problems with Joshua 4. We are familiar enough, like it or not, with different later approaches to the same scriptural material: be they Jewish and Christian, Catholic and Protestant, liberal and conservative, or spiritual and materialistic. And some Biblical scholars—to the delight of some and the despair of others—argue for a high degree of diversity and even contradiction within the Bible. Here at least is a good example for their case.

Behind this chapter we have a basic tradition of twelve memorial stones. Behind this chapter we also have a basic conviction that their memory must be preserved through the generations. But we have conflicting accounts of where they came from and where they were put. There is agreement only that the stones had something to do with the temporarily dry bed of the Jordan. A classic case of the importance of memory, but also of the vagaries of even *official* religious memory.

Corporate memory through the generations is especially highly valued in the Jewish tradition, and this goes back at least as far as the tradition in the Book of Deuteronomy. There we find a high concentration of terms for teaching, learning and instruction. God teaches Moses; Moses teaches Israel; and the generation of Israel that hears Moses is instructed to teach their children. This is neatly encapsulated in the following:

> "When your son asks you in time to come, 'What is the meaning of the testimonies and the statutes and the ordinances which the Lord our God has commanded you?' then you shall say to your son, 'We were Pharaoh's slaves in Egypt; and the Lord brought us out of Egypt with a mighty hand.'"

> (6:20–21)

And the Book of Exodus (12:26–27; 13:14–15) gives similar instructions for the questions still proudly put by a Jewish boy at every family Passover service: "Why all these laws?" "Why the service of the Passover?" "Why the redemption of the first-born?" And so also here: "What mean these twelve stones?"

Of course *we* have a question too. Why two accounts of these twelve stones? A later chapter of the Book of Joshua may furnish the clue. We shall deal in greater detail below with chapter 22 and its poignant account of how the building of an altar (also near the Jordan) almost resulted in civil war. Verses 24–28 of that chapter foresee the dangers ahead should the children of both sides learn a different significance for the same altar.

We have no further evidence about the twelve stones of chapter 4. They are no longer to be found. Different stories about them were told and taught. We can only hope they did not lead to blows. These explanations in all their contradiction now rest side by side in Holy Scripture. That in itself should give us food for thought.

Discrepant accounts of the past can often simply be allowed to co-exist especially if people have a fond attachment to their memory. Competing accounts of the present are much more difficult. But most dangerous of all are conflicts about what happened in the past, between those whose present is *completely* determined by what they *know* has gone before.

One last point. The wonder of the stopping of the waters may not have been needed to get Israel across the Jordan, but it still had strategic importance. Rahab had already reported the fear of Jericho on hearing of the exodus from Egypt, and what had happened to kings in Transjordan. Now the first verse of chapter 5 tells us that the drying of the waters sapped the courage of *all* the Amorite and Canaanite kings from the Jordan westwards to the Mediterranean Sea.

CIRCUMCISION: A REPROACH REMOVED

Joshua 5:2–9

²At that time the Lord said to Joshua, "Make flint knives and circumcise the people of Israel again the second time." ³So Joshua made flint knives, and circumcised the people of Israel at Gibeath-haaraloth. ⁴And this is the reason why Joshua circumcised them: all the males of the people who came out of Egypt, all the men of war, had died on the way in the wilderness after they had come out of Egypt. ⁵Though all the people who came out had been circumcised, yet all the people that

were born on the way in the wilderness after they had come out of Egypt had not been circumcised. 6For the people of Israel walked forty years in the wilderness, till all the nation, the men of war that came forth out of Egypt, perished, because they did not hearken to the voice of the Lord; to them the Lord swore that he would not let them see the land which the Lord had sworn to their fathers to give us, a land flowing with milk and honey. 7So it was their children, whom he raised up in their stead, that Joshua circumcised; for they were uncircumcised, because they had not been circumcised on the way.

8When the circumcising of all the nation was done, they remained in their places in the camp till they were healed. 9And the Lord said to Joshua, "This day I have rolled away the reproach of Egypt from you." And so the name of that place is called Gilgal to this day.

(i)

What we think about circumcision will depend a great deal on our culture and experience. Many Christians think of it only as the mark of a Jew. They recall Paul's arguments that a non-Jew need not first become a Jew in his very flesh before he can become a Christian; that trust in God, which was deemed righteous in Abraham, had preceded the patriarch's circumcision. His trust, his belief, was what was exemplary about Abraham.

In the Western world circumcision is not widely practised although it is occasionally fashionable in certain medical circles. In some other societies it is a matter of course and quite unremarkable. So it appears to have been in ancient Israel. The custom was common in almost all her neighbours, as it has been amongst traditional Muslims in the Middle East until very recently.

The Philistines, ancient Israel's arch-rivals for her land, were the striking exception to this rule. David scorns the uncircumcised Goliath; Saul prefers death by his own sword to being thrust through by the uncircumcised. These are not expressions of religious difference, but rather barrack-room taunts implying that an enemy is less than manly. With such a deformed foe co-existence would be impossible. (As an aside we may note the continuing resentment in modern Israel that the outside world still calls their land after their ancient foe, Palestine. Memories of the *ancient* clash still fuel the *present* struggle for the land and its name.)

Simply the arrival of Israel in Canaan was something to celebrate. The circumcision of the people is described *after* the setting up of the stones, and *before* the first Passover in the land. Yet in a sense what is celebrated is not something special, but a return to normal. To be in Canaan was a natural state. To have been in the desert involved a suspension of regular custom. At the end of Amos chapter 5 it is observed that during the forty years in the desert Israel's fathers had not practised sacrifice (v. 25). There Amos is making the point that sacrifice is *not* of the *very essence* of Israel's relationship with God. It might be held that sacrifice required a settled shrine. A shrine would not have been essential for circumcision; yet our text is clear that that practice too was in abeyance in the desert period.

(ii)

Before we say more we must return to the topic of divergent tradition that occupied us in chapter 4. Now, however, the differences are not side by side in the same text. Rather two different versions of the text have come down to us from ancient times. Particularly in some books of the Old Testament, the translation into Greek of the original Hebrew Scriptures (preserved for us by the ancient Greek Church) has some significant differences from the version of the Hebrew Scriptures preserved in the Jewish community. In a few books, including Joshua, the shorter Greek text is often to be preferred and so it is here. In place of the familiar and fuller verses 4 and 5 it reads simply:

And this is how Joshua circumcised the people of Israel: whoever was born on the way and whoever was uncircumcised of those who left Egypt—all these Joshua circumcised.

The tradition is uniform that circumcision was not practised for forty years in the desert; but it divides over whether the earlier practice in Egypt was standard or not. If we cannot be sure what went before, it is harder to decide the significance of what Joshua did.

(iii)

It is surprising just how little circumcision is discussed in the Old Testament. In both Deuteronomy (10:16; 30:6) and Jeremiah (4:4; 9:25–26) the rite has become just a form of speech: circumcision of the heart. However, the origins of the Biblical rite are shrouded in some mystery. Gen. 17 reports as an instruction of God to Abraham that every male in his household from eight days and upwards should be circumcised as a sign of the covenant between them. This precedes the promise of an heir through Sarah. The chapter ends with the circumcision of Abraham aged ninety-nine and Ishmael aged thirteen. Lev. 12:3 provides for the circumcision of an eight-day-old male in the context of various purificatory rites a mother should attend to after giving birth. However, it appears from the strange story in Exod. 4:24–26 that Moses' son was only circumcised to help ward off divine menace on his father's life; and indeed many commentators hold that when Zipporah applies that son's blood to Moses' "legs", she is trying to make it appear that Moses too is circumcised. The Genesis story will be more recent than the Exodus one—designed to give a greater antiquity to the practice. We may suppose that some scribes who knew Genesis 17 and whose community was faithful to the instruction in Leviticus 12 may have sought to rectify the *suggestion they found* in the first version of Joshua 5, that their forefathers in Egypt had been less than scrupulous about the rite.

Of course the shorter version in Joshua 5 quoted above *need not* mean that the forefathers in Egypt were less than scrupulous about practising circumcision. Those it describes leaving Egypt "uncircumcised" had been the boys and youngsters among the refugees: in those days we may suppose that the rite was performed at puberty, or before marriage—the normal time among most peoples who keep this custom.

Our text concludes in a pun, by noting that the name Gilgal is related to the Hebrew verb "to roll". We have already noted that the name may really mean a wheel or circle. Here our author plays on the meaning of the verb and notes that what has been "rolled away" to give the place its name is "the reproach of

Egypt". For him the whole desert period was but an extension of the bad times in Egypt. The Exodus to his mind had been not the liberation itself but only a *pledge* of what was *fully* paid by the delivery of Israel safe to Canaan.

PASSOVER AND THE LORD'S HOST

Joshua 5:10–15

[10]While the people of Israel were encamped in Gilgal they kept the passover on the fourteenth day of the month at evening in the plains of Jericho. [11]And on the morrow after the passover, on that very day, they ate of the produce of the land, unleavened cakes and parched grain. [12]And the manna ceased on the morrow, when they ate of the produce of the land; and the people of Israel had manna no more, but ate of the fruit of the land of Canaan that year.

[13]When Joshua was by Jericho, he lifted up his eyes and looked, and behold, a man stood before him with his drawn sword in his hand; and Joshua went to him and said to him, "Are you for us, or for our adversaries?" [14]And he said, "No; but as commander of the army of the Lord I have now come." And Joshua fell on his face to the earth, and worshipped, and said to him, "What does my lord bid his servant?" [15]And the commander of the Lord's army said to Joshua, "Put off your shoes from your feet; for the place where you stand is holy." And Joshua did so.

Before leaving the question of circumcision it may be well to develop a hint already dropped. Earlier practice in Israel may well have corresponded to widespread practice elsewhere in seeing circumcision as a preparation for adulthood or marriage. One interesting botanical regulation provides good evidence that this idea was current in ancient Israel also. Within a series of miscellaneous instructions, Lev. 19:23–25 (literally translated) commends gleaning and leaving unused the fruit of a young "uncircumcised" tree for the first three years. The crop in the fourth season is dedicated to God, as the official first-fruits. And from the fifth season it is available for general consumption. For the first three seasons it is "uncircumcised", in the sense of being immature, and not yet ready for the new future.

(i)

Although Joshua 5 does not spell this out in detail the very mention of circumcision immediately before Passover reminds us of another dimension. The extended regulations for Passover in Exodus 12 insist that only the circumcised may join in the Passover festival: even slaves and resident aliens must first be circumcised before partaking. In its brevity, Josh. 5 is certainly consistent with this. Although the record of the Passover is typical of this brevity and takes up only three verses (10–12) some comments can be fairly made. The first is that it was a communal festival. That may have been force of circumstances: all Israel was together in one place. But in later times it was practised as one of the three great pilgrim festivals, celebrated at a central sanctuary. Part of Josiah's reform (2 Kings 23:21–23) involved the celebration in Jerusalem of a Passover the like of which had not been kept since the days of the Judges.

But if our first comment is a positive one, stressing the communal context for this family festival, our other two are negative: there is no mention of either Egypt or lamb. We know the Passover as the great feast that celebrates the liberation from Egypt. Already in our reading of Joshua we have had that deliverance recalled more than once. But the opportunity to link them is *not* taken here. It is worth recalling that the initial request which Moses and Aaron lodge with Pharaoh (Exod. 5:1–3) is that their people may journey into the desert for three days to celebrate a festival, lest their God fall on them with pestilence or the sword. Passover was an annual feast to appease the destroyer—the destroyer of new life whether of crops or of herds or of the people themselves; and it was celebrated long before tradition linked it with that fateful night when the destroyer was unleashed on the Egyptians. Somewhat paradoxically again this account of Passover, like the earlier report of circumcision, may carry us back to Israelite thinking which is earlier than we now read in the Books of Moses. Anyone who is familiar with several different forms of the Communion Service or Eucharist will know well that solemn actions are much more constant over a long period than the words we use for explaining them.

The familiar sacrificed lamb too finds no mention. It may be that the unleavened cereal aspect of the festival is underscored in this brief report to make a better transition to the note about the manna. With the destroyer appeased they were able to enjoy the produce of the land for a year; and with that food stock assured, there was no longer need for the special provision of manna. In yet another sense the journey was now over and they were home.

(ii)

The crossing of the Jordan has reminded us of the crossing of the sea from Egypt. The subsequent Passover of the circumcised recalls that Passover which *preceded* the crossing of the sea. And the final three verses of our chapter complete this series of mirror-like reflections. For Joshua's removal of his shoes before the captain of the Lord's host inevitably carries us back to Moses before the burning bush. We might have supposed that Joshua himself was Yahweh's commander. However, it is well to be reminded, before we read the report of the taking of Jericho in chapter 6, that Yahweh disposes of forces independent of Israel's.

There is no other mention in the Bible of Yahweh's army or host or troop-muster, nor of its commander. Of course "the Lord of hosts" is a regular title for God in the Old Testament. Then Deuteronomy 4:19 describes sun, moon and stars collectively as "all the host of heaven" and warns against according them worship. We shall see later in Joshua how Yahweh uses sun and moon to Israel's benefit. On the other hand the idea is clearly represented in the Old Testament that Yahweh presided over a divine court. The Song of Moses tells how the nations of the world were divided according to the number of these divine beings (Deut. 32:8–9); and the later chapters of the Book of Daniel talk of a "Prince" (the Hebrew word is the same as commander here) who represents the interests of each people. (This is the origin of our own talk about "guardian angels".) The commander of the Lord's army is chief among these powerful beings. His appearance before Joshua at the start of the campaign will have been a potent, if terrifying, omen of success.

JERICHO'S WALLS CAME TUMBLING DOWN

Joshua 6:1–27

[1]Now Jericho was shut up from within and from without because of the people of Israel; none went out, and none came in. [2]And the Lord said to Joshua, "See, I have given into your hand Jericho, with its king and mighty men of valour. [3]You shall march around the city, all the men of war going around the city once. Thus shall you do for six days. [4]And seven priests shall bear seven trumpets of rams' horns before the ark; and on the seventh day you shall march around the city seven times, the priests blowing the trumpets. [5]And when they make a long blast with the ram's horn, as soon as you hear the sound of the trumpet, then all the people shall shout with a great shout; and the wall of the city will fall down flat, and the people shall go up every man straight before him." [6]So Joshua the son of Nun called the priests and said to them, "Take up the ark of the covenant, and let seven priests bear seven trumpets of rams' horns before the ark of the Lord." [7]And he said to the people, "Go forward; march around the city, and let the armed men pass on before the ark of the Lord."

[8]And as Joshua had commanded the people, the seven priests bearing the seven trumpets of rams' horns before the Lord went forward, blowing the trumpets, with the ark of the covenant of the Lord following them. [9]And the armed men went before the priests who blew the trumpets, and the rear guard came after the ark, while the trumpets blew continually. [10]But Joshua commanded the people, "You shall not shout or let your voice be heard, neither shall any word go out of your mouth, until the day I bid you shout; then you shall shout." [11]So he caused the ark of the Lord to compass the city, going about it once; and they came into the camp, and spent the night in the camp.

[12]Then Joshua rose early in the morning, and the priests took up the ark of the Lord. [13]And the seven priests bearing the seven trumpets of rams' horns before the ark of the Lord passed on, blowing the trumpets continually; and the armed men went before them, and the rear guard came after the ark of the Lord, while the trumpets blew continually. [14]And the second day they marched around the city once, and returned into the camp. So they did for six days.

[15]On the seventh day they rose early at the dawn of day, and marched around the city in the same manner seven times: it was only

on that day that they marched around the city seven times. ¹⁶And at the seventh time, when the priests had blown the trumpets, Joshua said to the people, "Shout; for the Lord has given you the city. ¹⁷And the city and all that is within it shall be devoted to the Lord for destruction; only Rahab the harlot and all who are with her in her house shall live, because she hid the messengers that we sent. ¹⁸But you, keep yourselves from the things devoted to destruction, lest when you have devoted them you take any of the devoted things and make the camp of Israel a thing for destruction, and bring trouble upon it. ¹⁹But all silver and gold, and vessels of bronze and iron, are sacred to the Lord; they shall go into the treasury of the Lord." ²⁰So the people shouted, and the trumpets were blown. As soon as the people heard the sound of the trumpet, the people raised a great shout, and the wall fell down flat, so that the people went up into the city, every man straight before him, and they took the city. ²¹Then they utterly destroyed all in the city, both men and women, young and old, oxen, sheep, and asses, with the edge of the sword.

²²And Joshua said to the two men who had spied out the land, "Go into the harlot's house, and bring out from it the woman, and all who belong to her, as you swore to her." ²³So the young men who had been spies went in, and brought out Rahab, and her father and mother and brothers and all who belonged to her; and they brought all her kindred, and set them outside the camp of Israel. ²⁴And they burned the city with fire, and all within it; only the silver and gold, and the vessels of bronze and of iron, they put into the treasury of the house of the Lord. ²⁵But Rahab the harlot, and her father's household, and all who belonged to her, Joshua saved alive; and she dwelt in Israel to this day, because she hid the messengers whom Joshua sent to spy out Jericho.

²⁶Joshua laid an oath upon them at that time, saying, "Cursed before the Lord be the man that rises up and rebuilds this city, Jericho.

At the cost of his first-born shall he lay its foundation,

and at the cost of his youngest son shall he set up its gates."

²⁷So the lord was with Joshua; and his fame was in all the land.

(i)

In this best-known and most sung of the stories of Joshua several themes of the whole conquest narrative in chapters 1 to 11 intersect. From one perspective, it is the first of a series of campaigns, each concerned with an important local centre. From this point of view the chapter looks forward to the end of chapter 11. In another sense, it is a culmination of several ideas already introduced in the earlier chapters. Chapter 2 dealt with the reconnaissance of the area. The Ark which leads Israel across the Jordan (Josh. 3–4) makes here its final appearance in the book. And then most immediately the instruction at the end of chapter 5 from the commander of the Lord's army, that Joshua should respect the sanctity of the place, is but a prelude to God himself giving Joshua the orders of the day at the beginning of chapter 6.

Different elements in the Book of Joshua criss-cross at this chapter. It is also true that it is very hard to estimate the character of the narrative. "Joshua fought the battle of Jericho" in only a very limited sense. From childhood we are told that it takes two to make a battle or a quarrel. Yet the people of Jericho hardly figure in the narrative. At the opening we read that "Jericho was shut up from within and from without because of the people of Israel; none went out and none came in." They appear next quite impersonally in the instruction that "the city and all that is within it shall be devoted to the Lord for destruction" (v. 17). This is not a *battle*. Jericho is not fought for by force of arms. Arms are used only in the final slaughter of all those taken. At least it is not described as a battle which *Joshua* fought.

(ii)

Readers have reinterpreted the narrative in one of a few ways. Joshua may have been aware of the physical forces latent in concerted shout and blast of trumpet. His circling of the city daily until the seventh procession on the seventh day may have been a forceful psychological stratagem in face of an already terrified city. Equally the repeated processions in a circle round the city may be supposed to have magical properties. But all of this is *our* reconstruction from the text. That talks simply of the Lord's gift accompanied by a shout (v. 16), and of a sudden collapse of the wall all round (v. 20) such that Jericho could be entered simply from every quarter.

I am not of course excluding as improper any reconstruction from this text. Indeed it is already clear, from our discussion of the twelve stones in chapter 4 and of circumcision in chapter 5, that the narratives in Joshua are not simple flat reports of what happened; but may embody reflection, discussion, change of mind and even disagreement about what has gone before. We are all entitled to make our own intelligent guesses.

Thus we know that Passover was an annually repeated rite at a central sanctuary. We also know that just south of Jericho lies a solitary Muslim shrine that bears Moses' name—*Nebi Musa*. In former times it was an annual custom to bring young teenage lads there and circumcise them at a large celebration. Despite the lack of other evidence we may suggest that this Palestinian Arab custom may go back to ancient Biblical times.

In this context and against this background, several scholars have argued that some aspects of the story in Josh. 6 owe more to later celebration than to any original event. The instructions for the Feast of Passover and Unleavened Bread (Deut. 16:1–8) show that it was a week-long festival. Those who in the early years of settlement held this feast at Gilgal may have included as part of their observation a ritual procession with Ark and priestly horns round a *long-ruined* Jericho (for, as we shall shortly see, it is highly improbable that Jericho was an inhabited city when Israel entered the land). From such a beginning, this reconstruction argues, the story as we now have it in chapter 6 evolved: it tells us more about what later generations believed happened than about what in fact happened.

Our chapter concludes with Joshua pronouncing a curse on whoever would rebuild the town; and the Bible (1 Kings 16:34) and the archaeological record are at one in documenting that this did not happen until the middle years of the ninth century B.C. Our following section but one will have more to say about archaeological work carried out at Jericho and at other sites mentioned in Israel's record of conquest. For the moment let us simply underscore (a) that the Jericho story follows immediately on religious celebrations; (b) that religious paraphernalia play a larger part in this story than those that follow it in the Book of

Joshua; and (c) that it is introduced with General Joshua being
commanded to remove his shoes from off his feet because he is on
holy ground.

JERICHO "DEVOTED"—RAHAB LIBERATED

Joshua 6:1–27 (*cont'd*)

(iii)

It would be quite wrong to suggest that the religious aspects of the
Jericho story are *all* pointers to later ceremonial celebration by
the congregation of Israel at or near old Jericho or Gilgal. There
is one much more drastic once-for-all terrible religious dimension
to this story. In fact this religious topic binds all of chapters 6 to 11
together; and it is summed up in the Hebrew word *herem*. This is
not a common word in the Hebrew Bible. But it is an important
term in some few texts outside the Book of Joshua.

The best place to start our discussion is in Lev. 27. This chapter
is concerned with various offerings and dedications to the Lord. It
is not easy for an English translator to do justice to the various
distinctions and nuances in the Hebrew regulations. It is in verses
21, 28 and 29 that *herem* appears both as a noun and as a verb. In
the RSV here, as at the end of Lev., the noun is translated
"devoted thing" and the verb either "devote" or "utterly destroy". Fortunately some other elements of Lev. 27 help to explain this difficulty of translation. There is something superlative
and extraordinary about the *herem*. The text notes that much
property which has been deposited "with the Lord" as the result
of a vow of dedication can also be re-acquired or redeemed—but
never what is *herem*. *Herem* is the limiting case, of an offering too
special to return. In a nutshell it is more than usually sacred: as
the end of verse 28 puts it, "every *herem* is holy of holy to
Yahweh".

Apart from Joshua 6 and 7 the other striking Biblical narrative
about malpractice over *herem* is the confrontation between
Samuel and Saul over the fate of Agag and his Amalekites (1
Sam. 15). In this chapter in the RSV our key Hebrew word is

always translated "utterly destroy" except in verse 21 where *herem* is rendered "the things devoted to destruction". It is not our business here to offer a commentary on 1 Sam. 15, but it helps to bring the enormity of Saul's offence into perspective if we realize that the king had violated instructions concerning a dedication so holy that there were not even sacred means of recalling it. It was not just a matter of simple disobedience to instructions, even divine instructions. The enormity is compounded when Saul blunders into a protest that, after all, he and his people were just on their way to offer the best of what had been saved from the *herem* in sacrifice at Gilgal! A brave attempt on the spur of the moment—but immediate "sacrifice" on the battlefield was what had been commanded.

Why should Israel's foes in Canaan suffer this bloody dedication to Israel's God? As we shall discuss in the next section, it may never have actually happened as described here. Yet why then should it have been told as happening? The clue may lie in one of the brief commands in Exod. 22: "whoever sacrifices to a god other than Yahweh will be made *herem*" (v. 20). The link between *herem* and sacrifice which we have just noted in 1 Sam. 15 is perfectly encapsulated in this brief Exodus injuction: the offerer will be offered; the dedicator will be dedicated; the sacrificer will be sacrificed.

Those readers familiar with Arabic Jerusalem may appreciate another illustration of the relationship between "holiness" and *herem*: that state of super-holiness. The city of Jerusalem as a whole is known in Arabic as *al-Quds*. But within it the great sacred precinct on the vast platform (originally constructed by Herod the Great for the Jewish Temple) which now contains the two great mosques and many subsidiary buildings as well, is named the *Haram ash-Sharif*—"the noble sanctuary". Jerusalem is holy—its sanctuary is *herem*. The Biblical use of this word may well appear less noble to the modern reader than that delightful devoted spot in Jerusalem.

War was firmly within the religious sphere. That is unwelcome to many Christians, but it should cause them no surprise. Battle happened either at God's command or despite his displeasure.

There were some sacrificial obligations on the fighters and the spoils of war belonged to God—they were *herem*. God's ownership of them could be renounced in favour of the people or at least partially renounced. But if his claim were maintained, as in the case of Jericho, then everything living was slaughtered, man and beast: it became God's, like a sacrifice became his. Everything combustible was burned and only the silver and gold and the vessels of bronze and of iron (v. 24), which would remain unscathed in the general conflagration, were reserved to become the property of the sanctuary.

(iv)

Of course the one exception in the case of Jericho is Rahab and her family. They were all to be saved because of her *practical* assistance to the cause. Because of the brevity with which her rescue is reported it is not easy to understand what her final status was. At Joshua's orders the spies rescue her and her family (v. 22). Verse 23 talks of them being set "outside the camp". Verse 25 talks of Rahab and all her father's household remaining in Israel "to this day". Outside Israel's camp (and Israel was only a camp at this time)—within Israel to this day? We surmised earlier that she may have been on the edges of Jericho society. It may be that she remained at the margins, protected but not absorbed.

ARCHAEOLOGY AND ISRAEL'S SETTLEMENT IN CANAAN

(i)

The settlement of Israel in Canaan is dated by most historians in the middle of the second half of the thirteenth century B.C.—i.e. around 1225 B.C. Several indicators converge to support this date. (1) Israel's independent development in Palestine is supposed to be mirrored in the emergence of Iron Age culture. And in the Levant, the transition from Late Bronze Age to Iron Age is set around 1200 B.C.

(2) From about 1225 there was a "power vacuum" in the Levant—that is the area occupied by today's Syria, Lebanon, Israel and Jordan. In the preceding period the area was under domination from both north and south: from the Hittites (based in the heartland of modern Turkey) and the Egyptians. The relations between these two imperial powers were varied: mostly uneasy co-existence, but also the extremes of marriage alliance, and of battle at Kadesh on the Orontes (famous because we now possess the conflicting assessments of both sides). In fact the area was effectively partitioned between two external forces, as it was at the end of World War I between France and Britain. In the latter half of the thirteenth century B.C. this situation came to an end, so permitting the development of small, separate, independent states. The Hittite Empire suddenly collapsed, for reasons that are far from clear. And Egypt, under double assault from Libya (again a modern parallel!) and various "Sea Peoples", had to concentrate her energies in her own heartland.

(3) An Egyptian standing stone, often dated to 1224 B.C., makes the earliest known mention of Israel. The inscription on this "stele" of Pharaoh Merneptah lists "Israel" as one of several peoples and places in Canaan. The precise significance is unclear: however it is at least manifest that "Israel" is not (yet) a name for Canaan as a whole.

(4) The immediately preceding Pharaoh, Rameses II, is widely held to be the Pharaoh of the Exodus from Egypt. Major building operations under him are known in the Delta region of Egypt—and these are correlated with the forced labour operations of which the opening chapters of Exodus tell (1:8–14; 5:1–21).

(5) Major archaeological excavations at a dozen representative sites across Israel have furnished evidence of substantial destruction caused to towns in Canaan in the second half of the thirteenth century B.C. It is possible to associate this too with the Bible's traditions of a military occupation of her land by Israel.

(ii)

Of course some general cautionary remarks have to be made. None of the destructions can be *positively* laid to *Israel's* blame or credit by archaeological means. Some at least may have been the fault of the Philistines, one of the "Sea Peoples", putting pressure on the coast of Egypt and the southern Levant in this period. Equally some may have resulted from local squabbles, as Egyptian rule was relaxed.

But the crucial archaeological problem for the historicity of the narrative in Joshua is this. Most of the dozen excavated sites are not towns mentioned in Joshua. And in at least three of the four most prominent towns in Joshua 2–11, a very different story has to be told by the archaeologists:

(1) At Ai (Josh. 7–8), whose very name interestingly means "the ruin", the situation is quite clear. It had been a very prominent place in the third millenium B.C.; but had ceased to be occupied well before the year 2000. The site was not rebuilt till around 1150 B.C.—and only as a minor village above part of the ruins of the major earlier town. In the years around 1225 it did not exist— except as the ruin its very name signifies.

(2) Gibeon also was unoccupied in the Late Bronze Age. It too was freshly settled in the twelfth century B.C. There was no home there then for the crafty Gibeonites who trapped Israel and Joshua into the bargain Josh. 9 describes.

(3) Only at Hazor in the north (Josh. 11) does the archaeologist bring any comfort to those who would wish to read the Book of Joshua as historical record. That most important of towns was continuously occupied throughout the relevant period, and frequently destroyed and rebuilt. Here at least is a settlement which could have suffered at Joshua's hands in the later thirteenth century. (We shall not complicate this discussion with the possibly discordant traditions of Judg. 4!)

(4) And what of Jericho, which gave rise to this whole review in the first place? Dame Kathleen Kenyon's excavations there in the 1950s are a useful reminder that what we call "ancient Israel" was a relative late-comer in the Middle East. By one definition of "city"—a walled settlement depending on domestic agriculture—the earliest Jericho she discovered ranks proudly as the oldest city in the world, and dates back *some ten thousand years*. It is a haunting experience to have the privilege of mounting the

steps (normally locked up) in one of the towers of its ancient perimeter wall. And it has made me cringe more than once to overhear unscrupulous guides tell eager but unwary visitors that they are looking at a tower on the wall of the Jericho which Joshua took! (That Josh. 6 tells of the complete collapse of the walls just doubles the horror!) As far as Joshua is concerned, Miss Kenyon's work showed too that the ruined fortifications which an earlier excavator (Professor Garstang) had associated with the Israelite conquest belonged some hundreds of years earlier than the thirteenth century B.C.

In fact Jericho too was experiencing one of the several long unsettled periods she documented over its extended history. And it remained unoccupied till the ninth century rebuilding (cf. the end of 1 Kings 16). This evidence too I find conclusive. But it has to be admitted that Miss Kenyon's excavations also produced a hostage for those scholars who insist on finding history here. Most of Jericho has always been built of mud-brick. Rain is very rare in that part of the Jordan valley, but often strong when it does occur; and considerable erosion is caused then to the very dry brick. Is it possible that all of the Jericho which Joshua took washed away in the four centuries before the site was re-occupied? Believe it if you will: but only if Jericho was a minor village, and not the major walled town of which the Bible tells in Josh. 6.

We shall return to some of the implications of these archaeological discoveries as we read more of the text.

"A SHAMEFUL THING IN ISRAEL"

Joshua 7:1–26

[1]But the people of Israel broke faith in regard to the devoted things; for Achan the son of Carmi, son of Zabdi, son of Zerah, of the tribe of Judah, took some of the devoted things; and the anger of the Lord burned against the people of Israel.

[2]Joshua sent men from Jericho to Ai, which is near Bethaven, east of Bethel, and said to them, "Go up and spy out the land." And the men went up and spied out Ai. [3]And they returned to Joshua, and said to

him, "Let not all the people go up, but let about two or three thousand men go up and attack Ai; do not make the whole poeple toil up there, for they are but few." ⁴So about three thousand went up there from the people; and they fled before the men of Ai, ⁵and the men of Ai killed about thirty-six men of them, and chased them before the gate as far as Shebarim, and slew them at the descent. And the hearts of the people melted, and became as water.

⁶Then Joshua rent his clothes, and fell to the earth upon his face before the ark of the Lord until the evening, he and the elders of Israel; and they put dust upon their heads. ⁷And Joshua said, "Alas, O Lord God, why hast thou brought this people over the Jordan at all, to give us into the hands of the Amorites, to destroy us? Would that we had been content to dwell beyond the Jordan! ⁸Oh Lord, what can I say, when Israel has turned their backs before their enemies! ⁹For the Canaanites and all the inhabitants of the land will hear of it, and will surround us, and cut off our name from the earth; and what wilt thou do for thy great name?"

¹⁰The Lord said to Joshua, "Arise, why have you thus fallen upon your face? ¹¹Israel has sinned; they have transgressed my covenant which I commanded them; they have taken some of the devoted things; they have stolen, and lied, and put them among their own stuff. ¹²Therefore the people of Israel cannot stand before their enemies; they turn their backs before their enemies, because they have become a thing for destruction. I will be with you no more, unless you destroy the devoted things from among you. ¹³Up, sanctify the people, and say, 'Sanctify yourselves for tomorrow; for thus says the Lord, God of Israel, "There are devoted things in the midst of you, O Israel; you cannot stand before your enemies, until you take away the devoted things from among you." ¹⁴In the morning therefore you shall be brought near by your tribes; and the tribe which the Lord takes shall come near by families; and the family which the Lord takes shall come near by households; and the household which the Lord takes shall come near man by man. ¹⁵And he who is taken with the devoted things shall be burned with fire, he and all that he has, because he has transgressed the covenant of the Lord, and because he has done a shameful thing in Israel.'"

¹⁶So Joshua rose early in the morning, and brought Israel near tribe by tribe, and the tribe of Judah was taken; ¹⁷and he brought near the families of Judah, and the family of the Zerahites was taken; and he brought near the family of the Zerahites man by man, and Zabdi was

taken; [18]and he brought near his household man by man, and Achan the son of Carmi, son of Zabdi, son of Zerah, of the tribe of Judah, was taken. [19]Then Joshua said to Achan, "My son, give glory to the Lord God of Israel, and render praise to him; and tell me now what you have done; do not hide it from me." [20]And Achan answered Joshua, "Of a truth I have sinned against the Lord God of Israel, and this is what I did: [21]when I saw among the spoil a beautiful mantle from Shinar, and two hundred shekels of silver, and a bar of gold weighing fifty shekels, then I coveted them, and took them; and behold, they are hidden in the earth inside my tent, with the silver underneath."

[22]So Joshua sent messengers, and they ran to the tent; and behold, it was hidden in his tent with the silver underneath. [23]And they took them out of the tent and brought them to Joshua and all the people of Israel; and they laid them down before the Lord. [24]And Joshua and all Israel with him took Achan the son of Zerah, and the silver and the mantle and the bar of gold, and his sons and daughters, and his oxen and asses and sheep, and his tent, and all that he had; and they brought them up to the Valley of Achor. [25]And Joshua said, "Why did you bring trouble on us? The Lord brings trouble on you today." And all Israel stoned him with stones; they burned them with fire, and stoned them with stones. [26]And they raised over him a great heap of stones that remains to this day; then the Lord turned from his burning anger. Therefore to this day the name of that place is called the Valley of Achor.

If *herem* was the fate of the inhabitants of Jericho and all they possessed, it also underlies the next chapter of Israel's story in the land. Israel suffers a rare reverse: defeat in battle by the inhabitants of Ai. The cause was not simply inadequate reconnaissance by spies (vv. 2–3) who had marked Ai down as a minor problem that need not involve the strength of the whole people. And, as so often in life, the reverse followed immediately on a high point.

(i)

The tables are completely turned on Israel: "the hearts of the people melted, and became as water" (7:5) is just what Rahab had said of the plight of her people before Israel (2:11). Joshua is desperate (7:9) lest the report of this reverse give the Canaanites back the very courage drained away at his crossing of the Jordan

(5:1). Having claimed speechlessness in face of the catastrophe (7:8), he moves immediately to make a clever attempt to link God's reputation with that of Israel: the Lord will suffer if they do; after all, it was he who had brought them west of Jordan in the first place. Exod. 32 and Deut. 9 report Moses trying a similar tactic when God threatened to annihilate Israel after the construction of the golden calf. There is a similar discussion at greater length in Num. 14. During that parley God threatens to make a new start with Moses of a people fit for himself.

Josh. 7 is a striking example of the principle of corporate involvement. Its opening words are that "the people of Israel broke faith", although it goes on immediately to specify that this was the action of one man. And when the price comes to be paid (vv. 24–26), that man's whole family suffers his fate. To an extent this just illustrates what we all know: that "no man is an island", that much of what we do has implications for others which we seldom glimpse at the time and often learn with horror some time afterwards.

What is not spelled out is how far Joshua himself is automatically implicated in this. When God says to the prostrate leader (vv. 10–11): "Arise, why have you thus fallen upon your face? Israel has sinned", is he noting the pointlessness of any sort of approach to himself, *including prayer*, until the public record has been set straight? If this is the intention of the story, then it is at one with those prophetic protests against religiosity like Isa. 1:10–17 which add prayer itself to the list of observances rendered null and void until the evil of people's doings is removed from before God's eyes.

The Bible is often at odds with us in its perception that we cannot cheat on ourselves, that an action leads inexorably to its result, and that if mischief has been undertaken the appropriate remedy must be applied to avoid spreading contagion. The warning had been given on the day of Jericho's capture (6:18) that any tampering with what was already *herem* would render those persons involved *herem* to the Lord, and would bring "trouble" (Hebrew *'achar*).

(ii)

"Trouble" is the key word of Josh. 7, and is altogether too tame a word to convey all that is meant. We talk so readily of troubles of many different sorts, that we may fail to hear the echoes of this rather uncommon Biblical word. It is plain enough that the action of Israel's defector is remembered in the valley called "Achor" at the end of the chapter (vv. 24–26). However, it is likely that the first hearers of this story heard this key word in the name of its unlucky hero too (7:1) for both 1 Chron. 2:7, which refers briefly to the story, and the Greek version of our chapter call him Acha*r* or "Troubler".

A quick look at the occasions the Bible uses this word will give some insight into its meaning. We will meet it later in this volume, in Jephthah's agonized gasp to his daughter as she welcomes him home: "you have become the cause of great trouble to me; for I have opened my mouth to the Lord, and I cannot take back my vow" (Judg. 11:35). The "trouble" is bound up in a vow to God, and it involves nothing less than a man having to offer up his daughter as a burnt offering. In similar vein, Jonathan who tastes honey, not having heard his father Saul's oath, "Cursed be the man who eats food until it is evening and I am avenged on my enemies" (1 Sam. 14:24), says when the truth comes out: "My father has troubled the land" (v. 29). And the victorious young prince is only saved from death because the people formally "ransom" their hero (vv. 43–46).

At their famous encounter before the contest on Mount Carmel, Elijah and King Ahab accuse each other of being "troubler of Israel": Elijah because his words have been instrumental in bringing a three-year famine on the kingdom; and Ahab because he has "forsaken the commandments of the Lord and followed the Baals" (1 Kings 18:17–18). Jacob complains in similar terms (Gen. 34:30) when two of his sons bring bad odour on him among his neighbours because of the havoc they wreak in Shechem in revenging the rape of their sister Dinah.

Of course it is the Book of Proverbs which contains the most abundant treasury of pithy examples of the principle that "whatever a man sows, that he will also reap"—though we have to go to

Paul (Gal. 6:7) for that particular proverb. Prov. 15:27 almost encapsulates Achar's "trouble":

> He who is greedy for unjust gain makes trouble for his household,
>   but he who hates bribes will live.

Josh. 7 gathers almost all these elements together. As in the case of Ahab, Israel had been given instructions, but had ignored them. Verse 11 makes the matter crystal clear: "covenant" is something commanded (we noted this sense of "covenant" in Josh. 3), and Israel "transgresses" it by a series of concrete acts of disobedience. As in the case of Jonathan, the sacred lot will have been the process used in securing the guilty and eliminating the innocent (vv. 16–18). In the case of all three passages, it is from what we might regard as quite independent and separate circumstances that the Biblical characters learn that something has been done amiss: failure in battle, famine, lack of response from the divine oracle—all these prompt the same questions: "where is our fault?" and "what must we do?".

TROUBLE AND GUILT

Joshua 7:1–26 (*cont'd*)

I have already argued that '*achar* is the key word in this chapter. It is reflected in the name of the hero mentioned at the outset, and of the valley at the end. And Joshua clearly holds (v. 25) that stoning the wretch is the fit response in the right place.

It is not clear how far this unhappy tale was known to other Biblical writers. The Valley of Achor itself helps to define the northern border of Judah in Josh. 15:7 (but not the corresponding southern frontier of Benjamin in 18:17). And then it figures twice in the prophets, as a baleful place in need of improvement:

> Sharon shall become a pasture for flocks,
>   and the Valley of Achor a place for herds to lie down,
>   for my people who have sought me.   (Isa. 65:10)

> And there I will give her her vineyards,
>   and make the Valley of Achor a door of hope.   (Hos. 2:15)

It jumps out from the text of Josh. 7 (vv. 1, 18) that Achar is from the great southern tribe: that the "troubler of Israel" is from Judah. In the genealogy of Judah in 1 Chron. 2, the tale is alluʃled to in great brevity in just six Hebrew words: *'achar 'achor yisra'el 'sher ma'al baherem*—"Achar, troubler-of Israel, who broke-faith in-the-*herem*". And that summary brings us to the other significant term for the understanding of Josh. 7—the Hebrew verb *ma'al*.

(i)

When wearing English dress, *ma'al* appears in several different guises. Even more difficult, scholars are quite divided over the basic meaning of the word in Hebrew. One starts from the intro-duction to Num. 5:11–31, perhaps the only Biblical example of a trial by ordeal. The proceedings are for a wife suspected of adultery, and the instructions open: "Say to the people of Israel, If any man's wife goes astray, and *acts unfaithfully* against him, if a man lies with her carnally, and it is hidden from the eyes of her husband..." Matrimonial unfaithfulness becomes an image, a figure of speech for human breach of faith towards God. The RSV translation of Josh. 7:1 ("But the people of Israel *broke faith*...") follows this account.

However, another scholar starts appropriately by noting that *ma'al* nearly always elsewhere concerns an offence against God, or at least some fault in sacred matters. Our verse in Joshua is a good example of this second aspect. This approach to *ma'al* holds the suspected adultery procedure to be the exception to the rule. The fact that adultery was branded throughout the ancient Near East as "the great sin" would have made it easier to use for that act a word that denoted a religious offence. While unable to pronounce on the merits of these two arguments, I am more sympathetic to the second. Clearly it has influenced the Jerusalem Bible at the beginning of Josh. 7:1—"But the sons of Israel *incurred guilt* by violating the ban..."

(ii)

But for our reflections on this passage, other details of the way *ma'al* is used in the OT may be even more important than its precise meaning. The first is that it appears (almost?) exclusively in late Old Testament books. It is used most frequently in the books of Chronicles and the related Ezra and Nehemiah. We find it several times in the book of the exilic prophet Ezekiel. And, within the books of Moses, it is used in sections of Leviticus and Numbers normally held to come from a similar date to the books just listed. It is used once in Deuteronomy—not in the main core of the book, but in the contribution of a late editor. (Num. 27:12–14 is repeated and more fully stated in Deut. 32:48–51; one of the added elements is the verb *ma'al*. So too 1 Chron. 10:13–14 recasts the earlier 1 Sam. 13:13–14 using *ma'al*.)

The next point is that when the whole community is accused of *ma'al*, it is usually referring to the causes of the exile in Babylon. This is true of Daniel 9:7 and it is always the case in Ezekiel. In Chronicles it characterizes that perfidy of king after king in Judah, starting with Solomon's successor, which culminates in the end of David's line on Jerusalem's throne.

In Josh. 7 we are dealing with an offence which could have led to the destruction of the whole community. The introduction to the report of the offence uses an idea developed quite late in Biblical thinking, which is often linked with the exile, *Judah's* exile. One purpose of this story will be to underline that there was disobedience from the very beginnings of life in the promised land—and nowhere other than in the often favoured tribe of Judah.

(iii)

We have already noted that it was by a system of drawing lots that the guilty party was detected (vv. 16–18). Joshua's words to Achar in verse 19 are surprisingly quite unique in the Old Testament: "My son, give glory to the Lord God of Israel, and render praise to him". It reminds me of the practice in some Muslim countries of carrying out the death penalty in public after morning public prayer in the mosque. However, something different is probably intended here. We have no information that evidence was given on formal oath during legal proceedings in Biblical times. A solemn doxology may have provided an alternative encouragement to tell the truth. The closest parallel is in the Book of Ezra (10:10–11) which, translated rather more literally than in the RSV, reads: "You have committed *ma'al*, and have brought back foreign wives, adding to the guilt of Israel. Now then, give thanks to Yahweh, God of your fathers, and do his pleasure . . ." And these words are followed, as in Achar's case, by a solemn confession of guilt.

Approving as we do of Jeremiah's promise for the future,

"In those days they shall no longer say:
  'The fathers have eaten sour grapes,
    and the children's teeth are set on edge.'
But every one shall die for his own sin; each man who eats sour grapes, his teeth shall be set on edge."

(31:29–30)

we are sensitive to the fact that the whole household of the miscreant is stoned and burned with him, man and beast. We have to remember that in Old Testament times sacred and profane alike were regarded as in a sense contagious. Achar and those in immediate contact with him were contaminated. Strict and decisive measures were necessary, as in dealing with a plague. Readers more in tune with this way of thinking than we are may have been relieved rather to find that *only* Achar's family had to die to restore sacral equilibrium—the deception had already cost thirty-six Israelite lives before the gates of Ai (vv. 4–5).

Readers of the Book of Acts in the New Testament will remember the fate of Ananias and Sapphira, the couple who cheated the early Church's treasury of part of the proceeds of land sold apparently for the common purse. Their death was not at men's hands. Achar's was no less inevitable.

A RUINOUS HEAP OF STONES

Joshua 8:1–29

¹And the Lord said to Joshua, "Do not fear or be dismayed; take all the fighting men with you, and arise, go up to Ai; see, I have given into

your hand the king of Ai, and his people, his city, and his land; ²and you shall do to Ai and its king as you did to Jericho and its king; only its spoil and its cattle you shall take as booty for yourselves; lay an ambush against the city, behind it."

³So Joshua arose, and all the fighting men, to go up to Ai; and Joshua chose thirty thousand mighty men of valour, and sent them forth by night. ⁴And he commanded them, "Behold, you shall lie in ambush against the city, behind it; do not go very far from the city, but hold yourselves all in readiness; ⁵and I, and all the people who are with me, will approach the city. And when they come out against us, as before, we shall flee before them; ⁶and they will come out after us, till we have drawn them away from the city; for they will say, 'They are fleeing from us, as before.' So we will flee from them; ⁷then you shall rise up from the ambush, and seize the city; for the Lord your God will give it into your hand. ⁸And when you have taken the city, you shall set the city on fire, doing as the Lord has bidden; see, I have commanded you." ⁹So Joshua sent them forth; and they went to the place of ambush, and lay between Bethel and Ai, to the west of Ai; but Joshua spent that night among the people.

¹⁰And Joshua arose early in the morning and mustered the people, and went up, with the elders of Israel, before the people to Ai. ¹¹And all the fighting men who were with him went up, and drew near before the city, and encamped on the north side of Ai, with a ravine between them and Ai. ¹²And he took about five thousand men, and set them in ambush between Bethel and Ai, to the west of the city. ¹³So they stationed the forces, the main encampment which was north of the city and its rear guard west of the city. But Joshua spent that night in the valley. ¹⁴And when the king of Ai saw this he and all his people, the men of the city, made haste and went out early to the descent toward the Arabah to meet Israel in battle; but he did not know that there was an ambush against him behind the city. ¹⁵And Joshua and all Israel made a pretence of being beaten before them, and fled in the direction of the wilderness. ¹⁶So all the people who were in the city were called together to pursue them, and as they pursued Joshua they were drawn away from the city. ¹⁷There was not a man left in Ai or Bethel, who did not go out after Israel; they left the city open, and pursued Israel.

¹⁸Then the Lord said to Joshua, "Stretch out the javelin that is in your hand toward Ai; for I will give it into your hand." And Joshua stretched out the javelin that was in his hand toward the city. ¹⁹And the

ambush rose quickly out of their place, and as soon as he had stretched out his hand, they ran and entered the city and took it; and they made haste to set the city on fire. [20]So when the men of Ai looked back, behold, the smoke of the city went up to heaven; and they had no longer power to flee this way or that, for the people that fled to the wilderness turned back upon the pursuers. [21]And when Joshua and all Israel saw that the ambush had taken the city, and that the smoke of the city went up, then they turned back and smote the men of Ai. [22]And the others came forth from the city against them; so they were in the midst of Israel, some on this side, and some on that side; and Israel smote them, until there was left none that survived or escaped. [23]But the king of Ai they took alive, and brought him to Joshua.

[24]When Israel had finished slaughtering all the inhabitants of Ai in the open wilderness where they pursued them and all of them to the very last had fallen by the edge of the sword, all Israel returned to Ai, and smote it with the edge of the sword. [25]And all who fell that day, both men and women, were twelve thousand, all the people of Ai. [26]For Joshua did not draw back his hand, with which he stretched out the javelin, until he had utterly destroyed all the inhabitants of Ai. [27]Only the cattle and the spoil of that city Israel took as their booty, according to the word of the Lord which he commanded Joshua. [28]So Joshua burned Ai, and made it for ever a heap of ruins, as it is to this day. [29]And he hanged the king of Ai on a tree until evening; and at the going down of the sun Joshua commanded, and they took his body down from the tree, and cast it at the entrance of the gate of the city, and raised over it a great heap of stones, which stands there to this day.

Despite the length of this passage I propose to comment very scantily on its details and then raise a rather large question. The heart of the action is a largely matter-of-fact ambush story. Attentive readers may scratch their heads as they try to reconstruct what might have happened. Even in ancient times rather different versions were available.

(i)

It is striking that Judges 20 reports at greater length a rather similar stratagem employed against another town in the same vicinity, in the southern part of the central hill country. There the

defenders are not foreigners but Benjaminites while their attackers represent the rest of Israel. The town in question is not Ai
but Gibeah. The repertory of ambush ruses cannot be very large.
A force whose confidence is already buoyed by success will generally be eager to offer its opponents another "bloody nose". The
same trick may even have worked more than once in the same
territory. Successful commanders have often been good historians. But coincidence is strained by the final link between
Judg. 20 and Josh. 7–8: in both cases an outrage has occurred
which menaces a whole community.

We see from Josh. 8:1–2 that God himself takes the initiative
and gives not only instructions to Joshua but a promise of success
as well. Contrast the opening of chapter 7 where in verses 2–5
Joshua, apparently on his own authority, sends out spies who
come back with the ill-fated report that Ai is a simple target. It
may be that Yahweh, having interrupted Israel's campaign to
receive satisfaction for the wrong done over the ban on Jericho,
has to restart matters himself. Alternatively it may be the case
that some criticism is implied in 8:1–2 of Joshua acting in 7:2
without first seeking divine clearance. In the similar case where
Jonathan fell foul of Saul's curse the problem came to light
exactly when Saul sought divine guidance (1 Sam. 14:37).

When we meet it first in verse 18 Joshua's outstretched javelin
might just be a pre-arranged signal for his troops to advance. But
when verse 26 tells us that "Joshua did not draw back his hand,
with which he stretched out the javelin, until he had utterly
destroyed all the inhabitants of Ai", we are reminded of Exod.
17. There Joshua leads Israel *in the field* against Amalek.
However, he is only the lieutenant. For all to go well with Israel
Moses has to keep his arms raised; and when he is tired, his
attendants have to prop them up. Joshua's javelin here has the
power over the tide of battle like the Ark or Elijah's mantle over
the waters of Jordan.

The section concludes with a ghastly pun. Joshua's spear was
not lowered until all the inhabitants of Ai were slain. Plunder had
however been divinely sanctioned. Verse 28 underscores the very
meaning of the name Ai, reporting its burning and that it was a

perpetual *tell* of total destruction. Except for the saving of the booty, Ai suffers the fate laid down in Deut. 13:12–18 for a city that has encouraged apostasy. However the word play is further twisted in verse 29. Not only does the word *talah* ("hang") jingle with the noun *tell* ("ruin"), but the great heap of stones piled over the king's corpse is but a reduced image of the city's pile. With such fine attention to detail, no wonder the king's corpse was properly cut down and buried before evening: again according to Deuteronomy (this time 21:22–23—the very instruction which saw Jesus removed from his cross before day was out).

(ii)

These last comments lead naturally to my general point. The careful framing of the closing verses sends the reader away with his impression fortified of an efficient and resolute Israelite force. Those for whom destruction can be an art show little regret or remorse about what they do. In my earlier note on archaeology and Israel's settlement in Canaan, I reported the excavated evidence that Israel's settlement in Canaan may not have taken place as the first half of the Book of Joshua reports. Some embarrassed readers of the Bible may be relieved. They no longer have the encumberance of a Biblical past which includes the bloody seizure of Israel's land: that was historical fiction. However, two points need to be made before this tradition is cut down and given pious burial.

(a) The first is that our earlier note, while documenting the historical difficulties at Jericho, Ai and Gibeon, also pointed out considerable evidence of destruction elsewhere in the country at the same time. Settlement may have been bloody enough, even if the blood was not shed quite as Joshua reports.

(b) But more important is this. Those whose faith and whose standards are closely related to the Bible must in the end pay more attention to *its* record, to *its* construction of events, to *its* values, than to *their own reconstruction* of what may have happened. If we have to make a distinction between the two, then it is the Book of Joshua and not what actually happened in the thirteenth century B.C. (or whenever else) that has influenced minds and affected attitudes ever since.

It is only *small* relief that Israel under Joshua did not ruin Ai and its king in ghastly symmetry. Any relief is lost in the cries of the many innocents whose destruction in God's name was made easier by the presence of narratives like Josh. 8 in Holy Writ. In British history (to draw examples from only the seventeenth century) the use of the more militaristic texts of the Old Testament by Cromwellians, Covenanters, and the Stuart monarchs alike, might well make us pause for thought.

AN ALTAR ON MOUNT EBAL

Joshua 8:30–35

[30]Then Joshua built an altar in Mount Ebal to the Lord, the God of Israel, [31]as Moses the servant of the Lord had commanded the people of Israel, as it is written in the book of the law of Moses, "an altar of unhewn stones, upon which no man has lifted an iron tool"; and they offered on it burnt offerings to the Lord, and sacrificed peace offerings. [32]And there, in the presence of the people of Israel, he wrote upon the stones a copy of the law of Moses, which he had written. [33]And all Israel, sojourner as well as homeborn, with their elders and officers and their judges, stood on opposite sides of the ark before the Levitical priests who carried the ark of the covenant of the Lord, half of them in front of Mount Gerizim and half of them in front of Mount Ebal, as Moses the servant of the Lord had commanded at the first, that they should bless the people of Israel. [34]And afterward he read all the words of the law, the blessing and the curse, according to all that is written in the book of the law. [35]There was not a word of all that Moses commanded which Joshua did not read before all the assembly of Israel, and the women, and the little ones, and the sojourners who lived among them.

This short account has all the marks of being a late insert into its context. It separates the report of Ai's fate and the practical response to it by the local confederacy. Indeed in some ancient versions of the Book of Joshua our six verses appear after 9:1–2 and not before. Yet that only solves one problem by creating another: then the concerted action of the kings no longer forms the immediate backdrop to the guile of Gibeon.

The account of this construction work on Mount Ebal claims to carry out instructions given by Moses. Before we comment any further it is worth quoting the relevant part of Deut. 27 in full.

> "Keep all the commandment which I command you this day. And on the day you pass over the Jordan to the land which the Lord your God gives you, you shall set up large stones, and plaster them with plaster; and you shall write upon them all the words of this law, when you pass over to enter the land which the Lord your God gives you, a land flowing with milk and honey, as the Lord, the God of your fathers, has promised you. And when you have passed over the Jordan, you shall set up these stones, concerning which I command you this day, on Mount Ebal, and you shall plaster them with plaster. And there you shall build an altar to the Lord your God, an altar of stones; you shall lift up no iron tool upon them. You shall build an altar to the Lord your God of unhewn stones; and you shall offer burnt offerings on it to the Lord your God; and you shall sacrifice peace offerings, and shall eat there; and you shall rejoice before the Lord your God. And you shall write upon the stones all the words of this law very plainly."

> (27:1*b*–8)

There can be no doubt of the close relationship between the beginnning of Deut. 27 and the end of Josh. 8. They share a number of distinctive expressions like the unhewn stones on which no iron tools have been used. Mention of Ebal and Gerizim is restricted to these two passages in the whole Bible except for the end of Deut. 11 to which we must shortly turn. Their relationship may be manifest; but it is far from simple.

The first concern of Deut. 27 is with stones which would be set up in Canaan after the crossing of the Jordan, on which at the same time a copy of the Mosaic Law would be inscribed (vv. 1–4). This memorial of the Law is then located on Mount Ebal and to it there is attached an altar (vv. 5–7). Verse 8 brings us back rather clumsily to the first theme: the Law on the stones should be very clearly written. Our passage in Joshua 8 starts with the altar of unhewn stones (vv. 30–31). When we read in verse 32 of Joshua writing on these stones a copy of the Law we must suppose that it was the altar which was so inscribed.

These traditions cannot be reconciled. This is further evidence that Israel's memory of her past was reshaped and refor-

mulated—that the Bible has no uniform account of how things
began. We have already met in Josh. 4 two accounts of stones set
up at or near Gilgal, after the crossing of the Jordan. These
commemorated that crossing, and we have no record of instructions concerning them from Moses. Deut. 27, however, has
Moses envisaging a stone memorial, though at Ebal, and celebrating the Law; and Josh. 8 brings inscribed stones into its
account of an altar built by Joshua at the latter place. To later
Israelite thinkers simple standing stones would have smacked of
some of the abhorrent cult places of their Canaanite neighbours
and predecessors. Just as such stones in Britain today, they would
have appeared to later Biblical traditions to be remnants of an
earlier religion. In the East many a Christian church is now a
mosque—and none is more famous than Constantine's great
basilica called Agia Sophia in Istanbul. The Christian mosaics
have been plastered over and texts from the Koran put in their
place. It looks as though something similar took place in the case
of Canaanite standing stones after the Israelite settlement and
these confused passages in Deuteronomy and Joshua reflect attempts to explain the presence of such objects in Israel's land.
(The end of Deut. 11 handles the problem rather differently:
taking liberties with geography, it actually locates Gilgal and
Ebal close together.)

   The altar is to be no mere symbol like the transjordanian one in
Josh. 22. It is to be the working altar for the two sorts of animal
sacrifice which ancient Israel knew. First mentioned are the
whole burnt offerings or holocausts which as the name suggests
were offered up to God by being burnt in their entirety. In the
second sort of sacrifice the slaughtered animal was divided: part
being offered to God with a due portion for the priest, and part
being a relatively rare non-vegetable meal for the worshipper and
his family and friends. Sacrifice was a celebration.

   Our section concludes with Joshua carrying out the instructions
in the second half of Deut. 27 with a public reading of Moses'
teaching. His audience is divided into two groups symbolizing the
choice between obedience and disobedience, symbolizing the
divine blessing and curse that would follow the nation's choice.

The ancient city of Shechem is not mentioned by name, and will not be named till Josh. 24 and Judg. 9. It figures in the Abraham traditions (Gen. 12) as a place with sacred associations. It is its position in a yoke-shaped pass between the peaks of Gerizim to the south and Ebal to the north that gives it its very name: "shoulder" in Hebrew. It is appropriate that blessing belongs to Gerizim in the south which in Hebrew is also the right-hand side (directions are worked out from the rising of the sun in the east), and that curse is associated with Ebal on the sinister left. Indeed a visitor to modern Nablus may notice that because of different geological structure, the southern hill has a more fruitful pleasant aspect while the northern is more bleak and forbidding. All the more surprising that the altar should have been on sinister Ebal. Or was it?

The present shrine of the Samaritans is on Mount Gerizim and we know that that has been true since at least more than a century before Jesus. It was towards Gerizim in the south that Jesus and the Samaritan woman were looking from the well of Jacob just outside Sychar (John 4) when the woman said to Jesus, "Our fathers worshiped on this mountain". In the Samaritan version of Deut. 27 it is for Mount Gerizim that Moses ordains the altar. A Samaritan alteration of Jewish tradition, or a Jewish alteration of Samaritan tradition? ·

Remembering the conclusion of our last section we must record again that our forefathers in the Jewish Christian tradition were more concerned with how their record of the past related to their own present with its tensions and disputes than with the straight facts of that past. It is rather like Shakespeare's "historical" themes. His *Julius Caesar* and his *Macbeth* have more to do with Tudor England than with ancient Rome or medieval Scotland.

HEWERS OF WOOD AND DRAWERS OF WATER

Joshua 9:1–27

[1]When all the kings who were beyond the Jordan in the hill country and in the lowland all along the coast of the Great Sea toward

Lebanon, the Hittites, the Amorites, the Canaanites, the Perizzites, the Hivites, and the Jebusites, heard of this, ²they gathered together with one accord to fight Joshua and Israel.

³But when the inhabitants of Gibeon heard what Joshua had done to Jericho and to Ai, ⁴they on their part acted with cunning, and went and made ready provisions, and took worn-out sacks upon their asses, and wineskins, worn-out and torn and mended, ⁵with worn-out, patched sandals on their feet, and worn-out clothes; and all their provisions were dry and mouldy. ⁶And they went to Joshua in the camp at Gilgal, and said to him and to the men of Israel, "We have come from a far country; so now make a covenant with us." ⁷But the men of Israel said to the Hivites, "Perhaps you live among us; then how can we make a covenant with you?" ⁸They said to Joshua, "We are your servants." And Joshua said to them, "Who are you? And where do you come from?" ⁹They said to him, "From a very far country your servants have come, because of the name of the Lord your God; for we have heard a report of him, and all that he did in Egypt, ¹⁰and all that he did to the two kings of the Amorites who were beyond the Jordan, Sihon the king of Heshbon, and Og king of Bashan, who dwelt in Ashtaroth. ¹¹And our elders and all the inhabitants of our country said to us, 'Take provisions in your hand for the journey, and go to meet them, and say to them, "We are your servants; come now, make a covenant with us."' ¹²Here is our bread; it was still warm when we took it from our houses as our food for the journey, on the day we set forth to come to you, but now, behold, it is dry and mouldy; ¹³these wineskins were new when we filled them, and behold, they are burst; and these garments and shoes of ours are worn out from the very long journey." ¹⁴So the men partook of their provisions, and did not ask direction from the Lord. ¹⁵And Joshua made peace with them, and made a covenant with them, to let them live; and the leaders of the congregation swore to them.

¹⁶At the end of three days after they had made a covenant with them, they heard that they were their neighbours, and that they dwelt among them. ¹⁷And the people of Israel set out and reached their cities on the third day. Now their cities were Gibeon, Chephirah, Beeroth, and Kiriath-jearim. ¹⁸But the people of Israel did not kill them, because the leaders of the congregation had sworn to them by the Lord, the God of Israel. Then all the congregation murmured against the leaders. ¹⁹But all the leaders said to all the congregation, "We have sworn to them by the Lord, the God of Israel, and now we may not

touch them. [20]This we will do to them, and let them live, lest wrath be upon us, because of the oath which we swore to them." [21]And the leaders said to them, "Let them live." So they became hewers of wood and drawers of water for all the congregation, as the leaders had said of them.

[22]Joshua summoned them, and he said to them, "Why did you deceive us, saying, 'We are very far from you,' when you dwell among us? [23]Now therefore you are cursed, and some of you shall always be slaves, hewers of wood and drawers of water for the house of my God." [24]They answered Joshua, "Because it was told to your servants for a certainty that the Lord your God had commanded his servant Moses to give you all the land, and to destroy all the inhabitants of the land from before you; so we feared greatly for our lives because of you, and did this thing. [25]And now, behold, we are in your hand: do as it seems good and right in your sight to do to us." [26]So he did to them, and delivered them out of the hand of the people of Israel; and they did not kill them. [27]But Joshua made them that day hewers of wood and drawers of water for the congregation and for the altar of the Lord, to continue to this day, in the place which he should choose.

(i)

One of the most potent causes of instability in today's world is tension between internationally *recognized* independent states on the one hand, and nations or national movements which are actively *claiming* independent status on the other. Many countries are currently locked in struggle with a minority seeking independence; and most of us find our sympathies varying from case to case.

Closely related to this are the different attitudes shown in many countries to internal and external relationships. Most of us are more sympathetic to the "freedom fighter" struggling for justice against *another* regime than we are to "terrorists" and "rebels" who wantonly unsettle the peace *at home*. Many of Britain's "friends" abroad profess to be scandalized at the level of military presence in Northern Ireland. On the other hand people in Britain "know" that even foreigners generally well disposed to them do not understand. It is easier for the super-powers to press in international bodies for the liberation of people outside their control than to welcome dissent and freedom of expression within their own alliances.

And of course different attitudes at home and abroad are no new phenomenon. Israel's attitude to other peoples depended on their geographical location. The most eloquent expression of an open attitude to other people is to be found in the course of Solomon's long prayer at the dedication of the Temple.

> "Likewise when a foreigner, who is not of thy people Israel, comes from a far country for thy name's sake (for they shall hear of thy great name, and thy mighty hand, and of thy outstretched arm), when he comes and prays toward this house, hear thou in heaven thy dwelling place and do according to all for which the foreigner calls to thee; in order that all the peoples of the earth may know thy name and fear thee, as do thy people Israel, and that they may know that this house which I have built is called by thy name."

(1 Kings 8:41–43)

This is the case which the Gibeonites make. They claim (vv. 9 and 10) to be from a far country and to have been attracted by the reputation of Israel's God.

Unfortunately it was all a ruse. The Gibeonites lived only a little to the south-west of Bethel and Ai in the very heart of the promised land just north of Jerusalem. Unfortunately it *had* to be a ruse: for according to Deuteronomy and Joshua the non-Israelite peoples of the promised land had no rights except the right to be slaughtered to make way for the incomers.

(ii)

The difference between external and internal relations is made perfectly explicit in the rules for making war contained in Deut. 20. The general rule is stated first. If a besieged city accepted Israel's terms then its people would live but would do forced labour for Israel. If peace was not made on Israel's offered terms and the city had to be reduced, then the adult males would be killed but the women and children and belongings of the city would be enjoyed by Israel as proper spoil (vv. 10–14). The general rules continue in verses 19 and 20 with an injunction against felling the fruit trees around the town for timber for siege work.

These general rules are interrupted in verses 15 to 18 as follows:

> "Thus you shall do to all the cities which are very far from you, which are not cities of the nations here. But in the cities of these peoples that the Lord your God gives you for an inheritance, you shall save alive nothing that breathes..."

The people of the promised land were too dangerous to Israel *by their very presence*, by their different religious practices, for them to be offered terms of peace. As we have noted such attitudes still bedevil the Israel/Palestine problem.

(iii)

Gibeon reappears later in the Old Testament story. When David sought a divine explanation for a serious three-year famine he was told there was blood guilt on Saul and his house because he had put the Gibeonites to death: despite the earlier oath to spare them, "Saul had sought to slay them in his zeal for the people of Israel and Judah" (2 Sam. 21:2). When David asked the survivors what he should do for them to "bless the heritage of the Lord" he found them deferential but firm:

> The Gibeonites said to him, "It is not a matter of silver or gold between us and Saul or his house; neither is it for us to put any man to death in Israel." And he said, "What do you say that I shall do for you?" They said to the king, "The man who consumed us and planned to destroy us, so that we should have no place in all the territory of Israel, let seven of his sons be given to us, so that we may hang them up before the Lord at Gibeon on the mountain of the Lord." And the king said, "I will give them."

> (2 Sam. 21:4–6)

Their initial polite reply reminds us of Josh. 9:8 where even more briefly they elicit support saying, "We are your servants". Denial of any status is often a good springboard for a big request!

What is only hinted at in Joshua 9 and 2 Samuel 21 becomes

rather clearer in 1 Kings 3. It was at the great sanctuary at Gibeon that Solomon was accustomed to offer large-scale sacrifice. It was while visiting that sanctuary that he had his famous vision by night.

Joshua 9 concludes discreetly with Joshua making the Gibeonites "hewers of wood and drawers of water for the congregation and for the altar of the Lord, to continue to this day, in the place which he should choose" (v. 27). From the discussion with David and the practice of Solomon it appears that the chosen place was Gibeon itself. Was this the reason for the religious fears of some about making peace with the inhabitants of the land?

One of the differences between the monarchy of Saul and the following kingdom of David and Solomon was over policy to other people in Canaan. Saul was more exclusivist. David and Solomon aimed for integration. When the kingdoms first of Israel and then of Judah finally fell, one explanation given for the fall was too much mixing with alien religious tradition.

The fourth town of the Gibeonite confederacy (9:17) is Kiriath-jearim. It will be no accident that it was precisely there that the Ark was lodged for some twenty years between its recovery from the Philistines and its final arrival in David's Jerusalem (1 Sam. 7:1–2). Wheels within wheels within wheels!

WHEN THE SUN STOOD STILL

Joshua 10:1–15

[1]When Adoni-zedek king of Jerusalem heard how Joshua had taken Ai, and had utterly destroyed it, doing to Ai and its king as he had done to Jericho and its king, and how the inhabitants of Gibeon had made peace with Israel and were among them, [2]he feared greatly, because Gibeon was a great city, like one of the royal cities, and because it was greater than Ai, and all its men were mighty. [3]So Adoni-zedek king of Jerusalem sent to Hoham king of Hebron, to Piram king of Jarmuth, to Japhia king of Lachish, and to Debir king of Eglon, saying, [4]"Come up to me, and help me, and let us smite Gibeon; for it has made peace with Joshua and with the people of Israel." [5]Then the five kings of the Amorites, the king of Jerusalem, the king of Hebron, the king of

Jarmuth, the king of Lachish, and the king of Eglon, gathered their forces, and went up with all their armies and encamped against Gibeon, and made war against it.

⁶And the men of Gibeon sent to Joshua at the camp in Gilgal, saying, "Do not relax your hand from your servants; come up to us quickly, and save us, and help us; for all the kings of the Amorites that dwell in the hill country are gathered against us." ⁷So Joshua went up from Gilgal, he and all the people of war with him, and all the mighty men of valour. ⁸And the Lord said to Joshua, "Do not fear them, for I have given them into your hands; there shall not a man of them stand before you." ⁹So Joshua came upon them suddenly, having marched up all night from Gilgal. ¹⁰And the Lord threw them into a panic before Israel, who slew them with a great slaughter at Gibeon, and chased them by the way of the ascent of Beth-horon, and smote them as far as Azekah and Makkedah. ¹¹And as they fled before Israel, while they were going down the ascent of Beth-horon, the Lord threw down great stones from heaven upon them as far as Azekah, and they died; there were more who died because of the hailstones than the men of Israel killed with the sword.

¹²Then spoke Joshua to the Lord in the day when the Lord gave the Amorites over to the men of Israel; and he said in the sight of Israel,

"Sun, stand thou still at Gibeon,

and thou Moon in the valley of Aijalon."

¹³And the sun stood still, and the moon stayed,

until the nation took vengeance on their enemies.

Is this not written in the Book of Jashar? The sun stayed in the midst of heaven, and did not hasten to go down for about a whole day. ¹⁴There has been no day like it before or since, when the Lord hearkened to the voice of a man; for the Lord fought for Israel.

¹⁵Then Joshua returned, and all Israel with him, to the camp at Gilgal.

We are given no further detailed information about joint action against Joshua and Israel taken by "all the kings who were beyond the Jordan in the hill country and in the lowland all along the coast of the Great Sea toward Lebanon" (9:1–2). Such harmony in practice over the whole country is perhaps improbable. Perhaps it was no more than a statement of intent. It is relatively easy to achieve a declaration from the European Community about the Middle East crisis or from the Organization of American States about the Falklands. However, joint action is another matter. This declaration encouraged the Gibeonites into their own devious plan and the success of their strategy coupled with the reports from Jericho and Ai provoked a more limited and more determined reaction.

Chapter 10 carries the action for the first time into the territory of Judah and its opening verse is the first explicit reference to Jerusalem in the whole Bible. Jerusalem, which like its partners was not just a city but a city state with dependent villages and lands round about, may have been neighbouring state to Gibeon and so most immediately threatened by its defection to the in-comers. Of the five confederates Jarmuth and Eglon (vv. 3, 5) are unknown outside this chapter and the account of Judah's territory in Joshua 15. But Hebron was David's capital before Jerusalem. Set in the heights of the hill country, in the heart of Judah, its Biblical associations go back to Abraham who purchased there a burial plot for his wife (Gen. 23). Lachish was prominent later as the second city of the kingdom of Judah. It lies on the edge of the hill country between Hebron and the coast; and it has been immortalized both in the magnificent Assyrian pictorial represen-tation of its capture in 701 B.C. and by Hebrew letters that came to light there a few decades ago which shed their own light on that campaign. It is widely supposed that Jerusalem too figures covertly in the Abraham traditions: when Melchiz*edek*, king of Salem and priest of God Most High, honoured victorious Abra-ham with an offering of bread and wine and a blessing (Gen. 14:18–20). The similarity in name of King Adoniz*edek* here in Joshua makes the link all the more plausible. The Hebrew word *tsedeq* appears in other significant Jerusalem names such as Zadok the priest and King Zedekiah.

Gibeon's status after her peace with Israel is described in Hebrew in the same phrase as is used of Rahab's household (6:25)—they "were among them" (10:1); they were in the midst of Israel. First and foremost this is a description of their diplo-matic status. Well might Jerusalem and its confederates express alarm, for the line from Jericho via Ai to Gibeon's four towns neatly bisects the country. Accordingly they muster all their troops and come in force against Gibeon.

Many of *our* questions about what transpires the *text* is not equipped to answer. Israel always seems to return to the base camp at Gilgal. The people of Gibeon dispatch a request there for protection from their new sworn overlords: "Come quickly and save us". This is a unique appeal in the pages of Joshua. We shall find that deliverance, salvation, and rescue are much more the stuff of the Book of Judges. In Joshua the land promised is transferred by force to new owners, but vulnerability is little expressed. However, Joshua is as good as his name ("Saviour") and brings his whole force from Gilgal.

Joshua responds to an urgent plea. What we read next is God's encouragement to him: "Do not fear them, for I have given them into your hands; there shall not a man of them stand before you." Had Joshua appealed to God after receiving Gibeon's request? Was God showing his support ahead of any appeal? Was God expressing quickly that he in fact had the initiative—*I* have given them into your hands? Joshua arrived suddenly after an overnight march. But it is God who is credited in the Hebrew of verse 10 with the slaying and chasing and smiting. And it is his heavenly forces (v. 11) which cause the larger number of casualties.

Verses 12 to 14 seem to be a separate piece of information. They read rather like an appendix, but what they report is far from peripheral. In fact it is rather like an alternative account. In verse 11 God's weapons are great hailstones; in verses 12–14, a stopping of sun and moon in their tracks. Of course it is possible to harmonize and rationalize. The violent hailstorm will have darkened the sky. Sometimes in a grey sky the sun is visible only very palely and resembles the moon. Alternatively a solar eclipse may be the natural event that lies behind these traditions. There is plenty of evidence from around the world of the awe and even panic caused by a darkening of the sun in daytime—especially since eclipses are natural events of such rarity. The panic and wonder regularly led pre-scientific man to exaggerate grossly the length of the eclipse.

However, it is safest to return to our earlier suggestion that we are dealing here with alternative memories of divine action, and this approach is even more to be recommended if I am right in supposing that the Bible prefers yet a third memory of how God acted at Gibeon. Isaiah offers a warning (28:21) that God who had proved his power at Gibeon and at Perazim, both times on behalf of his people, could turn that power against them in punishment. Perazim refers to an incident in one of David's campaigns (2 Sam. 5). Only in Joshua 10 does Gibeon figure in the Bible's military history and the interesting thing about Isaiah 28:21 is that the Hebrew verb which the RSV translates "will be wroth"more strictly means "will shudder" or "will quake". The third image of divine intervention at Gibeon is the earthquake.

Hail, ash, eclipse, earthquake: common to all three is the memory that divine forces were mightily engaged at Gibeon. The end of verse 14 sums it up as "the Lord fought for Israel." After the story of Jericho close to Gilgal it is surely not a coincidence that this second account of direct divine intervention is also associated with a shrine centre.

MOPPING UP IN THE SOUTH

Joshua 10:16–43

[16]These five kings fled, and hid themselves in the cave at Makkedah. [17]And it was told Joshua, "The five kings have been found, hidden in the cave at Makkedah." [18]And Joshua said, "Roll great stones against the mouth of the cave, and set men by it to guard them; [19]but do not stay there yourselves, pursue your enemies, fall upon their rear, do not let them enter their cities; for the Lord your God has given them into your hand." [20]When Joshua and the men of Israel had finished slaying them with a very great slaughter, until they were wiped out, and when the remnant which remained of them had entered into the fortified cities, [21]all the people returned safe to Joshua in the camp at Makkedah; not a man moved his tongue against any of the people of Israel.

[22]Then Joshua said, "Open the mouth of the cave, and bring those five kings out to me from the cave." [23]And they did so, and brought those five kings out to him from the cave, the king of Jerusalem, the king of Hebron, the king of Jarmuth, the king of Lachish, and the king of Eglon. [24]And when they brought those kings out to Joshua, Joshua summoned all the men of Israel, and said to the chiefs of the men of

war who had gone with him, "Come near, put your feet upon the necks of these kings." Then they came near, and put their feet on their necks. ²⁵And Joshua said to them, "Do not be afraid or dismayed; be strong and of good courage; for thus the Lord will do to all your enemies against whom you fight." ²⁶And afterward Joshua smote them and put them to death, and he hung them on five trees. And they hung upon the trees until evening; ²⁷but at the time of the going down of the sun, Joshua commanded, and they took them down from the trees, and threw them into the cave where they had hidden themselves, and they set great stones against the mouth of the cave, which remain to this very day.

²⁸And Joshua took Makkedah on that day, and smote it and its king with the edge of the sword; he utterly destroyed every person in it, he left none remaining; and he did to the king of Makkedah as he had done to the king of Jericho.

²⁹Then Joshua passed on from Makkedah, and all Israel with him, to Libnah, and fought against Libnah; ³⁰and the Lord gave it also and its king into the hand of Israel; and he smote it with the edge of the sword, and every person in it; he left none remaining in it; and he did to its king as he had done to the king of Jericho.

³¹And Joshua passed on from Libnah, and all Israel with him, to Lachish, and laid seige to it, and assaulted it: ³²and the Lord gave Lachish into the hand of Israel, and he took it on the second day, and smote it with the edge of the sword, and every person in it, as he had done to Libnah.

³³Then Horam king of Gezer came up to help Lachish; and Joshua smote him and his people, until he left none remaining.

³⁴And Joshua passed on with all Israel from Lachish to Eglon; and they laid seige to it, and assaulted it; ³⁵and they took it on that day, and smote it with the edge of the sword; and every person in it he utterly destroyed that day, as he had done to Lachish.

³⁶Then Joshua went up with all Israel from Eglon to Hebron; and they assaulted it, ³⁷and took it, and smote it with the edge of the sword, and its king and its towns, and every person in it; he left none remaining, as he had done to Eglon, and utterly destroyed it with every person in it.

³⁸Then Joshua, with all Israel, turned back to Debir and assaulted it, ³⁹and he took it with its king and all its towns; and they smote them with the edge of the sword, and utterly destroyed every person in it; he left none remaining; as he had done to Hebron and to Libnah and its king, so he did to Debir and to its king.

⁴⁰So Joshua defeated the whole land, the hill country and the Negeb and the lowland and the slopes, and all their kings; he left none remaining, but utterly destroyed all that breathed, as the Lord God of Israel commanded. ⁴¹And Joshua defeated them from Kadesh-barnea to Gaza, and all the country of Goshen, as far as Gibeon. ⁴²And Joshua took all these kings and their land at one time, because the Lord God of Israel fought for Israel. ⁴³Then Joshua returned, and all Israel with him, to the camp at Gilgal.

We return immediately to more matter-of-fact military history. The leaders of the southern coalition also lead their flight—doubtless on the principle beloved of leaders that they should live to fight another day. Incidentally we should ignore the identical verses 15 and 43. They are absent from some ancient versions of the book; and verse 15 in particular manifestly interrupts continuous action from the rout of Gibeon to its triple consequences.

(i)

In the case of all of the ignominious huddle of kings in the cave Joshua first took only "holding action". His immediate concern was the complete destruction of the opposition forces and in particular to prevent them returning to their own walled cities. Verse 20 reads rather oddly in the RSV translation—if their opponents were entirely wiped out then there could hardly have been a remnant to escape. The Hebrew is certainly ambiguous; but it gives me the impression that Israel completed all it could immediately after the battle and only when no more could be done (because any enemies still alive were now behind walls) did they return to their chief outside Makkedah. They returned "safe" (v. 21)—or more literally "in peace"; and that peace was so complete that it extended even to rhetoric and the war of words— "not a man *sharpened* his tongue against any of the people of Israel".

(ii)

Joshua could now turn his attention to the five spent kings in the cave. He encouraged his leaders and men to abuse them presumably to help remove any residual fear of the inhabitants of the land. To this end he repeated to his men God's opening assurance to himself (1:6)—"Be strong and of good courage". There may be another deliberate aspect to this disgrace of the five kings. That same divine introduction to the book had promised Joshua "every place that the sole of Israel's foot will tread upon". Here we have a particularly telling "ritual" of power and control. The main theme of these chapters in Joshua may be the hand over to new Israelite tenants of the divine estates in Canaan which involved forceful ejection of their predecessors. But a subsidiary theme is surely the hopeless inadequacy of kingship. Each *king*'s fate is reported along with the disaster to his people and the attention to this detail is so meticulous that it must have a significance, even although that it not spelt out to us. After this abuse the kings were executed, strung up on five trees and, like the king of Ai, duly buried by sunset. Their hiding place became in turn their tomb and, as with Ai, the tradition of their burial associated with the cave was already an ancient one when our Book of Joshua was written.

(iii)

The follow-up to the battle at Gibeon now enters its third phase (vv. 28–39). However, it is not a simple matter of visiting each of the five confederate towns in turn. Makkedah close to which the five kings had taken refuge was the first to be reduced, and then its king suffered the fate of the king of Jericho (although in fact that fate was never described in chapter 6). And the same happened to not far distant Libnah. Then Joshua turns to three further confederates. Lachish is taken in two days and put to the sword and the helping force from Gezer is totally destroyed along with Horam, Gezer's king (it is a suprise to find a thriving Gezer a little later in the book—16:10). Eglon and Hebron who enjoy no outside support apparently fall more quickly. Joshua and all Israel then turn back to Debir and it too suffers the standard fate. Talk of Debir after Hebron is not surprising in itself. They are paired again in 15:13–19. Rather more surprising is that the attentive reader will already have noticed the name Debir in chapter 10 (in v. 3). There Debir is *king* of confederate Eglon.

But the main surprise is that Jerusalem, closer both to Gibeon and to Gilgal than any of the other towns dealt with—Jerusalem, whose king Adonizedek had set up the confederacy in the first place, is bypassed without comment. It escapes the punitive round-up. It does not share its king's fate. In fact it is an unadmitted exception to the omnibus claim of verses 40 and 41, where we learn that Joshua captured all of the later Judah, both its hill country and the southern Negeb wilderness, from Gibeon itself south to Kadesh which is still today close to the Egyptian/Israeli frontier.

Joshua's ability to reduce all these small states in a single campaign is conventionally and dutifully ascribed to divine help in verse 42. But the talk in this verse of God fighting for Israel appears to be more a religious commonplace than an awed testimony to his spectacular help according to verses 12 to 14.

CONQUEST COMPLETE

Joshua 11:1–12:24

¹When Jabin king of Hazor heard of this, he sent to Jobab king of Madon, and to the king of Shimron, and to the king of Achshaph, ²and to the kings who were in the northern hill country, and in the Arabah south of Chinneroth, and in the lowland, and in Naphoth-dor on the west, ³to the Canaanites in the east and the west, the Amorites, the Hittites, the Perizzites, and the Jebusites in the hill country, and the Hivites under Hermon in the land of Mizpah. ⁴And they came out, with all their troops, a great host, in number like the sand that is upon the seashore, with very many horses and chariots. ⁵And all these kings joined their forces, and came and encamped together at the waters of Merom, to fight with Israel.

⁶And the Lord said to Joshua, "Do not be afraid of them, for tomorrow at this time I will give over all of them, slain, to Israel; you shall hamstring their horses, and burn their chariots with fire." ⁷So Joshua came suddenly upon them with all his people of war, by the waters of Merom, and fell upon them. ⁸And the Lord gave them into the hand of Israel, who smote them and chased them as far as Great Sidon and Misrephoth-maim, and eastward as far as the valley of

Mizpeh; and they smote them, until they left none remaining. ⁹And Joshua did to them as the Lord bade him; he hamstrung their horses, and burned their chariots with fire.

¹⁰And Joshua turned back at that time, and took Hazor, and smote its king with the sword; for Hazor formerly was the head of all those kingdoms. ¹¹And they put to the sword all who were in it, utterly destroying them; there was none left that breathed, and he burned Hazor with fire. ¹²And all the cities of those kings, and all their kings, Joshua took, and smote them with the edge of the sword, utterly destroying them, as Moses the servant of the Lord had commanded. ¹³But none of the cities that stood on mounds did Israel burn, except Hazor only; that Joshua burned. ¹⁴And all the spoil of these cities and the cattle, the people of Israel took for their booty; but every man they smote with the edge of the sword, until they had destroyed them, and they did not leave any that breathed. ¹⁵As the Lord had commanded Moses his servant, so Moses commanded Joshua, and so Joshua did; he left nothing undone of all that the Lord had commanded Moses.

¹⁶So Joshua took all that land, the hill country and all the Negeb and all the land of Goshen and the lowland and the Arabah and the hill country of Israel and its lowland ¹⁷from Mount Halak, that rises toward Seir, as far as Baalgad in the valley of Lebanon below Mount Hermon. And he took all their kings, and smote them, and put them to death. ¹⁸Joshua made war a long time with all those kings. ¹⁹There was not a city that made peace with the people of Israel, except the Hivites, the inhabitants of Gibeon; they took all in battle. ²⁰For it was the Lord's doing to harden their hearts that they should come against Israel in battle, in order that they should be utterly destroyed, and should receive no mercy but be exterminated, as the Lord commanded Moses.

²¹And Joshua came at that time, and wiped out the Anakim from the hill country, from Hebron, from Debir, from Anab, and from all the hill country of Judah, and from all the hill country of Israel; Joshua utterly destroyed them with their cities. ²²There was none of the Anakim left in the land of the people of Israel; only in Gaza, in Gath, and in Ashdod, did some remain. ²³So Joshua took the whole land, according to all that the Lord had spoken to Moses; and Joshua gave it for an inheritance to Israel according to their tribal allotments. And the land had rest from war.

¹Now these are the kings of the land, whom the people of Israel defeated, and took possession of their land beyond the Jordan toward the sunrising, from the valley of the Arnon to Mount Hermon, with all

the Arabah eastward: ²Sihon king of the Amorites who dwelt at Heshbon, and ruled from Aroer, which is on the edge of the valley of the Arnon, and from the middle of the valley as far as the river Jabbok, the boundary of the Ammonites, that is, half of Gilead, ³and the Arabah to the Sea of Chinneroth eastward, and in the direction of Bethjeshimoth, to the sea of the Arabah, the Salt Sea, southward to the foot of the slopes of Pisgah; ⁴and Og king of Bashan, one of the remnant of the Rephaim, who dwelt at Ashtaroth and at Edrei ⁵and ruled over Mount Hermon and Salecah and all Bashan to the boundary of the Geshurites and the Maacathites, and over half of Gilead to the boundary of Sihon king of Heshbon. ⁶Moses, the servant of the Lord, and the people of Israel defeated them; and Moses the servant of the Lord gave their land for a possession to the Reubenites and the Gadites and the half-tribe of Manasseh.

⁷And these are the kings of the land whom Joshua and the people of Israel defeated on the west side of the Jordan, from Baalgad in the valley of Lebanon to Mount Halak, that rises toward Seir (and Joshua gave their land to the tribes of Israel as a possession according to their allotments, ⁸in the hill country, in the lowland, in the Arabah, in the slopes, in the wilderness, and in the Negeb, the land of the Hittites, the Amorites, the Canaanites, the Perizzites, the Hivites, and the Jebusites): ⁹the king of Jericho, one; the king of Ai, which is beside Bethel, one; ¹⁰the king of Jerusalem, one; the king of Hebron, one; ¹¹the king of Jarmuth, one; the king of Lachish, one; ¹²the king of Eglon, one; the king of Gezer, one; ¹³the king of Debir, one; the king of Geder, one; ¹⁴the king of Hormah, one; the king of Arad,one; ¹⁵the king of Libnah, one; the king of Adullam, one; ¹⁶the king of Makkedah, one; the king of Bethel, one; ¹⁷the king of Tappuah, one; the king of Hepher, one; ¹⁸the king of Aphek, one; the king of Lasharon, one; ¹⁹the king of Madon, one; the king of Hazor, one; ²⁰the king of Shimron-meron, one; the king of Achshaph, one; ²¹the king of Taanach, one; the king of Megiddo, one; ²²the king of Kedesh, one; the king of Jokneam in Carmel, one; ²³the king of Dor in Naphathdor, one; the king of Goiim in Galilee, one; ²⁴the king of Tirzah, one: in all, thirty-one kings.

(i)

At first hearing the opening of Joshua 11 makes a rather similar impression to the opening of chapter 10. Both start with the initiative of an apparently prominent king, here Jabin king of

Hazor, there Adonizedek, king of Jerusalem. In each case reports of Joshua's prowess prompt the king in question to organize an anti-Israelite alliance. But to the attentive listener these two stories have a somewhat different ring. While Hazor, like Jerusalem, Lachish and Eglon, will reappear in Biblical history, the towns to which Jabin sends are known only in the town lists of Joshua 12 and 19. Only one of the kings is named (contrast 10:3), and after mention of three minor places the report turns to generalities.

Hazor lies well north of the Sea of Galilee about three miles west of the Jordan and almost as far north as the southern border of modern Lebanon. Near it at the Jordan is an ancient ford where until 1948 the main highway from Jerusalem to Damascus crossed a narrow bridge with the romantic name "Daughters of Jacob". From here Jabin's emissaries went beyond the south end of the Sea of Galilee (Chinneroth, v. 2) and south of modern Haifa on the Mediterranean coast (Naphoth-dor, v. 2). For good measure the stereotyped list of Canaanites, Amorites, Hittites, Perizites and even the Jebusites (who belong in Jerusalem) and Hivites are given a mention. As a result Israel was faced by a vast force as numerous as the grains of sand by the sea!

Despite this multitude Joshua is again given the divine exhortation not to be afraid. What took place at the waters of Merom is impossible to reconstruct. The site of the battle is just west of the present hilltop town of Safad, long important for its links with Jewish mysticism and the Cabbala—in fact about eight miles west of Hazor. The all too brief report (11:6–9) talks of Israel's sudden arrival on the scene and a punitive chase of her enemies northwestwards towards what is now the Lebanese coast and eastwards to the upper Jordan valley. Again no prisoners were taken. This short report is bracketed by a double mention of the only novel element in this story (apart of course from the names). Along with his promise to deliver the enemy into Joshua's hands (v. 6), God instructs him to destroy the Canaanite armaments, by disabling the horses and burning the war chariots, and this Joshua did (v. 9). At first reading this destruction of the superior Canaanite weaponry is to follow the victory and perhaps this is what the report intends: Israel may have seen no need for new technology. Yet the very fact of the double mention within the confines of a short story, coupled with the habit of Biblical narrators not to tell their stories in what we would regard as strict chronological order, has led some readers of Joshua 11 to another account of the matter. The disabling of the armaments was not a consequence of the victory but its cause. The divine offer of victory (v. 6) was expressed concretely in a plan. Part of Israel's surprise arrival (v. 7) had involved her covert disabling of the chariotry. This provoked panic and headlong flight; and for a modern middle eastern comparison, we might compare Israel's surprise disablement of her neighbours' air forces at the beginning of the 1967 Six Day War. That this was the key to the whole victory is then underscored in verse 9. The divine contribution to this battle becomes the brilliant tactical insight communicated to General Joshua.

(ii)

Hazor and its allied cities meet the usual fate. Populations are put to the sword, each with its king, and their property taken as spoil. However, Hazor alone is burned. The other towns which like it were built on the mounds of previous cities were left standing.

One suspects that an early version of Joshua's campaigns in Canaan once ended with verse 15: "As the Lord had commanded Moses his servant, so Moses commanded Joshua, and so Joshua did; he left nothing undone of all that the Lord commanded Moses." The next five verses make a series of general comments on the whole campaign. First of all, and in terms that resemble the end of chapter 10, the *geographical* extent of Israel's success is made plain: from the Egyptian border to Mount Hermon (at which the modern frontiers of Israel, Lebanon and Syria meet). Again the execution of the kings of the whole region is given special mention. But the next comment comes as a surprise. After ten chapters which have reported unqualified victory in four strategically placed campaigns in which first the centre of the country was secured and then large coalitions slashed in north and south, we do not expect the comment (v. 18): "Joshua made war *a long time* with all those kings." If not easier, it had at least appeared swifter. There is an ambivalence in the Book of Joshua over just how complete Israel's conquest was. We have touched on the matter before and will have to discuss it again. In Judges 2 and 3 we shall find two *divine* reasons to justify a less than complete conquest.

"IT WAS THE LORD'S DOING"

Joshua 11:1–12:24 (*cont'd*)

The last of the general remarks in 11:16–20 deserves a little more attention. The religious issue at stake is partly camouflaged by a very familiar but (I think) rather tendentious translation.

(i)

We are all familiar with the Old Testament God who hardened the heart of Pharaoh so that he persistently refused Moses' repeated requests to "Let my people go"; but there is an unnecessary and unfair edge to the polemic here. It reminds me of that irregular English verb about which we joke, which goes like this: I am *firm*—you are *obstinate*—he or she is *pig-headed*. About a third party we tend to be gratuitously insulting and especially when that third party is an enemy of our cause. The Hebrew verb *hazaq* is rather more open and much more interesting. We can detect its flavour in one or two other Biblical texts before returning to Exodus and Joshua. A good beginning is in the Book of Job near the start of Eliphaz's opening speech:

> "Behold, you have instructed many,
>   and *you have strengthened* the weak hands.
> Your words have upheld him who was stumbling,
>   and you have made firm the feeble knees."

(Job 4:3–4)

The verb in question is used in a similarly positive sense in Isaiah 35:

Strengthen the weak hands,
   and make firm the feeble knees.
Say to those who are of a fearful heart,
   "Be strong, fear not!"

(Isaiah 35:3–4)

Similarly Ezekiel pictures God promising to replace the existing shepherd of Israel:

"I myself will be the shepherd of my sheep, and I will make them lie down, says the Lord God. I will seek the lost, and I will bring back the strayed, and I will bind up the crippled, and I will *strengthen* the weak, and the fat and the strong I will watch over; I will feed them in justice."
(Ezekiel 34:15–16)

In all of these cases the word means to boost morale, to give encouragement. Support can be given to one party and denied to another, as we see in Ezekiel 30:24:

And *I will strengthen* the arms of the king of Babylon, and put my sword in his hand; but I will break the arms of Pharaoh, and he will groan before him like a man mortally wounded.

All this said, we do better justice both to Pharaoh of the Exodus and to this Hebrew word if we talk of God boosting his morale and giving him encouragment not to let Israel go. "Hard-hearted", like "stiff-necked", has bad overtones in modern English. In fact on their own, both "hard" and "stiff" have unfortunate associations. Yet in a military context we do speak positively of "hardening young recruits" and of "stiffening resolve".

The Egyptian monarch whom Moses confronted may well have been personally "hard-hearted" but that was not *God's* contribution according to the Hebrew text of the Book of Exodus. It is most clearly in Exodus 14 that what I have been saying makes better sense as a text. Israel is already moving out of Egypt. The issue is not whether to allow them but whether to pursue them.

When the king of Egypt was told that the people had fled, the mind of Pharaoh and his servants was changed toward the people, and they said, "What is this we have done, that we have let Israel go from serving us?" So he made ready his chariot and took his army with him, and took six hundred picked chariots and all the other chariots of Egypt with officers over all of them. And the Lord *stiffened the resolve* of Pharaoh king of Egypt and he pursued the people of Israel as they went forth defiantly.

(14:5–8)

Similarly,

"Lift up your rod, and stretch out your hand over the sea and divide it, that the people of Israel may go on dry ground through the sea. And I will *stiffen the resolve* of the Egyptians, so that they shall go in after them, and I will get glory over Pharaoh and all his host, his chariots, and his horsemen."
(14:16–17)

(ii)

To return to where we started, this is what Joshua 11:20 is also saying. It was God's doing to encourage, to boost the resolve of Canaan's kings to oppose Israel. And it may help to bring the theological issue into focus if I say that the word we have been discussing in this verse, in Exodus, in Job, Isaiah and Ezekiel, is the same as the word used of Joshua in Josh. 1 where in four verses (6, 7, 9, 18) he is instructed by God to "be strong and of good courage". God is doing the same, not something different, to both sides. Joshua and the kings of Canaan alike are egged on—in order that a battle will take place which he will win and they will lose.

Many will find this notion intolerable. We can cope with notions of people paying the price of their mistakes or falling victim to their weaknesses. We are not too squeamish over the idea of God helping *us* and not *them*. But that God should help us by helping them, that they should fall victim to their God-given strengths is a different matter. Divine even-handedness would be one thing; but this smacks rather of manipulation and puppetry.

The reader must decide whether he is in the hands here of a reliable or a cynical narrator. Believers must consider whether God's concerns are only other-worldly and how far God is a realistic politician (with all that that involves).

We might suppose that something is being said here about the nature of the contest, about the quality of the struggle, for the land of Canaan. The story-teller may want to suggest that there was high motivation and even religious fanaticism on both sides. He draws attention to this by stating that both sides were encouraged by God. The problem we are noting might also result from an attempt to be consistent. Israel had been enthused by Yahweh and the Canaanites by their own gods. However, a later and more reflective Biblical story-teller who knew that God was One and undivided was bound to attribute *all* divine motivation to the *one* God.

The religious difficulties caused by this passage cannot just be talked into going away. However, it may help to suggest that this is not the main story-teller but a later commentator at work. We have already seen that 11:15 makes a good conclusion. Then there are other tensions too between verses 16–20 and earlier parts of the book. Gibeon's peace-making is presented as deserving some praise (11:19), while in chapter 9 her duplicity is condemned as is Israel's faithlessness in not seeking divine guidance. All the others are said to have been encouraged by God to come out against Israel and be destroyed, yet chapter 6 has depicted a terrified Jericho towering behind its walls and locked gates. All in all, as we have noticed before, the Book of Joshua does not offer us one straightforward account of what happened in the conquest.

Chapter 11 ends with Joshua's annihilation of the remnants of the Anakim, one of two or three clans of giants that people Israel's memories of her early past. We will meet them again in Joshua and they appear also in the first two chapters of Deuteronomy.

Chapter 12 rounds off the first half of the Book of Joshua with a summary of Israel's conquests on both sides of the Jordan. The first 6 verses recall the opening 3 chapters of Deuteronomy describing the extent of Israel's holdings gained by Moses in Transjordan—largely the territories of Sihon, king of Heshbon and Og, king of Bashan. The remaining eighteen verses offer less detailed territorial description of Israel west of the Jordan (vv. 7–8) and list instead about thirty defeated cities, states and their kings, most of whom have not explicitly figured in the earlier eleven chapters (vv. 9–24). We have already noted the way the Book of Joshua insists on the fate of Canaan's kings. This may be a hint that Israel can do well without kings, and indeed might herself be better without one.

DEVELOPING THE LAND—FIRST PRINCIPLES

Joshua 13:1–14:5

¹Now Joshua was old and advanced in years; and the Lord said to him, "You are old and advanced in years, and there remains yet very much land to be possessed. ²This is the land that yet remains: all the regions of the Philistines, and all those of the Geshurites ³(from the Shihor, which is east of Egypt, northward to the boundary of Ekron, it is reckoned as Canaanite; there are five rulers of the Philistines, those of Gaza, Ashdod, Ashkelon, Gath, and Ekron), and those of the Avvim, ⁴in the south, all the land of the Canaanites, and Me-arah which belongs to the Sidonians, to Aphek, to the boundary of the Amorites, ⁵and the land of the Gebalites, and all Lebanon, toward the sunrising, from Baal-gad below Mount Hermon to the entrance of Hamath, ⁶all the inhabitants of the hill country from Lebanon to Misrephoth-maim, even all the Sidonians. I will myself drive them out from before the people of Israel; only allot the land to Israel for an inheritance, as I have commanded you. ⁷Now therefore divide this land for an inheritance to the nine tribes and half the tribe of Manasseh."

⁸With the other half of the tribe of Manasseh the Reubenites and the Gadites received their inheritance, which Moses gave them, beyond the Jordan eastward, as Moses the servant of the Lord gave them: ⁹from Aroer, which is on the edge of the valley of the Arnon, and the city that is in the middle of the valley, and all the tableland of Medeba as far as Dibon; ¹⁰and all the cities of Sihon king of the Amorites, who reigned in Heshbon, as far as the boundary of the Ammonites; ¹¹and Gilead, and the region of the Geshurites and Ma-acathites, and all Mount Hermon, and all Bashan to Salecah; ¹²all the kingdom of Og in Bashan, who reigned in Ashtaroth and in Edre-i (he alone was left of the remnant of the Rephaim); these Moses had defeated and driven out. ¹³Yet the people of Israel did not drive out the Geshurites or the Ma-acathites; but Geshur and Maacath dwell in the midst of Israel to this day.

¹⁴To the tribe of Levi alone Moses gave no inheritance; the offerings by fire to the Lord God of Israel are their inheritance, as he said to him.

¹⁵And Moses gave an inheritance to the tribe of the Reubenites according to their families. ¹⁶So their territory was from Aroer, which is on the edge of the valley of the Arnon, and the city that is in the middle of the valley, and all the tableland by Medeba; ¹⁷with Heshbon, and all its cities that are in the tableland; Dibon, and Bamoth-baal, and Beth-baal-meon, ¹⁸and Jahaz, and Kedemoth, and Mepha-ath, ¹⁹and Kiriathaim, and Sibmah, and Zereth-shahar on the hill of the valley, ²⁰and Beth-peor, and the slopes of Pisgah, and Beth-jeshimoth, ²¹that is, all the cities of the tableland, and all the kingdom of Sihon king of the Amorites, who reigned in Heshbon, whom Moses defeated with the leaders of Midian, Evi and Rekem and Zur and Hur and Reba, the princes of Sihon, who dwelt in the land. ²²Balaam also, the son of Beor, the soothsayer, the people of Israel killed with the sword among the rest of their slain. ²³And the border of the people of Reuben was the Jordan as a boundary. This was the inheritance of the Reubenites, according to their families with their cities and villages.

²⁴And Moses gave an inheritance also to the tribe of the Gadites, according to their families. ²⁵Their territory was Jazer, and all the cities of Gilead, and half the land of the Ammonites, to Aroer, which is east of Rabbah, ²⁶and from Heshbon to Ramath-mizpeh and Betonim, and from Mahanaim to the territory of Debir, ²⁷and in the valley Beth-haram, Beth-nimrah, Succoth, and Zaphon, the rest of the kingdom of Sihon king of Heshbon, having the Jordan as a boundary, to the lower end of the Sea of Chinnereth, eastward beyond the Jordan. ²⁸This is the inheritance of the Gadites according to their families, with their cities and villages.

²⁹And Moses gave an inheritance to the half-tribe of Manasseh; it was allotted to the half-tribe of the Manassites according to their families. ³⁰Their region extended from Mahanaim, through all Bashan, the whole kingdom of Og king of Bashan, and all the towns of Jair, which are in Bashan, sixty cities, ³¹and half Gilead, and Ash-taroth, and Edre-i, the cities of the kingdom of Og in Bashan; these were allotted to the people of Machir the son of Manasseh for the half of the Machirites according to their families.

³²These are the inheritances which Moses distributed in the plains of Moab, beyond the Jordan east of Jericho. ³³But to the tribe of Levi Moses gave no inheritance; the Lord God of Israel is their inheritance, as he said to them.

¹And these are the inheritances which the people of Israel received in the land of Canaan, which Eleazar the priest, and Joshua the son of Nun, and the heads of the fathers' houses of the tribes of the people of Israel distributed to them. ²Their inheritance was by lot, as the Lord had commanded Moses for the nine and one-half tribes. ³For Moses had given an inheritance to the two and one-half tribes beyond the Jordan; but to the Levites he gave no inheritance among them. ⁴For the people of Joseph were two tribes, Manasseh and Ephraim; and no portion was given to the Levites in the land, but only cities to dwell in, with their pasture lands for their cattle and their substance. ⁵The people of Israel did as the Lord commanded Moses; they allotted the land.

(i)

It is not easy to systematize the laws of property in Biblical Israel. And of course any time we discuss the people of the Old Testament we are talking about a people in changing conditions and over a long time. We are dealing in the middle period with the relatively settled conditions of two neighbouring and more or less independent monarchies. Earlier we have the picture of the settlement and consolidation of a much less centralized and more tribally based people. Then the Jews of the later Biblical period are either spread thinly over much of the Middle East or resident in a tiny rump of the old Judea round about Jerusalem, in a small administrative section of a very extended empire. Attitudes to ownership and property changed accordingly.

The texture is certainly very varied. However, two threads do reappear regularly. The one is that there is a communal aspect to land ownership and the "commune" is the wider family or clan. This is naturally obvious in the earliest period when the structure was tribal. However the later customary law too enjoined the wider family to come to the aid of any members in danger of forfeiting their land (we shall see a sample of this as we read the Book of Ruth).

The other constant thread showing through these next chapters runs in a different direction. Sometimes it seems to conflict with what I have just said, sometimes to highlight it. This is the view that the land is neither individual nor communal property, but all land belongs to God. He is the ultimate holder of the title-deeds and it is he who makes it available to his kindred people.

These are the leading ideas which control the second section of the Book of Joshua (chs. 13–19). It is not just God as God, but God as owner of the land, who takes the initiative and reminds Joshua of unfinished business. Or, perhaps better stated, part of being God of Israel was responsibility for the land of Israel. A large element in the conflict with local Canaanite religion was over proper title to the land. Baal's very name means Holder/Owner/Husband/Master.

(ii)

God prompts the ageing Joshua: "You are old and advanced in years, and there remains yet very much land to be possessed" (v. 1). The possession will be real but not absolute. God gives but without giving away. As the collect says of his grace, "It is neither diminished by his giving nor increased by his withholding". "Possession" to the people of Israel will mean something much more active than mere titular ownership. Josh. 13:7 talks of possession in terms of dividing the land for an inheritance or better dividing the land into (heritable) holdings. The land is to be farmed and worked.

I linked verses 1 and 7 together quite deliberately; but now I must explain why. It is widely acknowledged by scholars that the following chapters of Joshua have been subject to most complex development—to the extent that there is very little agreement over the main route through the material. The first draft seems to have been considerably expanded and frequently interrupted. Often too the interruptions themselves are interrupted and in the process some key ideas are modified. We have only to read a few words of chapter 13 before finding our first example.

The first draft (most of v. 1 then v. 7) followed the talk in chapters 1–12 of Joshua taking the whole land, by noting that full possession would mean dividing and getting on with the job. The rewrite in vv. 2–6 develops a minor theme which we have already explored, namely that Joshua did not in fact *complete* the military take-over of Canaan. And of course the phrase at issue is ambiguous. It can be differently interpreted both in Hebrew and in English. "Complete possession" can refer either to "having it all" or to "having it thoroughly". Then the arithmetic of the allocation has to be explained. The division is not by twelve, the number of the tribes, but by nine and a half; and so another interruption has to remind us that two and a half tribes were already settled in the east of the Jordan. Their territory is briefly sketched in vv. 8–12 (the next verse notes that there were exceptions and enclaves in the east too). Yet the arithmetic is still not clear. The Bible knows two main ways of counting the tribes of Israel to make twelve. One includes Levi and Joseph, the other excludes the Levites and makes up the number by reckoning Joseph as two: Ephraim and Manasseh. The second method holds in the Book of Joshua. The Levites do not require a land holding. Their business is with altars and sacred fire. Yet that job description too may represent yet another rethink in our text. Verse 14 is repeated in verse 33. Such repetition is common in the Bible to allow the reader to pick up the thread after a major interruption—and vv. 15–32 have held us up in order to say at much greater length what was said in vv. 8–12. The first draft of our text mentions the Transjordanians in passing, simply to note that they are already taken care of. That was not good enough for the later Biblical tradition. If the Book of Joshua was to have complete records of the western holdings of Israel then it had better contain a full account of the east as well, hence vv. 15–32. However, when Levi brings us back to the point again, it is striking that God himself is now said to be their holding. Levi has a stake in the divine.

The beginning of chapter 14 returns us to the main point. It sets us facing the direction in which the beginning of chapter 13 had tried to point us—the division of Canaan west of the Jordan. It is now specified that Joshua is to be assisted by a representative group. The job will be done *by lot* and it is now explained how two and a half plus nine and a half still make twelve after the exclusion of Levi. Yet in case their sacred business had seemed to us too other-worldly for real life in the land, we are reassured that they had towns and common pasture within the holdings of their secular brothers.

JUDAH FIRST AND CALEB

Joshua 14:6–15:63

⁶Then the people of Judah came to Joshua at Gilgal; and Caleb the son of Jephunneh the Kenizzite said to him, "You know what the Lord said to Moses the man of God in Kadesh-barnea concerning you and me. ⁷I was forty years old when Moses the servant of the Lord sent me from Kadesh-barnea to spy out the land; and I brought him word again as it was in my heart. ⁸But my brethren who went up with me made the heart of the people melt; yet I wholly followed the Lord my God. ⁹And Moses swore on that day, saying, 'Surely the land on which your foot has trodden shall be an inheritance for you and your children for ever, because you have wholly followed the Lord my God.' ¹⁰And now, behold, the Lord has kept me alive, as he said, these forty-five years since the time that the Lord spoke this word to Moses, while Israel walked in the wilderness; and now, lo, I am this day eighty-five years old. ¹¹I am still as strong to this day as I was in the day that Moses sent me; my strength now is as my strength was then, for war, and for going and coming. ¹²So now give me this hill country of which the Lord spoke on that day; for you heard on that day how the Anakim were there, with great fortified cities: it may be that the Lord will be with me, and I shall drive them out as the Lord said."

¹³Then Joshua blessed him; and he gave Hebron to Caleb the son of Jephunneh for an inheritance. ¹⁴So Hebron became the inheritance of Caleb the son of Jephunneh the Kenizzite to this day, because he wholly followed the Lord, the God of Israel. ¹⁵Now the name of Hebron formerly was Kiriath-arba; this Arba was the greatest man among the Anakim. And the land had rest from war.

¹The lot for the tribe of the people of Judah according to their families reached southward to the boundary of Edom, to the wilderness of Zin at the farthest south. ²And their south boundary ran from the end of the Salt Sea, from the bay that faces southward; ³it goes out southward of the ascent of Akrabbim, passes along to Zin, and goes up south of Kadesh-barnea, along by Hezron, up to Addar, turns about to Karka, ⁴passes along to Azmon, goes out by the Brook of Egypt, and comes to its end at the sea. This shall be your south boundary. ⁵And the east boundary is the Salt Sea, to the mouth of the Jordan. And the boundary on the north side runs from the bay of the sea at the mouth of the Jordan; ⁶and the boundary goes up to Beth-hoglah, and passes

along north of Beth-arabah; and the boundary goes up to the stone of Bohan the son of Reuben; [7]and the boundary goes up to Debir from the Valley of Achor, and so northward, turning toward Gilgal, which is opposite the ascent of Adummim, which is on the south side of the valley; and the boundary passes along to the waters of En-shemesh, and ends at En-rogel; [8]then the boundary goes up by the valley of the son of Hinnom at the southern shoulder of the Jebusite (that is, Jerusalem); and the boundary goes up to the top of the mountain that lies over against the valley of Hinnom, on the west, at the northern end of the valley of Rephaim; [9]then the boundary extends from the top of the mountain to the spring of the Waters of Nephtoah, and from there to the cities of Mount Ephron; then the boundary bends round to Baalah (that is, Kiriath-jearim); [10]and the boundary circles west of Baalah to Mount Seir, passes along to the northern shoulder of Mount Jearim (that is, Chesalon), and goes down to Beth-shemesh, and passes along by Timnah; [11]the boundary goes out to the shoulder of the hill north of Ekron, then the boundary bends round to Shikkeron, and passes along to Mount Baalah, and goes out to Jabneel; then the boundary comes to an end at the sea. [12]And the west boundary was the Great Sea with its coast-line. This is the boundary round about the people of Judah according to their families.

[13]According to the commandment of the Lord to Joshua, he gave to Caleb the son of Jephunneh a portion among the people of Judah, Kiriath-arba, that is, Hebron (Arba was the father of Anak). [14]And Caleb drove out from there the three sons of Anak, Sheshai and Ahiman and Talmai, the descendants of Anak. [15]And he went up from there against the inhabitants of Debir; now the name of Debir formerly was Kiriath-sepher. [16]And Caleb said, "Whoever smites Kiriath-sepher, and takes it, to him will I give Achsah my daughter as wife." [17]And Othni-el the son of Kenaz, the brother of Caleb, took it; and he gave him Achsah his daughter as wife. [18]When she came to him, she urged him to ask her father for a field; and she alighted from her ass, and Caleb said to her, "What do you wish?" [19]She said to him, "Give me a present; since you have set me in the land of the Negeb, give me also springs of water." And Caleb gave her the upper springs and the lower springs.

[20]This is the inheritance of the tribe of the people of Judah according to their families. [21]The cities belonging to the tribe of the people of Judah in the extreme South, toward the boundary of Edom, were Kabzeel, Eder, Jagur, [22]Kinah, Dimonah, Adadah, [23]Kedesh, Hazor,

Ithnan, 24Ziph, Telem, Bealoth, 25Hazor-hadattah, Kerioth-hezron
(that is, Hazor), 26Amam, Shema, Moladah, 27Hazar-gaddah,
Heshmon, Beth-pelet, 28Hazar-shual, Beer-sheba, Biziothiah,
29Baalah, Iim, Ezem, 30Eltolad, Chesil, Hormah, 31Ziklag, Mad-
mannah, Sansannah, 32Lebaoth, Shilhim, Ain, and Rimmon; in all,
twenty-nine cities, with their villages.

33And in the lowland, Eshta-ol, Zorah, Ashnah, 34Zanoah,
En-gannim, Tappu-ah, Enam, 35Jarmuth, Adullam, Socoh, Azekah,
36Sha-araim, Adithaim, Gederah, Gederothaim: fourteen cities with
their villages.

37Zenan, Hadashah, Migdal-gad, 38Dilean, Mizpeh, Joktheel,
39Lachish, Bozkath, Eglon, 40Cabbon, Lahmam, Chitlish,
41Gederoth, Beth-dagon, Naamah, and Makkedah: sixteen cities with
their villages.

42Libnah, Ether, Ashan, 43Iphtah, Ashnah, Nezib, 44Keilah,
Achzib, and Mareshah: nine cities with their villages.

45Ekron, with its towns and its villages; 46from Ekron to the sea, all
that were by the side of Ashdod, with their villages.

47Ashdod, its towns and its villages; Gaza, its towns and it villages;
to the Brook of Egypt, and the Great Sea with its coast-line.

48And in the hill country, Shamir, Jattir, Socoh, 49Dannah, Kiriath-
sannah (that is, Debir), 50Anab, Eshtemoh, Anim, 51Goshen, Holon,
and Giloh: eleven cities with their villages.

52Arab, Dumah, Eshan, 53Janim, Beth-tappu-ah, Aphekah,
54Humtah, Kiriath-arba (that is, Hebron), and Zior: nine cities with
their villages.

55Maon, Carmel, Ziph, Juttah, 56Jezreel, Jokde-am, Zanoah,
57Kain, Gibe-ah, and Timnah: ten cities with their villages.

58Halhul, Beth-zur, Gedor, 59Ma-arath, Beth-anoth, and Eltekon:
six cities with their villages.

60Kiriath-baal (that is, Kiriath-jearim), and Rabbah: two cities with
their villages.

61In the wilderness, Beth-arabah, Middin, Secacah, 62Nibshan, the
City of Salt, and En-gedi: six cities with their villages.

63But the Jebusites, the inhabitants of Jerusalem, the people of
Judah could not drive out; so the Jebusites dwell with the people of
Judah at Jerusalem to this day.

We are informed about Judah's holdings in southern Canaan not
just first but in greatest detail also. The family information about

Jacob/Israel in Genesis lists Reuben, Simeon, and Levi before it reaches Judah. Judah's pre-eminence not just here but in many other Biblical traditions reflects her position as survivor when the northern kingdom of Israel fell and then, after her own collapse and exile, as heritor and executor of all Israelite and Biblical tradition. The Old Testament in a real sense is a *Jewish*—and that means Judean-book. Judah stars with first-born Reuben in the rescue and sale into Egypt of dreamer Joseph (Gen. 37)—and then independently in the scandalous episode with Tamar in the following chapter. Yet only seldom is Judah's future role hinted at in the traditions about the early past.

The second half of the Book of Joshua features Judah not just first but quite the most fully. First of all in 15:1–12 her outer borders are grandly sketched. Judah's southern neighbour is Edom. We often think of Edom as belonging in southern Transjordan. However, in many periods both the earlier kingdom and the much later Roman province called Idumaea extended considerably westwards from its mountain fastnesses between the Dead Sea and Petra. To the east Judah was bounded by the Dead Sea. Her northern frontier she shared with the tribe of Benjamin (see on 18:15–19). Readers familiar with the various routes out of present Jerusalem will find the east half of this northern border near the road from Jerusalem to Jericho, while the west part is pretty much the railway line out of Jerusalem down to the coastal plain. Giving Judah the Mediterranean Sea as her western boundary is the grandest claim of all, for it ignores the allied structure of Philistine city states in the coastal plain. When making territorial claims it is often convenient to suppose that others do not exist.

This full outline of Judah's territory is then filled in with a comprehensive list of localities in verses 20–62. These are either a gold mine or a minefield for present-day historical geographers—according to taste. Many of Judah's towns we never read of again in the Bible, but Beersheba (15:28) is still a principal Bedouin market and a main town in southern Israel. Ziklag (31) was a personal gift to David for his service to the Philistines (1 Sam. 27:6). A cave near Adullam (35) provided sanctuary for David

(1 Sam. 22:1). Lachish (39) and Hebron (54) we met in chapter 10. Kiriath-jearim (60) played host to the Ark (1 Sam. 7:1) after its return from the Philistines and before David brought it to Jerusalem and its alternative name Kiriath-*Baal* or *Baal*ah (9) helps us see that some people were more scrupulous and some less about the hostile associations of place-names. (We might compare Irish nationalist resentment over the name *London*-derry.) Finally verse 62 mentions the lovely oasis at Engedi just north of Masada by the Dead Sea; and the City of Salt may be a small older town by the site we now know as Qumran where the Dead Sea Scrolls were found in 1947.

Two exceptions are noted in the chapter: one explicitly and the other rather more quietly. The last verse of the chapter admits that Jerusalem *could* not be taken and that its original Jebusite inhabitants formed an enclave amongst the people of Judah (this again reminds us of our discussion of chapter 10). Then the careful reader will note that no totals are given after the towns listed in verses 45–47. Ekron, Ashdod and Gaza and all the associated territory are not counted in but they are mentioned as being there. The word Philistine is not breathed; but at least these town lists are more honest than the frontier description in recognizing this massive coastal presence.

And that leaves us with Caleb. The association of Caleb with Hebron in the midst of Judah's hill country seems to have been a contentious matter. The relevant Biblical traditions hardly agree with each other. It is *Caleb* who drags out of Hebron the descendants of the Giants according to Joshua 15:14 and proceeds from there against the inhabitants of Debir. However, *Judah* is credited with these actions in Judges 1:10–11. Then we have already read in Joshua 10:36–37 of *Joshua's* total destruction of Hebron and all its inhabitants, and in 11:21 that Joshua "wiped out the Anakim from the hill country, from Hebron, from Debir, from Anab, and from all the hill country of Judah." The Bible is far from clear about where the credit belongs. Little wonder that those who advance Caleb's claim do it twice and at length (14:6–15 and 15:13–19), and in the first passage quote the authority of Moses himself (reminding us of Num. 14:24 and Deut. 1:36). It was Caleb and Joshua—and some would say that Caleb was the leading spirit—who first saved Israel from that dread of their enemies in Canaan which so afflicted the Canaanites once Israel crossed the Jordan. Hebron, later first capital of David, was his reward.

JOSEPH AND THE NORTHERNERS

Joshua 16:1–19:51

16 ¹The allotment of the descendants of Joseph went from the Jordan by Jericho, east of the waters of Jericho, into the wilderness, going up from Jericho into the hill country to Bethel; ²then going from Bethel to Luz, it passes along to Ataroth, the territory of the Archites; ³then it goes down westward to the territory of the Japhletites, as far as the territory of Lower Beth-horon, then to Gezer, and it ends at the sea.

⁴The people of Joseph, Manasseh and Ephraim, received their inheritance.

⁵The territory of the Ephraimites by their families was as follows: the boundary of their inheritance on the east was Ataroth-addar as far as Upper Beth-horon, ⁶and the boundary goes thence to the sea; on the north is Michmethath; then on the east the boundary turns round toward Taanath-shiloh, and passes along beyond it on the east to Janoah, ⁷then it goes down from Janoah to Ataroth and to Naarah, and touches Jericho, ending at the Jordan. ⁸From Tappu-ah the boundary goes westward to the brook Kanah, and ends at the sea. Such is the inheritance of the tribe of the Ephraimites by their families, ⁹together with the towns which were set apart for the Ephraimites within the inheritance of the Manassites, all those towns with their villages. ¹⁰However they did not drive out the Canaanites that dwelt in Gezer: so the Canaanites have dwelt in the midst of Ephraim to this day but have become slaves to do forced labour.

17 ¹Then allotment was made to the tribe of Manasseh, for he was the first-born of Joseph. To Machir the first-born of Manasseh, the father of Gilead, were allotted Gilead and Bashan, because he was a man of war. ²And allotments were made to the rest of the tribe of Manasseh, by their families, Abi-ezer, Helek, Asri-el, Shechem, Hepher, and Shemida; these were the male descendants of Manasseh the son of Joseph, by their families.

3Now Zelophe-had the son of Hepher, son of Gilead, son of Machir, son of Manasseh, had no sons, but only daughters; and these are the names of his daughters: Mahlah, Noah, Hoglah, Milcah, and Tirzah. 4They came before Eleazar the priest and Joshua the son of Nun and the leaders, and said, "The Lord commanded Moses to give us an inheritance along with our brethren." So according to the commandment of the Lord he gave them an inheritance among the brethren of their father. 5Thus there fell to Manasseh ten portions, besides the land of Gilead and Bashan, which is on the other side of the Jordan; 6because the daughters of Manasseh received an inheritance along with his sons. The land of Gilead was allotted to the rest of the Manassites.

7The territory of Manasseh reached from Asher to Michmethath, which is east of Shechem; then the boundary goes along southward to the inhabitants of En-tappu-ah. 8The land of Tappu-ah belonged to Manasseh, but the town of Tappu-ah on the boundary of Manasseh belonged to the sons of Ephraim. 9Then the boundary went down to the brook Kanah. The cities here, to the south of the brook, among the cities of Manasseh, belong to Ephraim. Then the boundary of Manasseh goes on the north side of the brook and ends at the sea; 10the land to the south being Ephraim's and that to the north being Manasseh's, with the sea forming its boundary; on the north Asher is reached, and on the east Issachar. 11Also in Issachar and in Asher Manasseh had Beth-shean and its villages, and Ible-am and its villages, and the inhabitants of Dor and its villages, and the inhabitants of En-dor and its villages, and the inhabitants of Taanach and its villages, and the inhabitants of Megiddo and its villages; the third is Naphath. 12Yet the sons of Manasseh could not take possession of those cities; but the Canaanites persisted in dwelling in that land. 13But when the people of Israel grew strong, they put the Canaanites to forced labour, and did not utterly drive them out.

14And the tribe of Joseph spoke to Joshua, saying, "Why have you given me but one lot and one portion as an inheritance, although I am a numerous people, since hitherto the Lord has blessed me?" 15And Joshua said to them, "If you are a numerous people, go up to the forest, and there clear ground for yourselves in the land of the Perizzites and the Rephaim, since the hill country of Ephraim is too narrow for you." 16The tribe of Joseph said, "The hill country is not enough for us; yet all the Canaanites who dwell in the plain have chariots of iron, both those in Beth-shean and its villages and those in the Valley of Jezreel." ¹⁷Then Joshua said to the house of Joseph, to Ephraim and Manasseh, "You are a numerous people, and have great power; you shall not have one lot only, ¹⁸but the hill country shall be yours, for though it is a forest, you shall clear it and possess it to its farthest borders; for you shall drive out the Canaanites, though they have chariots of iron, and though they are strong."

18 ¹Then the whole congregation of the people of Israel assembled at Shiloh, and set up the tent of meeting there; the land lay subdued before them.

²There remained among the people of Israel seven tribes whose inheritance had not yet been apportioned. ³So Joshua said to the people of Israel, "How long will you be slack to go in and take possession of the land, which the Lord, the God of your fathers, has given you? ⁴Provide three men from each tribe, and I will send them out that they may set out and go up and down the land, writing a description of it with a view to their inheritances, and then come to me. ⁵They shall divide it into seven portions, Judah continuing in his territory on the south, and the house of Joseph in their territory on the north. ⁶And you shall describe the land in seven divisions and bring the description here to me; and I will cast lots for you here before the Lord our God. ⁷The Levites have no portion among you, for the priesthood of the Lord is their heritage; and Gad and Reuben and half the tribe of Manasseh have received their inheritance beyond the Jordan eastward, which Moses the servant of the Lord gave them."

⁸So the men started on their way; and Joshua charged those who went to write the description of the land, saying, "Go up and down and write a description of the land, and come again to me; and I will cast lots for you here before the Lord in Shiloh." ⁹So the men went and passed up and down in the land and set down in a book a description of it by towns in seven divisions; then they came to Joshua in the camp at Shiloh, ¹⁰and Joshua cast lots for them in Shiloh before the Lord; and there Joshua apportioned the land to the people of Israel, to each his portion.

¹¹The lot of the tribe of Benjamin according to its families came up, and the territory allotted to it fell between the tribe of Judah and the tribe of Joseph. ¹²On the north side their boundary began at the Jordan; then the boundary goes up to the shoulder north of Jericho, then up through the hill country westward; and it ends at the wilderness of Beth-aven. ¹³From there the boundary passes along southward in the direction of Luz, to the shoulder of Luz (the same is Bethel),

then the boundary goes down to Ataroth-addar, upon the mountain that lies south of Lower Beth-horon. [14]Then the boundary goes in another direction, turning on the western side southward from the mountain that lies to the south, opposite Beth-horon, and it ends at Kiriath-baal (that is, Kiriath-jearim), a city belonging to the tribe of Judah. This forms the western side. [15]And the southern side begins at the outskirts of Kiriath-jearim; and the boundary goes from there to Ephron, to the spring of the Waters of Nephtoah; [16]then the boundary goes down to the border of the mountain that overlooks the valley of the son of Hinnom, which is at the north end of the valley of Rephaim; and it then goes down the valley of Hinnom, south of the shoulder of the Jebusites, and downward to En-rogel; [17]then it bends in a northerly direction going on to Enshemesh, and thence goes to Geliloth, which is opposite the ascent of Adummim; then it goes down to the Stone of Bohan the son of Reuben; [18]and passing on to the north of the shoulder of Beth-arabah it goes down to the Arabah; [19]then the boundary passes on to the north of the shoulder of Beth-hoglah; and the boundary ends at the northern bay of the Salt Sea, at the south end of the Jordan: this is the southern border. [20]The Jordan forms its boundary on the eastern side. This is the inheritance of the tribe of Benjamin, according to its families, boundary by boundary round about.

[21]Now the cities of the tribe of Benjamin according to their families were Jericho, Beth-hoglah, Emek-keziz, [22]Beth-arabah, Zemaraim, Bethel, [23]Avvim, Parah, Ophrah, [24]Chepharammoni, Ophni, Geba—twelve cities with their villages: [25]Gibeon, Ramah, Be-eroth, [26]Mizpeh, Chephirah, Mozah, [27]Rekem, Irpeel, Taralah, [28]Zela, Ha-eleph, Jebus (that is, Jerusalem), Gibe-ah and Kiriath-jearim—fourteen cities with their villages. This is the inheritance of the tribe of Benjamin according to its families.

19 [1]The second lot came out for Simeon, for the tribe of Simeon, according to its families; and its inheritance was in the midst of the inheritance of the tribe of Judah. [2]And it had for its inheritance Beer-sheba, Sheba, Moladah, [3]Hazar-shual, Balah, Ezem, [4]Eltolad, Bethul, Hormah, [5]Ziklag, Beth-marcaboth, Hazar-susah, [6]Beth-lebaoth, and Sharuhen—thirteen cities with their villages; [7]Enrimmon, Ether, and Ashan—four cities with their villages; [8]together with all the villages round about these cities as far as Baalath-beer, Ramah of the Negeb. This was the inheritance of the tribe of Simeon according to its families. [9]The inheritance of the tribe of Simeon formed part of

the territory of Judah; because the portion of the tribe of Judah was too large for them, the tribe of Simeon obtained an inheritance in the midst of their inheritance.

¹⁰The third lot came up for the tribe of Zebulun, according to its families. And the territory of its inheritance reached as far as Sarid; ¹¹then its boundary goes up westward, and on to Mareal, and touches Dabbesheth, then the brook which is east of Jokne-am; ¹²from Sarid it goes in the other direction eastward toward the sunrise to the boundary of Chisloth-tabor; thence it goes to Daberath, then up to Japhia; ¹³from there it passes along on the east toward the sunrise to Gath-hepher, to Eth-kazin, and going on to Rimmon it bends toward Neah; ¹⁴then on the north the boundary turns about to Hannathon, and it ends at the valley of Iphtahel; ¹⁵and Kattath, Nahalal, Shimron, Idalah, and Bethlehem—twelve cities with their villages. ¹⁶This is the inheritance of the tribe of Zebulun, according to its families—these cities with their villages.

¹⁷The fourth lot came out for Issachar, for the tribe of Issachar, according to its families. ¹⁸Its territory included Jezreel, Chesulloth, Shunem, ¹⁹Haphara-im, Shion, Anaharath, ²⁰Rabbith, Kishion, Ebez, ²¹Remeth, En-gannim, En-haddah, Beth-pazzez; ²²the boundary also touches Tabor, Shahazumah, and Beth-shemesh, and its boundary ends at the Jordan—sixteen cities with their villages. ²³This is the inheritance of the tribe of Issachar, according to its families—the cities with their villages.

²⁴The fifth lot came out for the tribe of Asher according to its families. ²⁵Its territory included Helkath, Hali, Beten, Achshaph, ²⁶Allammelech, Amad, and Mishal; on the west it touches Carmel and Shihor-libnath, ²⁷then it turns eastward, it goes to Beth-dagon, and touches Zebulun and the valley of Iphtah-el northward to Beth-emek and Neiel; then it continues in the north to Cabul, ²⁸Ebron, Rehob, Hammon, Kanah, as far as Sidon the Great; ²⁹then the boundary turns to Ramah, reaching to the fortified city of Tyre; then the boundary turns to Hosah, and it ends at the sea; Mahalab, Achzib, ³⁰Ummah, Aphek and Rehob—twenty-two cities with their villages. ³¹This is the inheritance of the tribe of Asher according to its families—these cities with their villages.

³²The sixth lot came out for the tribe of Naphtali, for the tribe of Naphtali, according to its families. ³³And its boundary ran from Heleph, from the oak in Za-anannim, and Adami-nekeb, and Jabneel, as far as Lakkum; and it ended at the Jordan; ³⁴then the boundary

turns westward to Aznoth-tabor, and goes from there to Hukkok, touching Zebulun at the south, and Asher on the west, and Judah on the east at the Jordan. ³⁵The fortified cities are Ziddim, Zer, Hammath, Rakkath, Chinnereth, ³⁶Adamah, Ramah, Hazor, ³⁷Kedesh, Edre-i, En-hazor, ³⁸Yiron, Migdal-el, Horem, Beth-anath, and Beth-shemesh—nineteen cities with their villages. ³⁹This is the inheritance of the tribe of Naphtali according to its families—the cities with their villages.

⁴⁰The seventh lot came out for the tribe of Dan, according to its families. ⁴¹And the territory of its inheritance included Zorah, Eshta-ol, Ir-shemesh, ⁴²Sha-alabbin, Aijalon, Ithlah, ⁴³Elon, Timnah, Ekron, ⁴⁴Eltekeh, Gibbethon, Baalath, ⁴⁵Jehud, Bene-berak, Gath-rimmon, ⁴⁶and Me-jarkon and Rakkon with the territory over against Joppa. ⁴⁷When the territory of the Danites was lost to them, the Danites went up and fought against Leshem, and after capturing it and putting it to the sword they took possession of it and settled in it, calling Leshem, Dan, after the name of Dan their ancestor. ⁴⁸This is the inheritance of the tribe of Dan, according to their families—these cities with their villages.

⁴⁹When they had finished distributing the several territories of the land as inheritances, the people of Israel gave an inheritance among them to Joshua the son of Nun. ⁵⁰By command of the Lord they gave him the city which he asked, Timnath-serah in the hill country of Ephraim; and he rebuilt the city, and settled in it.

⁵¹These are the inheritances which Eleazar the priest and Joshua the son of Nun and the heads of the fathers' houses of the tribes of the people of Israel distributed by lot at Shiloh before the Lord, at the door of the tent of meeting. So they finished dividing the land.

(i)

The *basic* information in Josh. 16–17 is given about Ephraim and Manasseh *separately*, in 16:5–8 and 17:7–9 (with supplements and modifications in 16:9–10 and 17:10–13). However, these details of claims and partial retractions are now only the centre-piece of a larger picture about the house of Joseph. The new frame is supplied in the form of a southern base line, described in 16:1–3, and a note in the following verse that for purposes such as this Joseph is two units and not one; then a closing conversation between representatives of Joseph and Joshua explains that this unique concession was due to Joseph's size (17:14–18). The new middle verses (17:1–6) are also untypical: they offer a contorted explanation (in terms of Num. 27:1–11) of the division of Manasseh east and west of the Jordan.

(ii)

There is a sudden change of scene in chapters 18 and 19. *Gilgal* has been the base for all action described in the book to this point; and its status was reinforced as recently as Josh. 14:6, when Judah pled Caleb's case *there* to Joshua. Now we are at *Shiloh* between Bethel and Shechem in the central hill country, which will remain the significant centre until the end of chapter 22, which reappears at the end of the Book of Judges, but perhaps is best known in the Bible as the scene of Samuel's vision and the demise of the house of Eli (1 Sam. 1–6). Accompanying this is a new stress on a method of *allotting* the land (18:1–10). The ideas which this introduction to the allocation to the northern tribes (Josh. 18–19) shares with the preceding section (Josh. 16–17) are located precisely in the new Joseph framework already mentioned: that Joseph is *one* (18:5), and that successful settlement has cost effort (18:3 and 17:15,18).

These connections persuade me that the combination of Ephraim and Manasseh into one was part of a whole new edition of the traditions of land allocation: in two stages, at two places, at two times—*and by two methods*. It is only here in 18:1–10 and the following seven descriptions that details are clearly spelt out of a method of *allotting* the land. The holdings of Benjamin (18:11–28) and the six tribes listed in 19:1–48 are summarily described, in a manner not unlike the "original" information about Ephraim (16:5–8) and Manasseh (17:7–9). That will have been the first shorter draft of the tradition. The unity of Joseph, and the contrast between Judah, Joseph and the rest, and the *emphasis* on "lot", are the themes of an expansion and reformulation of this more summary information.

Drawing or casting lots was not leaving a matter to chance or random decision. The activity was a sacral one "before the Lord" (18:1,10). The principle is most clearly expressed in the Book of Proverbs:

The lot is cast into the lap,
　　but the decision is wholly from the Lord.

(16:33)

The lot puts an end to disputes
　　and decides between powerful contenders.

(18:18)

Various sacred offices are assigned to different priestly families by lot according to 1 Chron. 24–26; and the opening of Neh. 11 catches nicely the attitudes of willing acceptance of the divine decision.

Now the leaders of the people lived in Jerusalem; and the rest of the people cast lots to bring one out of ten to live in Jerusalem the holy city, while nine tenths remained in the other towns. And the people blessed all the men who willingly offered to live in Jerusalem.

(11:1–2)

Another fine example ends the first chapter of the Book of Acts, where prayer for divine guidance precedes the apostolic casting of lots to select a replacement for Judas the betrayer. Altogether this is a much more positive approach to the "luck of the draw" than our society's casual or desperate recourse to spinning coins or pulling straws.

Our section closes as the previous one had begun. Joshua is given a personal holding in the hill country heartland of Ephraim just as Caleb had been granted one in the hill country heartland of Judah.

ASYLUM AND LEVI

Joshua 20:1–21:42

¹Then the Lord said to Joshua, ²"Say to the people of Israel, 'Appoint the cities of refuge, of which I spoke to you through Moses, ³that the manslayer who kills any person without intent or unwittingly may flee there; they shall be for you a refuge from the avenger of blood. ⁴He shall flee to one of these cities and shall stand at the entrance of the gate of the city, and explain his case to the elders of that city; then they shall take him into the city, and give him a place, and he shall remain with

them. [5]And if the avenger of blood pursues him, they shall not give up the slayer into his hand; because he killed his neighbour unwittingly, having had no enmity against him in times past. [6]And he shall remain in that city until he has stood before the congregation for judgment, until the death of him who is high priest at the time: then the slayer may go again to his own town and his own home, to the town from which he fled.'"

[7]So they set apart Kedesh in Galilee in the hill country of Naphtali, and Shechem in the hill country of Ephraim, and Kiriath-arba (that is, Hebron) in the hill country of Judah. [8]And beyond the Jordan east of Jericho, they appointed Bezer in the wilderness on the tableland, from the tribe of Reuben, and Ramoth in Gilead, from the tribe of Gad, and Golan in Bashan, from the tribe of Manasseh. [9]These were the cities designated for all the people of Israel, and for the stranger sojourning among them, that any one who killed a person without intent could flee there, so that he might not die by the hand of the avenger of blood, till he stood before the congregation.

[1]Then the heads of the fathers' houses of the Levites came to Eleazar the priest and to Joshua the son of Nun and to the heads of the fathers' houses of the tribes of the people of Israel; [2]and they said to them at Shiloh in the land of Canaan, "The Lord commanded through Moses that we be given cities to dwell in, along with their pasture lands for our cattle." [3]So by command of the Lord the people of Israel gave to the Levites the following cities and pasture lands out of their inheritance.

[4]The lot came out for the families of the Kohathites. So those Levites who were descendants of Aaron the priest received by lot from the tribes of Judah, Simeon, and Benjamin, thirteen cities.

[5]And the rest of the Kohathites received by lot from the families of the tribe of Ephraim, from the tribe of Dan and the half-tribe of Manasseh, ten cities.

[6]The Gershonites received by lot from the families of the tribe of Issachar, from the tribe of Asher, from the tribe of Naphtali, and from the half-tribe of Manasseh in Bashan, thirteen cities.

[7]The Merarites according to their families received from the tribe of Reuben, the tribe of Gad, and the tribe of Zebulun, twelve cities.

[8]These cities and their pasture lands the people of Israel gave by lot to the Levites, as the Lord had commanded through Moses.

[9]Out of the tribe of Judah and the tribe of Simeon they gave the following cities mentioned by name, [10]which went to the descendants

of Aaron, one of the families of the Kohathites who belonged to the Levites; since the lot fell to them first. [11]They gave them Kiriath-arba (Arba being the father of Anak), that is Hebron, in the hill country of Judah, along with the pasture lands round about it. [12]But the fields of the city and its villages had been given to Caleb the son of Jephunneh as his possession.

[13]And to the descendants of Aaron the priest they gave Hebron, the city of refuge for the slayer, with its pasture lands, Libnah with its pasture lands, [14]Jattir with its pasture lands, Eshtemoa with its pasture lands, [15]Holon with its pasture lands, Debir with its pasture lands, [16]Ain with its pasture lands, Juttah with its pasture lands, Beth-shemesh with its pasture lands—nine cities out of these two tribes; [17]then out of the tribe of Benjamin, Gibeon with its pasture lands, Geba with its pasture lands, [18]Anathoth with its pasture lands, and Almon with its pasture lands—four cities. [19]The cities of the descendants of Aaron, the priests, were in all thirteen cities with their pasture lands.

[20]As to the rest of the Kohathites belonging to the Kohathite families of the Levites, the cities allotted to them were out of the tribe of Ephraim. [21]To them were given Shechem, the city of refuge for the slayer, with its pasture lands in the hill country of Ephraim, Gezer with its pasture lands, [22]Kibzaim with its pasture lands, Beth-horon with its pasture lands—four cities; [23]and out of the tribe of Dan, Elteke with its pasture lands, Gibbethon with its pasture lands, [24]Aijalon with its pasture lands, Gath-rimmon with its pasture lands—four cities; [25]and out of the half-tribe of Manasseh, Taanach with its pasture lands, and Gath-rimmon with its pasture lands—two cities. [26]The cities of the families of the rest of the Kohathites were ten in all with their pasture lands.

[27]And to the Gershonites, one of the families of the Levites, were given out of the half-tribe of Manasseh, Golan in Bashan with its pasture lands, the city of refuge for the slayer, and Be-eshterah with its pasture lands—two cities; [28]and out of the tribe of Issachar, Kishion with its pasture lands, Daberath with its pasture lands, [29]Jarmuth with its pasture lands, En-gannim with its pasture lands—four cities; [30]and out of the tribe of Asher, Mishal with its pasture lands, Abdon with its pasture lands, [31]Helkath with its pasture lands, and Rehob with its pasture lands—four cities; [32]and out of the tribe of Naphtali, Kedesh in Galilee with its pasture lands, the city of refuge for the slayer, Hammoth-dor with its pasture lands, and Kartan with its pasture

lands—three cities. [33]The cities of the several families of the Gershonites were in all thirteen cities with their pasture lands.

[34]And to the rest of the Levites, the Merarite families, were given out of the tribe of Zebulun, Jokne-am with its pasture lands, Kartah with its pasture lands, [35]Dimnah with its pasture lands, Nahalal with its pasture lands—four cities; [36]and out of the tribe of Reuben, Bezer with its pasture lands, Jahaz with its pasture lands, [37]Kedemoth with its pasture lands, and Mepha-ath with its pasture lands—four cities, [38]and out of the tribe of Gad, Ramoth in Gilead with its pasture lands, the city of refuge for the slayer, Mahanaim with its pasture lands, [39]Heshbon with its pasture lands, Jazer with its pasture lands—four cities in all. [40]As for the cities of the several Merarite families, that is, the remainder of the families of the Levites, those allotted to them were in all twelve cities.

[41]The cities of the Levites in the midst of the possession of the people of Israel were in all forty-eight cities with their pasture lands. [42]These cities had each its pasture lands round about it; so it was with all these cities.

(i)

Although they apparently concern different institutions, these chapters are closely intertwined. The material in both chapters is closely related to the discussion of the same two topics (though in reverse order) in Num. 35: there Moses ordains; here Joshua carries out.

The background to the situation sketched in the nine verses of Joshua 20 is most economically provided in Exod. 21:12–14:

"Whoever strikes a man so that he dies shall be put to death. But if he did not lie in wait for him, but God let him fall into his hand, then I will appoint for you a place to which he may flee. But if a man wilfully attacks another to kill him treacherously, you shall take him from my altar, that he may die."

All the legal systems of which I am aware attempt to distinguish clearly between deliberate murder and varying degrees of accidental manslaughter or homicide. Since few of us harbour murderous passions but all of us recognize that we could cause the death of a fellow—whether by our carelessness at the car wheel or through leaving a machine unattended, or without any blame because we were only the unwitting instrument of a person taking his own life—we need no persuasion over the rightness of this thinking.

Blood feud is not a regular part of our society. But again we all recognize at least some of its components. We feel instinctively that there is something *wrong* about the sudden death of anyone. If premature illness is the cause we may curse fate or question God; but if a *human* agent is involved in the death of someone close to us, however much or little to blame, our anger is readily focused there.

The actual practice of the blood feud, or family vengeance killing, may be restricted to occasional outbursts among ethnic or religious minorities in our society—people who in extremis cannot trust the procedures of society as a whole. Indeed the nearest approximation in many modern societies is tit-for-tat reprisal killing by political terrorists: when there is complete polarization between "us" and "them", planned vengeance becomes the norm.

The debate about the rights and wrongs of capital punishment rumbles on in many countries which have abolished it and in some states judicial killing is re-introduced. Many see it as an appropriate expression of proper vengeance and certainly the Bible is in no doubt about the proper fate of the wilful killer. Whatever our views as citizens about having a person killed in our name, we may recognize that when it exacts the death penalty society offers itself as the extended family of the murderer's victim and renounces its relationship to the murderer.

The custom is widespread since ancient times that sanctuary or asylum or refuge is to be had in a holy place and especially by grasping hold of an altar. History and literature both are replete with instances of the killing of the unarmed in church or mosque or temple. Note the strong adverbs in the exceptional ruling quoted above from Exodus:

> "But if a man *wilfully* attacks another to kill him *treacherously*, you shall take him from my altar, that he may die."

The burden of proof is on those who set sanctuary aside.

(ii)

Josh. 21 supplies the detail already hinted at in 14:3–4. Levi is not part of the twelve-tribe system of the Book of Joshua, yet the Levites are not overlooked. Towns and adjoining pasture-lands are provided from within all twelve tribes to four Levitical clans. Scholars are seriously divided over the historical worth of this record. On the one side the numerical symmetry seems too idealized to be true. On the other the fact that it is not quite perfectly achieved leads some to suppose a factual basis for the ideal structure—perhaps the thirteen cities assigned to the full Aaronite priests from Judah, Simeon and Benjamin (who represent the territory of the southern kingdom of Judah; see v. 19).

According to Josh. 21, these forty-eight towns simply grant residence and livelihood to the Levites, though it is noted that six of them are also the refuge towns listed in Josh. 20 (in accordance with Deut. 19:1–13 and 4:41–43). However, in its own briefer presentation of the same material, 1 Chron. 6:54–81 designates *all* these places as "cities of refuge" (vv. 57, 67). This conflict of information makes it all the harder to treat Josh. 20–21 as a reliable, historical source.

(iii)

Our last comment is reserved for the so-called "avenger of blood" (Josh. 20:3,9). The Hebrew phrase *go'el haddam* is the more striking to anyone who knows that *go'el* on its own is regularly translated in the Bible as "redeemer". We should not suppose that in vengeance killing anyone's blood is being "bought back". The basic meaning of *go'el* is "kinsman". Society expected and depended upon family solidarity, especially in times of crisis. When we come to read Ruth we shall see that it is the kinsman's duty both to rescue alienated land and to provide family for a member who has died without heir. Here *go'el haddam* means "the blood kinsman"—the family representative with the responsibility for exacting the ultimate penalty. We should remember that when the Bible calls God our *go'el* it is thinking first and foremost not of what he *does* for us but about the *relationship* in which he stands to us. We are his family and he shoulders the responsibility for us.

CAMPAIGN OVER—RESERVES SENT HOME

Joshua 21:43–22:6

43Thus the Lord gave to Israel all the land which he swore to give to their fathers; and having taken possession of it, they settled there. 44And the Lord gave them rest on every side just as he had sworn to their fathers; not one of all their enemies had withstood them, for the Lord had given all their enemies into their hands. 45Not one of all the good promises which the Lord had made to the house of Israel had failed; all came to pass.

1Then Joshua summoned the Reubenites, and the Gadites, and the half-tribe of Manasseh, 2and said to them, "You have kept all that Moses the servant of the Lord commanded you, and have obeyed my voice in all that I have commanded you; 3you have not forsaken your brethren these many days, down to this day, but have been careful to keep the charge of the Lord your God. 4And now the Lord your God has given rest to your brethren, as he promised them; therefore turn and go to your home in the land where your possession lies, which Moses the servant of the Lord gave you on the other side of the Jordan. 5Take good care to observe the commandment and the law which Moses the servant of the Lord commanded you, to love the Lord your God, and to walk in all his ways, and to keep his commandments, and to cleave to him, and to serve him with all your heart and with all your soul." 6So Joshua blessed them, and sent them away; and they went to their homes.

(i)

There is no hesitation here about the success and completeness of the task. Canaan had been promised to Israel's ancestors. God had delivered the goods. Israel had not just received formal title to the territory, she was now actually settled there. The military success had been total. God himself had participated to ensure that.

However, the situation was not like the one familiar to us, with modern Israel winning every war but never achieving peace. It was not a matter of an ongoing "fortress Israel". They held that God had achieved for them "rest on every side" (21:44). The fortress could be dismantled, the troops sent home, the swords returned to ploughs and the spears to pruning hooks. "Not one of all of the good promises which the Lord had made to the house of Israel had failed; all came to pass" (21:45). Solomon was to say the same at the end of his great prayer when the new Temple in Jerusalem was dedicated (1 Kings 8:56).

We began to explore the theme of God's "rest" in connection with Josh. 1:15. Later in this volume when we come to the Book of Ruth we shall find that the same Hebrew word is translated "home" in Ruth 1:9 and 3:1; and that translation is appropriate here too. Their Lord is giving them a home or, perhaps better, is bringing them back to a home their fathers had received in promise. Longing to return home to the promised land has of course been a powerful element in both ancient and modern Zionism. Only in *that* land is authentic existence possible for God's people. Many Christian traditions, in contrast, have tended to accept alienation and homelessness as a condition of this world, or at least as a condition of serving a homeless and alienated master in this world. Hope in God's promised rest is then deferred to another fuller life. It is in this context that songs like the powerful Negro spirituals have sung of crossing Jordan and returning home. In such songs the Jordan waters merge with the great waters of the powerful river of death which all of us must cross.

(ii)

Joshua dispatches his Transjordanian helpers with a very formal speech which also nicely underscores his own authority. They have followed all Moses' instructions: keeping with the campaign until the very end. They have followed all Joshua's instructions during the campaign; and all this loyalty to their brothers now settled in Israel's heartlands west of the Jordan is nothing less than being "careful to keep the charge of the Lord their God" (22:3). Moses-Me-God: it is when Joshua speaks in this way and claims such authority that we understand how Jewish tradition reckons this book as the first of the Former Prophets.

Some interesting language is used in the Hebrew text of verses 4 and 5. Where the RSV translates "go to your home" the Hebrew literally reads "go to your tents". Tents in the Old

Testament are associated with a people on the move, or under arms, or in festal assembly. Sometimes it is hard to disentangle these uses. When Solomon dedicates his new Temple he is assisted by a great assembly gathered from the whole of Israel at an eight-day festival: "On the eighth day he sent the people away; and they blessed the king, and went to their tents [RSV homes] joyful and glad of heart for all the goodness that the Lord had shown to David his servant and to Israel his people" (1 Kings 8:66). Jeroboam and all Israel confront the bombastic Rehoboam at Shechem in the famous words, "What portion have we in David? We have no inheritance in the son of Jesse. To your tents, O Israel! Look now to your own house, David" (1 Kings 12:16). So too in the desert before Mount Horeb Israel are sent to their tents after God has disclosed himself to them in the Ten Commandments in case further exposure to the divine should prove fatal; and Moses is given the role of intermediary (Deut. 5:30). The Letter to the Hebrews remembers that Abraham "sojourned in the land of promise, as in a foreign land, living in tents with Isaac and Jacob" (11:9).

Tents suggest what is transitory, impermanent, *rest*less. I can only see a contrast between the Transjordanians who, duty done, may return to their families and their tents; and their brothers in the west, who have now entered their rest. The RSV has camouflaged this by calling tents "home". To be fair, Josh. 1:15 and Deut. 3:20 have both talked of "rest" for the Transjordanians; but here a different point is being made, as our next term confirms.

"Possession" in Josh. 22:4 translates a different Hebrew word from that rendered possession earlier in the book (it is anticipated once in 21:41). Often in the Bible this new term at the end of Joshua has no difference in sense. Where it is different, it specifies a holding that belongs to you *properly* although not *naturally*—to rights that have been specially acquired. Two good examples in Genesis are Abraham's purchase of a tomb for his wife (23:4), and the offering Hamor makes to Jacob of trade, inter-marriage and *property* (34:10).

Joshua's carefully chosen words underline that the Trans-jordanians are returning to second best—to *tents* in properly *acquired* property instead of *rest* in the *promised land*. A third detail of this speech will introduce our next section.

AN ALTAR NAMED WITNESS

Joshua 22:7–34

7Now to the one half of the tribe of Manasseh Moses had given a possession in Bashan; but to the other half Joshua had given a posses-sion beside their brethren in the land west of the Jordan. And when Joshua sent them away to their homes and blessed them, 8he said to them, "Go back to your homes with much wealth, and with very many cattle, with silver, gold, bronze, and iron, and with much clothing; divide the spoil of your enemies with your brethren." 9So the Reubenites and the Gadites and the half-tribe of Manasseh returned home, parting from the people of Israel at Shiloh, which is in the land of Canaan, to go to the land of Gilead, their own land of which they had possessed themselves by command of the Lord through Moses.

10And when they came to the region about the Jordan, that lies in the land of Canaan, the Reubenites and the Gadites and the half-tribe of Manasseh built there an altar by the Jordan, an altar of great size. 11And the people of Israel heard say, "Behold, the Reubenites and the Gadites and the half-tribe of Manasseh have built an altar at the frontier of the land of Canaan, in the region about the Jordan, on the side that belongs to the people of Israel." 12And when the people of Israel heard of it, the whole assembly of the people of Israel gathered at Shiloh, to make war against them.

13Then the people of Israel sent to the Reubenites and the Gadites and the half-tribe of Manasseh, in the land of Gilead, Phinehas the son of Eleazar the priest, 14and with him ten chiefs, one from each of the tribal families of Israel, every one of them the head of a family among the clans of Israel. 15And they came to the Reubenites, the Gadites, and the half-tribe of Manasseh, in the land of Gilead, and they said to them, 16"Thus says the whole congregation of the Lord, 'What is this treachery which you have committed against the God of Israel in turning away this day from following the Lord, by building yourselves an altar this day in rebellion against the Lord? 17Have we not had enough of the sin at Peor from which even yet we have not cleansed ourselves, and for which there came a plague upon the congregation of the Lord, ¹⁸that you must turn away this day from following the Lord? And if you rebel against the Lord today he will be angry with the whole congregation of Israel tomorrow. ¹⁹But now, if your land is unclean, pass over into the Lord's land where the Lord's tabernacle stands, and take for yourselves a possession among us; only do not rebel against the Lord, or make us as rebels by building yourselves an altar other than the altar of the Lord our God. ²⁰Did not Achan the son of Zerah break faith in the matter of the devoted things, and wrath fell upon all the congregation of Israel? And he did not perish alone for his iniquity.'"

²¹Then the Reubenites, the Gadites, and the half-tribe of Manasseh said in answer to the heads of the families of Israel, ²²"The Mighty One, God, the Lord! The Mighty One, God, the Lord! He knows; and let Israel itself know! If it was in rebellion or in breach of faith toward the Lord, spare us not today ²³for building an altar to turn away from following the Lord; or if we did so to offer burnt offerings or cereal offerings or peace offerings on it, may the Lord himself take vengeance. ²⁴Nay, but we did it from fear that in time to come your children might say to our children, 'What have you to do with the Lord, the God of Israel? ²⁵For the Lord has made the Jordan a boundary between us and you, you Reubenites and Gadites; you have no portion in the Lord.' So your children might make our children cease to worship the Lord. ²⁶Therefore we said, 'Let us now build an altar, not for burnt offering, nor for sacrifice, ²⁷but to be a witness between us and you, and between the generations after us, that we do perform the service of the Lord in his presence with our burnt offerings and sacrifices and peace offerings; lest your children say to our children in time to come, "You have no portion in the Lord."' ²⁸And we thought, If this should be said to us or to our descendants in time to come, we should say, 'Behold the copy of the altar of the Lord, which our fathers made, not for burnt offerings, nor for sacrifice, but to be a witness between us and you.' ²⁹Far be it from us that we should rebel against the Lord, and turn away this day from following the Lord by building an altar for burnt offering, cereal offering, or sacrifice, other than the altar of the Lord our God that stands before his tabernacle!"

³⁰When Phinehas the priest and the chiefs of the congregation, the heads of the families of Israel who were with him, heard the words that the Reubenites and the Gadites and the Manassites spoke, it pleased

them well. [31]And Phinehas the son of Eleazar the priest said to the Reubenites and the Gadites and the Manassites, "Today we know that the Lord is in the midst of us, because you have not committed this treachery against the Lord; now you have saved the people of Israel from the hand of the Lord."

[32]Then Phinehas the son of Eleazar the priest, and the chiefs, returned from the Reubenites and the Gadites in the land of Gilead to the land of Canaan, to the people of Israel, and brought back word to them. [33]And the report pleased the people of Israel; and the people of Israel blessed God and spoke no more of making war against them, to destroy the land where the Reubenites and the Gadites were settled. [34]The Reubenites and the Gadites called the altar Witness; "For," said they, "it is a witness between us that the Lord is God."

(i)

Joshua blesses the eastern tribes as they set off to re-cross the Jordan. In an almost conventional way he underscores their success and wishes them well in their good fortune:

> "Go back to your homes [literally "tents"] with much wealth, and with very many cattle, with silver, gold, bronze, and iron, and with much clothing; divide the spoil of your enemies with your brethren."
>
> (22:8)

But before this he strings together more typical exhortations from Deuteronomy than that book ever includes in a single verse:

> "Take good care to observe the commandment and the law which Moses the servant of the Lord commanded you, to love the Lord your God, and to walk in all his ways, and to keep his commandments, and to cleave to him, and to serve him with all your heart and with all your soul."
>
> (22:5)

A selection of similar expressions is found in Deut. 11:22 and 30:20. In the first of these passages, loyalty to the Lord will lead to Israel dispossessing nations greater and mightier than themselves. In the second, summing up the great alternatives of Deut. 27–30 of blessing and cursing, death and life, it is observed that only love of God will result in *life*: and that means a long stay on the land given.

We should note in Josh. 22:5 the way in which emotive and down-to-earth practical expressions mutually reinforce each other. We start with careful observance of Commandment and Law—*individual* Commandment and *whole* Law. That's what it is to love the Lord. But equally love is something much richer than scrupulous observance. Yet again strong love is not just emotion and passion, it requires learning and accommodating. Israel, after her desert honeymoon with Yahweh of which Hosea and Jeremiah speak, has now been brought into her new home. She must learn "to walk in all his ways"—the lover has still a lot to learn about the loved one. Part of that will be reasonably straightforward—a matter of keeping his commandments. But the most distinctive and perhaps the most important element in the whole catalogue is what follows—"to cleave to him". It can mean both "cling to passionately" and "stay firmly loyal". We shall see later in this volume that when Orpah kissed her mother-in-law (farewell) Ruth by contrast "clung to her".

Love and loyalty are not enough. King Solomon's downfall is depicted in very similar terms:

> Now King Solomon loved many foreign women: the daughter of Pharaoh, and Moabite, Ammonite, Edomite, Sidonian, and Hittite women, from the nations concerning which the Lord had said to the people of Israel, "You shall not enter into marriage with them, neither shall they with you, for surely they will turn away your heart after their gods"; Solomon clung to these in love.
>
> (1 Kings 11:1–2)

And so our verse comes to its climax in an expression that perfectly blends the practical and the emotional: the engagement of the whole self in specific obedience—"and to serve him with all your heart and with all your soul".

If they heed all this then they will have deserved the blessing with which he sends them away—that very material blessing of wealth and cattle and precious metals and clothing and all the spoil of their enemies (22:8). But it is a very big "if" for Joshua. Various parts of his careful speech of farewell go together to emphasize the precariousness of the Transjordanian situation. It is exactly because they are going back to tents outside the promised land that they have all the more need of maintaining passionate fidelity to Yahweh. The very terms of his dispatch make us wonder if this brave experiment *can* work even if its programme was given by Moses. And certainly his more hot-headed brothers in the west are very quick to cry treachery (22:16) and to reach for their weapons at the first suspicion of religious deviation.

(ii)

We shall savour in our next section some of the details of the delightful dialogue between eastern and western brothers. Here I want simply to draw attention to a place, and a name, and another Biblical story. Apart from the mention of half-Manasseh in Bashan (22:7), Gilead is the name this story calls the territory across the Jordan for the two-and-a-half tribes (verses 9, 13, 15, 32). The altar at issue in the story the easterners finally name "witness".

The troubled tale of Jacob and Laban comes to an end in Genesis 31, with Laban suggesting a covenant and a witness between them. Jacob responds by setting up a stone pillar and a cairn of stones. The pillar is called "Outlook"—in Hebrew *Mizpah*—a relatively common name in the hilly Holy Land. The name of the cairn is also a geographical pun: for in Hebrew cairn (*gl*) and witness (*'d*) are both two-letter words, and when their four letters are strung together they spell "Gilead".

Laban invokes these two monuments in the haunting words

"The Lord watch between you and me, when we are absent one from the other. If you ill-treat my daughters, or if you take wives besides my daughters, although no man is with us, remember, God is witness between you and me."

(Genesis 31:49–50)

The stones will also act as a boundary marker between Israelite Jacob and Aramaean Laban.

Our story in Josh. 22 is also a boundary story. Our story is also about stones of silent witness. Our story also puns on the name

Gilead with "witness" at its end and yet another word spun out of the letters *gl* at its beginning (the word translated "region" in v. 10). There are several echoes in Genesis on the one side and Joshua and Judges on the other between actions of Israel when settling in her land and actions of her forefathers when they were first there.

"HE KNOWS; AND LET ISRAEL ITSELF KNOW!"

Joshua 22:7–34 (*cont'd*)

There is humour in plenty in this story of the altar. It has many typical elements of a family quarrel and it offers almost a carica-ture of the process of oriental bargaining—or do I mean inter-national diplomacy? The dialogue deserves to be read aloud by two voices—and even over-acted.

On reaching the Jordan the easterners build an altar. Not any miniature replica but "an altar of great size" (22:10). This act is immediately noised about the west; and the gut response is to muster at Shiloh for punitive war. Fortunately they dispatch first a representative embassy headed appropriately by the the son of the leading priest. It is after all a religious matter. They do not ask what the easterners have done or what they meant by it. All that they know already without investigation. They speak after all for "the whole congregation of the Lord"!

> "What is this treachery which you have committed against the God of Israel in turning away this day from following the Lord, by building yourselves an altar this day in rebellion against the Lord?"
>
> (22:16)

The westerners claim to speak for *all* Israel. They shout *ma'al* (Josh. 7) and quote Peor (Num. 25) and Achar (Josh. 7) as awful precedents. And when they say, "if you rebel against the Lord today he will be angry with the whole congregation of Israel tomorrow", the easterners must wonder whether or not they are part of that congregation. The hidden western assumption which we have already detected in Joshua's more sober farewell speech is let slip in verse 19:

". . . if your land is unclean, pass over into the Lord's land where the Lord's tabernacle stands, and take for yourselves a possession among us; only do not rebel against the Lord, or make us as rebels by building yourselves an altar other than the altar of the Lord our God."

They know that the others are in the wrong place. Nothing they can do will be right.

Reuben, Gad and half-Manasseh respond in a classic shriek of innocence. "How could you possibly have assumed that our altar was intended for sacrifice? Of course we agree that that would have been apostasy. May God himself take vengeance if that was in our minds . . ." And we readers must judge their innocence. Protestations to a hostile embassy backed by a mustered army are not always truthful. It is at the end of their speech too that their real fear is expressed. "The time may come when your descendants declare the Jordan a divinely sanctioned border, and so too an exclusive border. That will effectively stop our descendants worshipping Yahweh. Our symbolic copy of your altar simply testifies to our loyalty, not to our treachery."

Mercifully a bargain is struck: "Ours is the proper altar—you are dangerous apostates." "We'll keep ours, but we won't use it." "If you don't use it, we won't pull it down."

An interesting symbol of compromise—an altar without sacrifice. A slaughter *place* but no *slaughter*. How long did it work? Was it a stable compromise? We have absolutely no historical confirmation. Possibly it is only a story; and if that story does reflect a historical situation it may be much later conflicts after Judah's exile that it mirrors. In many periods since then—and it is especially true today—there has been great tension within Judaism between those who hold you can be a Jew anywhere and those who hold that only in Israel can you be a good Jew.

More specifically we know that some time after Jerusalem fell to the Babylonians some Jewish mercenaries in Egypt had a temple on an island in the Nile. For them that was clearly acceptable. In Jerusalem they were considered a crowd of heretics.

An empty altar is a useful symbol of compromise if it recognizes that others have rights too and that ours are less absolute than we would like to claim. It is the kind of compromise that Israel and the Palestinians are needing. An altar but no sacrifice on it might be a good symbol for sovereignty without defence, for territorial rights without an army. Might a demilitarized state on the West Bank and in Gaza be the kind of altar without sacrifice to which those who today speak for the whole community of Israel should agree?

Yet we are much too well protected if *we* see this story simply as caricature or as a piece of oriental bargaining that has nothing to do with our culture. "Born again" Christians, episcopally confirmed Christians, spirit-filled Christians, Christians led by Peter's successor in Rome—all of us, when we get the chance, "speak for the whole community of the Lord"; and history is littered with Christian conflict backed by a show of force. All of us need to cultivate the symbolic unused altar.

JOSHUA'S "FIRST" FAREWELL

Joshua 23:1–16

[1]A long time afterward, when the Lord had given rest to Israel from all their enemies round about, and Joshua was old and well advanced in years, [2]Joshua summoned all Israel, their elders and heads, their judges and officers, and said to them, "I am now old and well advanced in years; [3]and you have seen all that the Lord your God has done to all these nations for your sake, for it is the Lord your God who has fought for you. [4]Behold, I have allotted to you as an inheritance for your tribes those nations that remain, along with all the nations that I have already cut off, from the Jordan to the Great Sea in the west. [5]The Lord your God will push them back before you, and drive them out of your sight; and you shall possess their land, as the Lord your God promised you. [6] Therefore be very steadfast to keep and do all that is written in the book of the law of Moses, turning aside from it neither to the right hand nor to the left, [7]that you may not be mixed with these nations left here among you, or make mention of the names of their gods, or swear by them, or serve them, or bow down yourselves to them, [8]but cleave to the Lord your God as you have done to this day. [9]For the Lord has driven out before you great and strong nations; and

as for you, no man has been able to withstand you to this day. [10]One man of you puts to flight a thousand, since it is the Lord your God who fights for you, as he promised you. [11]Take good heed to yourselves, therefore, to love the Lord your God. [12]For if you turn back, and join the remnant of these nations left here among you, and make marriages with them, so that you marry their women and they yours, [13]know assuredly that the Lord your God will not continue to drive out these nations before you; but they shall be a snare and a trap for you, a scourge on your sides, and thorns in your eyes, till you perish from off this good land which the Lord your God has given you.

[14]"And now I am about to go the way of all the earth, and you know in your hearts and souls, all of you, that not one thing has failed of all the good things which the Lord your God promised concerning you; all have come to pass for you, not one of them has failed. [15]But just as all the good things which the Lord your God promised concerning you have been fulfilled for you, so the Lord will bring upon you all the evil things, until he have destroyed you from off this good land which the Lord your God has given you, [16]if you transgress the covenant of the Lord your God, which he commanded you, and go and serve other gods and bow down to them. Then the anger of the Lord will be kindled against you, and you shall perish quickly from off the good land which he has given to you."

Chapters 23 and 24 of the Book of Joshua both contain farewell speeches from the leader. The first of these may well really be the second from the point of view of the literary history of the book. It picks up and develops more consistently themes from earlier chapters in the book. Two of these, meditation on the Law (from 1:7–9) and the nations that remain (from 13:2–6), help us to be certain that this chapter was not part of the original conclusion of the book. Instead it was an element in a major revision of the Joshua traditions. (Earlier sections of this volume have pointed out why Joshua 1:7–9 and 13:2–6 are developed from the passages close to them and not original elements of those passages.)

In a manner typical of a certain style of sermon, this chapter on one level is a string of Biblical quotations. It would be too pedantic to take space to point this out in detail. Yet like the best of such sermons it uses these familiar and authoritative words to great effect in making its own few main points.

(i) Joshua first expresses his confidence in what has happened under his leadership. His people have seen how God has fought for them. They have already taken up the land God granted to them—and there is more to come. What they have seen started should give them confidence that it may be continued. Yet the consistency of action they may expect from their God should be matched by their own loyalty. The Mosaic inheritance does not tolerate deviation, and the kernel of that inheritance is the opening of the Ten Commandments: NO OTHER GODS. Even when the future is unclear, "cleave to the Lord your God as you have done to this day" (23:8). Hold on tight even with your eyes shut. He has looked after you before; don't go anywhere else for help. "Faith" as a word is rare in the Old Testament but many of its books describe very eloquently the components of rich and mature faith.

(ii) Intermarriage is the preacher's particular fear. It is striking how quickly his confidence in what has been achieved disappears. Whether Israel's men marry women from the other nations or Israel's women are given in marriage to their men, the result will be the same: a diminishing of Israel. There is no easy pluralistic optimism here that in mixed marriages you win some and you lose some. It is in the Books of Ezra and Nehemiah, which describe the reconstruction of the Jewish community after the return from exile in Babylon, that we find the most forceful opposition to mixed marriages (see especially Ezra 9–10). Perhaps it was this same situation that Joshua 23 first addressed. Fear and suspicion of mixed marriage belongs better to an uprooted community seeking to maintain its identity in a strange land or trying to reconstruct a small city state around Jerusalem within the Persian Empire. It is not easy to square with Israel's thrusting confidence in her new land, with God's promises all fulfilled and no enemies able to withstand. Reluctance over intermarriage, and laws prohibiting sexual union between races, belong to societies on the defensive, not to communities in the first enthusiasm of settlement and development.

(iii) The dangers of both apostasy and intermarriage are just aspects of the preacher's concern for Moses' teaching as a whole.

One of the paradoxes of the Old Testament is that, although Moses himself is set early in Israel's story, mention of him and of his inheritance is found outside the Pentateuch mainly if not wholly in the *latest* strands of the Bible. Concern for *Torah* has been a vital element in keeping Judaism intact over two thousand years of dispersion. Yet one of the most striking aspects of the modern state of Israel is just how quickly many of the most characteristic features of dispersed, observant Judaism have lapsed. Many Israelis who are gladly making common cause as a nation on (what they at least hold to be) their own land, observe neither Sabbath nor food laws, and would gladly be rid of more rabbinic control if only the state permitted. All these things, they say, belong to the shameful past.

(iv) The key word of the last four verses of chapter 23 is "good". Good has been spoken by Yahweh to Israel. Good promises and positive encouragement. The land itself was the principal promise; and the land itself is the physical context in which the good life can be lived.

"For the Lord your God is bringing you into a good land, a land of brooks of water, of fountains and springs, flowing forth in valleys and hills, a land of wheat and barley, of vines and fig trees and pomegranates, a land of olive trees and honey, a land in which you will eat bread without scarcity, in which you will lack nothing, a land whose stones are iron, and out of whose hills you can dig copper. And you shall eat and be full, and you shall bless the Lord your God for the good land he has given you."

(Deut. 8:7–10)

God has uttered what is good and has given what is good. We are inevitably reminded of the repeated emphasis at the beginning of Genesis that everything that God created by speaking was good—very good. It is not just "good" that is common to both texts. Just as "earth" in English can mean both "soil" and "world" so *ha-arets* in Hebrew refers both to the *land* (of Israel) and the *world*. God gives Israel in Canaan the same opportunity as he gave mankind at the beginning—a fresh start in a good place. Unhappily in both contexts evil too has soon to be mentioned.

JOSHUA'S REVIEW

Joshua 24:1–13

¹Then Joshua gathered all the tribes of Israel to Shechem, and summoned the elders, the heads, the judges, and the officers of Israel; and they presented themselves before God. ²And Joshua said to all the people, "Thus says the Lord, the God of Israel, 'Your fathers lived of old beyond the Eu-phrates, Terah, the father of Abraham and of Nahor; and they served other gods. ³Then I took your father Abraham from beyond the River and led him through all the land of Canaan, and made his offspring many. I gave him Isaac; ⁴and to Isaac I gave Jacob and Esau. And I gave Esau the hill country of Seir to possess, but Jacob and his children went down to Egypt. ⁵And I sent Moses and Aaron, and I plagued Egypt with what I did in the midst of it; and afterwards I brought you out. ⁶Then I brought your fathers out of Egypt, and you came to the sea; and the Egyptians pursued your fathers with chariots and horsemen to the Red Sea. ⁷And when they cried to the Lord, he put darkness between you and the Egyptians, and made the sea come upon them and cover them; and your eyes saw what I did to Egypt; and you lived in the wilderness a long time. ⁸Then I brought you to the land of the Amorites, who lived on the other side of the Jordan; they fought with you, and I gave them into your hand, and you took possession of their land, and I destroyed them before you. ⁹Then Balak the son of Zippor, king of Moab, arose and fought against Israel; and he sent and invited Balaam the son of Beor to curse you, ¹⁰but I would not listen to Balaam; therefore he blessed you; so I delivered you out of his hand. ¹¹And you went over the Jordan and came to Jericho, and the men of Jericho fought against you, and also the Amorites, the Perizzites, the Canaanites, the Hittites, the Girgashites, the Hivites, and the Jebusites; and I gave them into your hand. ¹²And I sent the hornet before you, which drove them out before you, the two kings of the Amorites; it was not by your sword or by your bow. ¹³I gave you a land on which you had not laboured, and cities which you had not built, and you dwell therein; you eat the fruit of vineyards and oliveyards which you did not plant.'"

The end of the Book of Joshua tells of a convocation at *Shechem*. We are hardly prepared for this, for Gilgal and Shiloh have been Joshua's centres up to this point (the altar between Gerizim and

Ebal mentioned in 8:30–35 does of course hint at Shechem—but it is a late tradition which rather presupposes chapter 24 than prepares for it). Shechem must be the appropriate place of *religious* assembly at the time; for 24:1 says not that they responded to Joshua's invitation but that "they presented themselves before God". It is explicitly in his name that Joshua speaks (v. 2).

The main element in this solemn address is an extended review of Israel's remote and recent past. We are taken from Abraham's call beyond the Euphrates to his travels through the length of Canaan and the report of his many offspring. Isaac, and then Jacob and Esau, are quickly mentioned. Esau was settled in his own mountain land east of the Dead Sea, but Jacob continued the family wanderings out of Canaan to Egypt. The familiar story is recalled of oppression and plague and deliverance at the sea, and of a long period in the wilderness.

There is almost a family of such historical reviews in the Bible. Some are shorter, some are longer. The two closest to Josh. 24 are in the Book of Deuteronomy. The first we mentioned earlier in connection with the end of Josh. 4. The child's question, "Why the Law?" will be answered:

> "We were Pharaoh's slaves in Egypt; and the Lord brought us out of Egypt with a mighty hand; and the Lord showed signs and wonders, great and grievous, against Egypt and against Pharaoh and all his household, before our eyes; and he brought us out from there, that he might bring us in and give us the land which he swore to give to our fathers. And the Lord commanded us to do all these statutes . . ."
> (6:20–24)

Then Deut. 26:5–10 ordains that the basket of first-fruits will be taken annually to the sanctuary and presented there with the famous words:

> "A wandering Aramean [AV, A Syrian ready to perish] was my father; and he went down into Egypt and sojourned there, few in number; and there he became a nation, great, mighty, and populous. and the Egyptians treated us harshly . . ."

Psalms 135 and 136 are good examples of how such reviews of the past could be sung in praise of Yahweh; and Psalms 105 and 106 demonstrate just how detailed these historical hymns could become.

However, Joshua's main purpose is teaching rather than praise. What is often most interesting about the teacher's craft is how he adapts the tradition he shares with his audience in order to serve the particular purpose in hand. Joshua's review of the past, especially the most recent past, is very interesting for the different perspective it offers on some familiar topics. It is strikingly at odds with earlier portions of the Book of Joshua. Certainly the fate of Sihon and Og, kings of Heshbon and Bashan, who had made war on an Israel offering peace in Transjordan, is fairly summarized in verse 8. So too is the tale of Balaam in the following two verses. However, "you went over the Jordan and came to Jericho, and the lords [RSV men] of Jericho fought against you ... and I gave them into your hand" is hardly the impression we received from Joshua 2 and 6. In those chapters espionage is directed from before the Jordan crossing and Jericho is cowering behind closed gates in terror of its fate. An impression is given here of Israel's innocence in what took place—"It was self-defence m'Lud! I just happened to be there. It was quite unprovoked." We all know this wide-eyed ploy well enough. Divinely inspired terror is credited with the rest of the task, "personified" as the hornet (as it is also in Exod. 23:28 and Deut. 7:20). It may remind us of the striking image in Isaiah of swarms of insects representing hostile foreign hordes:

> In that day the Lord will whistle for the fly which is at the sources of the streams of Egypt, and for the bee which is in the land of Assyria. And they will all come and settle in the steep ravines, and in the clefts of the rocks, and on all the thornbushes, and on all the pastures.
>
> (7:18–19)

It is impossible to decide who is meant by the two kings of the Amorites (v. 12)—the Greek translation has "twelve" which is no easier. In any case—and this *does* square with the main Joshua tradition—God is given the credit and not Israel's own military prowess: "It was not by your sword or by your bow."

Amos castigates the wicked rich of his own day for unjustly acquiring too much property:

Therefore because you trample upon the poor
   and take from him exactions of wheat,
you have built houses of hewn stone,
   but you shall not dwell in them;
you have planted pleasant vineyards,
   but you shall not drink their wine.   (5:11)

This fate has apparently befallen the inhabitants of the land and Israel are the beneficiaries. Of those to whom much has been given, much also is expected.

"CHOOSE THIS DAY WHOM YE WILL SERVE"

Joshua 24:14–33

[14]"Now therefore fear the Lord, and serve him in sincerity and in faithfulness; put away the gods which your fathers served beyond the River, and in Egypt, and serve the Lord. [15]And if you be unwilling to serve the Lord, choose this day whom you will serve, whether the gods your fathers served in the region beyond the River, or the gods of the Amorites in whose land you dwell; but as for me and my house, we will serve the Lord."

[16]Then the people answered, "Far be it from us that we should forsake the Lord, to serve other gods; [17]for it is the Lord our God who brought us and our fathers up from the land of Egypt, out of the house of bondage, and who did those great signs in our sight, and preserved us in all the way that we went, and among all the peoples through whom we passed; [18]and the Lord drove out before us all the peoples, the Amorites who lived in the land; therefore we also will serve the Lord, for he is our God."

[19]But Joshua said to the people, "You cannot serve the Lord; for he is a holy God; he is a jealous God; he will not forgive your transgressions or your sins. [20]If you forsake the Lord and serve foreign gods, then he will turn and do you harm, and consume you, after having done you good." [21]And the people said to Joshua, "Nay; but we will serve the Lord." [22]Then Joshua said to the people, "You are witnesses against yourselves that you have chosen the Lord, to serve him." And they said, "We are witnesses." [23]He said, "Then put away the foreign gods which are among you, and incline your heart to the Lord, the God of Israel." [24]And the people said to Joshua, "The Lord our God we

will serve, and his voice we will obey." ²⁵So Joshua made a covenant with the people that day, and made statutes and ordinances for them at Shechem. ²⁶And Joshua wrote these words in the book of the law of God; and he took a great stone, and set it up there under the oak in the sanctuary of the Lord. ²⁷And Joshua said to all the people, "Behold, this stone shall be a witness against us; for it has heard all the words of the Lord which he spoke to us; therefore it shall be a witness against you, lest you deal falsely with your God." ²⁸So Joshua sent the people away, every man to his inheritance.

²⁹After these things Joshua the son of Nun, the servant of the Lord, died, being a hundred and ten years old. ³⁰And they buried him in his own inheritance at Timnath-serah, which is in the hill country of Ephraim, north of the mountain of Gaash.

³¹And Israel served the Lord all the days of Joshua, and all the days of the elders who outlived Joshua and had known all the work which the Lord did for Israel.

³²The bones of Joseph which the people of Israel brought up from Egypt were buried at Shechem, in the portion of ground which Jacob bought from the sons of Hamor the father of Shechem for a hundred pieces of money; it became an inheritance of the descendants of Joseph.

³³And Eleazar the son of Aaron died; and they buried him at Gibeah, the town of Phinehas his son, which had been given him in the hill country of Ephraim.

(i)

Choice is seldom offered to the people of the Bible in so many words. When it is offered it is something of a privilege. Usually it is *God's* business to choose. Deuteronomy talks regularly about him choosing a "place"—a sanctuary. He chooses David and his house, the city of Jerusalem, and a line of priests from Aaron; and of course he chooses the Biblical people as a whole:

> Blessed is the nation whose God is the Lord,
> the people whom he has chosen as his heritage!

> (Psalm 33:12)

Even *human* choice when it is offered is normally something lordly. A military commander chooses his front line troops—whether it be Moses or Joshua or David or Joab. Following his fateful census David is allowed to select which of three punishments will be allowed (2 Sam. 24). Then "the sons of God saw that the daughters of men were fair; and they took to wife such of them as they chose" (Gen. 6:2)

Choice belongs properly to the divine and the mighty. When it is exercised by others in the Old Testament, the stakes are large. Lot, when separating from Abraham, looked down on the Jordan Valley and saw it well watered like Egypt by the Nile. This territory he chose in preference to the land of Canaan which he left for Abraham—and fatefully the land of his choice included the cities of Sodom and Gomorrah.

Choice belonged to the privileged, and choice was something momentous. Alternatives are part of the stuff of the Book of Deuteronomy. These are reinforced in the blessings and curses of Deuteronomy 27–29. But it is only in the climax of the following chapter—that great culmination of Moses' long speech—that our key term of "choice" is first used.

> "I call heaven and earth to witness against you this day, that I have set before you life and death, blessing and curse; therefore choose life, that you and your descendants may live, loving the Lord your God, obeying his voice, and cleaving to him; for that means life to you and length of days, that you may dwell in the land which the Lord swore to your fathers, to Abraham, to Isaac, and to Jacob, to give them."
> (Deut. 30:19–20)

(ii)

What Joshua offers Israel at the end of their settlement process is even more momentous: choice of a god! Joshua 24 is a well-known text and that takes away from the surprise of this offer. Then again, those of us who live in modern pluralist societies expect the freedom to choose our religion, as well as our homes and our schools and our television sets. We do not readily sense the privilege offered Israel.

The "either/or" is there; but its terms are not for bargaining over. These are quite clearly laid out. The choice could be for the gods of Mesopotamia whom Abraham had known before his call, or the gods of Egypt worshipped by Israel's fathers despite Abraham's call, or the gods of the Amorites (Canaanites) in whose land Israel is now at home. On the other side there is Yahweh—the God of the radical break: Yahweh, who called Abraham out of Mesopotamia, and who called Israel "his son" out of Egypt. Israel may choose: but Joshua has already chosen (v. 15).

The people respond that they are already indebted to a God who has worked on their behalf—who has freed them from Egypt, who has preserved them in spectacular manner, and who has made room for them in a land. Yahweh, of whom all this ongoing story is true, is more worthy of their service than the local god of any country they may be in. "Far be it from us that we should forsake the Lord . . . we also will serve the Lord, for he is our God" (vv. 16–18).

The choice is a quite exclusive one and Joshua warns them plainly of the dangers of making it. Choosing Yahweh means serving a God who tolerates no other gods in his presence (the first of the Ten Commandments). When they persist in their loyalty he cites two different witnesses to their decision: (1) they themselves are witness against themselves; and (2) a great stone is set up in the sanctuary which silently hears their solemn protestations.

We all know only too well that *we* possess much more evidence to bring against ourselves than any other who would testify against us. We often treasure fond memories of places and sanctuaries in which we have loved to worship. When we attend a wedding or a baptism, we are rightly challenged by the memory of the stones that heard us make great declarations as we professed our faith, dedicated our children, and promised life-long fidelity. If stones could talk!

HOLY AND JEALOUS GOD

Joshua 24:14–33 (*cont'd*)

(i)

Joshua makes to discourage his people's commitment to Yahweh with a warning about his character (v. 19). We may not think there is much wrong with "holiness". However that is often a rather more unnerving quality in the Old Testament than in traditional Christian theology or piety. Christian ideas of God are shaped—and sometimes perhaps tamed—by the conviction that there is no more to say about God than can be learned by meditation on the figure of Jesus Christ and on his teaching about God. This attractively simple statement overlooks the fact that there is remarkably little detailed teaching about God from Jesus: much of what he must have believed has simply to be deduced from the Old Testament, whose fundamental ideas were common to him and his followers.

Joshua is concerned to warn an over-eager Israel that God can be a dangerous force, and is not to be trifled with. The sort of holiness he has in mind we find again at the end of the story of the return of the Ark of the Lord from Philistine territory to Beth-shemesh in Israel. Some of the men of that town looked into the Ark and died.

> Then the men of Bethshemesh said, "Who is able to stand before the Lord, this holy God? And to whom shall he go up away from us?"
> (1 Sam. 6:20)

Holiness is like a *force*—protective of God and destructive of those who meddle.

(ii)

If it has been our business to point out that holiness in the Old Testament is sometimes a more frightening and dangerous concept than we often suppose, our problem with God's "jealousy" is a different one. Here our task is to rehabilitate an idea. One element in this next problem results from a quirk of the English language. Although they have different opening letters, "jealous" and "zealous" are both descended from the same Greek word *zelos*. There are many stranger oddities in the history of language. One of the oddest known to me is that "cow" and "beef" can both be traced back through the European languages to the same parent word. Since both words are available to us English speakers, we have learnt to operate with a distinction:

between the cow that eats grass in our fields and the beef that
appears on our dinner plates. (In French, by contrast, *boeuf* and
mouton both graze and are roasted.)

Zealous and jealous share the same quality of burning passionate concern. But we tend to use each word in a different context.
Someone is "zealous" in work, or for a cause; while "jealousy"
may be part of a strong love. If anything, in modern English,
"zeal" is more acceptable, while "jealousy" is rather suspect.
However, in the more traditional language of even modern Bible
translations or revisions, this distinction is not clear. Elijah claims
to "have been very *jealous* for the Lord, the God of hosts"
(1 Kings 19:10), while a psalmist complains as follows:

> For it is for thy sake that I have borne reproach,
>   that shame has covered my face.
> I have become a stranger to my brethren,
>   an alien to my mother's sons.
> For *zeal* for thy house has consumed me,
>   and the insults of those who insult thee have fallen on me.
>
>   (Psalm 69:7–9)

Hardly a very big difference.

(iii)

God's "holiness" speaks of his otherness, his "jealousy" (or his
"zeal"), of his single-mindedness. A character with these
qualities brooks no hostile opposition. Again the English translation in front of us is not fully helpful. The Hebrew sentence
translated "he will not forgive your transgressions" (v. 19) is
unusual and a little difficult; but I am clear that "he will not
tolerate your rebellion" comes closer to its sense. That is the sort
of "sin" which God cannot allow to obstruct his purposes. So the
text continues: "If you forsake the Lord and serve foreign gods,
then he will turn and do you harm, and consume you, after having
done you good" (24:20). This may also help to explain the exposi-
tion within the Ten Commandments of the prohibition of images
and their worship. When we read "you shall not bow down to
them or serve them; for I the Lord your God am a jealous God,
visiting the iniquity of the fathers upon the children to the third

and fourth generation of those who hate me", we are not dealing with a petty, spiteful figure but rather (as the very last words quoted show) with God reacting to being *hated* by those from whom *love* was expected.

This quality of "wholly other" zeal or enthusiasm brooks no outright opposition. It is easy to mock and decry as partial, blinkered, outdated—just as the jealous lover may be the object of some cruel amusement. But there remains a place for jealousy of the truth and of high standards. There remains a place for intolerant commitment—provided it is still to the right cause. And there's the rub! But remember Jesus arriving in Jerusalem at Passover:

> In the temple he found those who were selling oxen and sheep and pigeons, and the money-changers at their business. And making a whip of cords, he drove them all, with the sheep and oxen, out of the temple . . . His disciples remembered that it was written, "Zeal for thy house will consume me." (John 2:14–17)

COVENANT: STATUTES AND ORDINANCES

Joshua 24:14–33 (*cont'd*)

(i)

Joshua has offered his people an unusual and solemn choice. The gravity of the choice is underscored by a character sketch of Yahweh, the God involved. After the nature of the choice has been elaborated, the people respond, saying to Joshua, "The Lord our God we will serve, and his voice we will obey" (24:24).

Quite a lot hangs on how the following verse, which includes the words in our title, is understood. A decision about this already influences how the verse is translated into English, and so the reader must bear with me as I talk a little about the Hebrew verse.

The RSV reads: "So Joshua made a covenant with the people that day, and made statutes and ordinances for them at Shechem" (24:25). The translators, it seems to me, have departed needlessly, if not heedlessly, from the shape of the Hebrew in two ways. First, although "statutes and ordinances" is a very common

Biblical phrase, especially in Deuteronomy, here the Hebrew has the singular "a statute and an ordinance"—or "a statutory ordinance". This singular phrase is very much rarer. We find it again in Hebrew only in Ezra 7:10 (where RSV again offers us the plural) and in Exodus 15:25 (where uniquely the translators have got it right). Then "*with* the people" and "*for* them" translate the same Hebrew preposition. Now, as I shall go on to argue, this preposition, and so the whole verse with it, may be taken in different ways—but hardly in two different ways at the same time.

What this boils down to is the following. Either our verse is saying that Joshua established a covenant *for* the people and made a statute and an ordinance *for* them, or that he imposed a covenant *on* the people and laid *on* them a statute and an ordinance. "Covenant with" is not the plain sense of this verse in Hebrew (we shall find a different situation at the beginning of Judges 2) and the balance of the verse properly translated is such that we must understand covenant and statutory ordinance very closely together.

Much depends on just *how* this passage pictures Joshua's role between God and people. Either from a position of solidarity with them, but conscious also of God's touchy unpredictability (his holy jealousy), he secures for the people some firm intimation of what sort of conduct will be deemed adequate service of this God. Or alternatively, as God's spokesman, he imposes on the people God's solemn demand.

The passage we have already quoted from Exodus is not too much help here, for as the footnote in the RSV makes clear the Hebrew does not specify whether it is the Lord or Moses who made for the people a statute and an ordinance at Marah. However, it does clearly associate this giving of statute and ordinance with testing and proving the people. God's covenant is a public standard. Adherence to its principles is a test of loyalty, a proof of courage, and so God's covenant here in Joshua 24 (or his ordained statute) is simply his revealed will. When we discussed Joshua 3 we saw that the "Ark of the Covenant" was so called because it was a box bearing his commandments. Josh. 24 too closes with tangible symbols like the Ark of the Covenant. Joshua makes a written copy of the statute and ordinance but he also sets up a stone in the sanctuary of the Lord at Shechem: a stone which has been silent witness to the whole transaction and to all the solemn declarations.

(ii)

If this act of Joshua underscores his links with Moses and the giving of the Law, and the traditions of Exodus and Deuteronomy, then the piece of filial piety described in verse 32 links the taking of the land to yet more remote traditions. Joseph, like Joshua, had died at a hundred and ten years after a life that had known success; but he had died outside the land promised to his father, the land of his own youth, and he pledged his descendants (Gen. 50:24–25) to bear his bones to the plot of land his father had purchased from the people of Hamor at Shechem. And so it is that while some of the patriarchal tombs (and pre-eminently those of Abraham and Sarah) can be visited at the great shrine of Hebron on land purchased by Abraham from Ephron, so Joseph's Tomb and Jacob's Well—the well where Jesus was to have his momentous conversation with the woman of Samaria— lie side by side to the east of modern Nablus and ancient Shechem.

Joshua himself was buried in the land granted to him at the end of the distribution of the land to all Israel (Josh. 19:49–50). And that almost marked the end of the good days; for when his leadership was removed and with it that of the elders of his own generation, Israel no longer served Yahweh despite all solemn promises, all written copies of the Law and all silent stones of witness. Just to underscore that the *whole* generation had passed away, Aaron's son, the priest Eleazar, also died and was buried in the land granted to his son Phinehas. The Book of Judges tells a very different story.

JUDGES

JUDAH'S SETTLEMENT—A SUCCESS?

Judges 1:1–21

¹After the death of Joshua the people of Israel inquired of the Lord, "Who shall go up first for us against the Canaanites to fight against them?" ²The Lord said, "Judah shall go up; behold, I have given the land into his hand." ³And Judah said to Simeon his brother, "Come up with me into the territory allotted to me, that we may fight against the Canaanites; and I likewise will go with you into the territory allotted to you." So Simeon went with him. ⁴Then Judah went up and the Lord gave the Canaanites and the Perizzites into their hand; and they defeated ten thousand of them at Bezek. ⁵They came upon Adoni-bezek at Bezek, and fought against him, and defeated the Canaanites and the Perizzites. ⁶Adoni-bezek fled; but they pursued him, and caught him, and cut off his thumbs and his great toes. ⁷And Adoni-bezek said, "Seventy kings with their thumbs and their great toes cut off used to pick up scraps under my table; as I have done, so God has requited me." And they brought him to Jerusalem, and he died there.

⁸And the men of Judah fought against Jerusalem, and took it, and smote it with the edge of the sword, and set the city on fire. ⁹And afterward the men of Judah went down to fight against the Canaanites who dwelt in the hill country, in the Negeb, and in the lowland. ¹⁰And Judah went against the Canaanites who dwelt in Hebron (now the name of Hebron was formerly Kiriath-arba); and they defeated Sheshai and Ahiman and Talmai.

¹¹From there they went against the inhabitants of Debir. The name of Debir was formerly Kiriath-sepher. ¹²And Caleb said, "He who attacks Kiriath-sepher and takes it, I will give him Achsah my daughter as wife." ¹³And Othni-el the son of Kenaz, Caleb's younger brother, took it; and he gave him Achsah his daughter as wife. ¹⁴When she came to him, she urged him to ask her father for a field; and she

alighted from her ass, and Caleb said to her, "What do you wish?" [15]She said to him, "Give me a present; since you have set me in the land of the Negeb, give me also springs of water." And Caleb gave her the upper springs and the lower springs.

[16]And the descendants of the Kenite, Moses' father-in-law, went up with the people of Judah from the city of palms into the wilderness of Judah, which lies in the Negeb near Arad; and they went and settled with the people. [17]And Judah went with Simeon his brother, and they defeated the Canaanites who inhabited Zephath, and utterly destroyed it. So the name of the city was called Hormah. [18]Judah also took Gaza with its territory, and Ashkelon with its territory, and Ekron with its territory. [19]And the Lord was with Judah, and he took possession of the hill country, but he could not drive out the inhabitants of the plain, because they had chariots of iron. [20]And Hebron was given to Caleb, as Moses had said; and he drove out from it the three sons of Anak. [21]But the people of Benjamin did not drive out the Jebusites who dwelt in Jerusalem; so the Jebusites have dwelt with the people of Benjamin in Jerusalem to this day.

(i)

In many respects the opening chapter of this book represents an odd introduction to the Judges. The business of judging comes nowhere into discussion. Not a judge is mentioned.

This silence is surprising, especially as we move from the Book of Joshua which began with a divine address to its hero and closed with his death and burial. However, it jolts us very quickly into noticing that this so-called "Book of Judges" is not simply a series of narratives about Israel's judges. Such narratives do form the substantial core of the book (chapters 3–16) and they have given the book its name. Their own proper introduction takes up much of chapter 2. However, the book begins, and even more substantially ends, by exploring different concerns. Just one aspect of the contrast between the main contents of the book and its outer casing is the greater prominence of Judah in the latter.

(ii)

In fact these opening verses of the first chapter concentrate exclusively on Greater Judah. However, the passage is built up of tiny separate scraps of information, some of which appear to contradict each other, some of which make surprisingly extravagant claims, and some of which the attentive reader will notice have already appeared in rather different forms scattered through the Book of Joshua.

Judah's precedence is signalled right at the beginning (vv. 1–2). These verses anticipate the rather fuller questioning of God before and during the battle against Benjamin in chapter 20 (see especially vv. 18, 23 and 27–28). Who will have pride of place in the front line? Who will have the honour of making a beginning? This interest in priority, initiative, and getting things going is echoed at other points in the book too, like 10:18—"Who is the man that will *begin* to fight against the Ammonites? He shall be head over all the inhabitants of Gilead." Then it is said during the promise of Samson's birth: "he shall *begin* to deliver Israel from the hand of the Philistines" (13:5).

Judges 1 describes an almost complete muster of Israel according to the traditional twelve-tribe pattern. Typically that means a mention, but no more than a mention, of Simeon (vv. 3, 17). Simeon was only known in later historical times as a part of southern Judah. Josh. 19:1–9 makes the matter quite clear, and lists as belonging to Simeon towns already attributed to Judah in 15:21–32. Accordingly, Judg. 1 pays occasional lip-service to co-operation between the two unequal partners; but mostly it talks simply of Judah.

Verses 4–7 provide our first brief anecdote. This is one which is not straight from the Book of Joshua. The story starts in Bezeq, possibly situated about half way between Tel Aviv and Jerusalem, close to the modern highway, and finishes in Jerusalem. Judah's unfortunate victim is effectively mutilated to prevent his bearing arms again: a fate he bears philosophically enough, even managing a boast as he reflects on his come-uppance. But who is he? And why is he taken to Jerusalem to die? Adoni*bezeq* means "the master of Bezeq", and he is otherwise unknown. The Jerusalem Bible suggests we should read his name as Adoni*zedeq*. The confusion is as easy to make in Hebrew as

English, especially when Bezeq appears as a place-name in the story. The large number of seventy vanquished kings certainly fits the proud city of Jerusalem better than the unknown Bezeq.

If all this is plausible so far, then we may suppose we are dealing here with the same Adonizedeq of Jerusalem who led an anti-Israelite coalition in Josh. 10. Indeed this will be the first—and strategically placed—instance in Judg. 1 where successes attributed to others in the Book of Joshua are claimed for Judah. Verse 8 in fact outdoes the record in Josh. 10 by claiming a capture and sacking of Jerusalem itself—more reliable tradition reports that King David was the first to achieve that (2 Sam. 5: 6–10). The next verse again follows the model in Josh. 10 by noting a general mopping-up expedition to the south.

The next short section (vv. 10–16) takes us over ground we have already traversed two or three times in the Book of Joshua! The Anakites, former inhabitants of Hebron, fell victim to Caleb according to Josh. 14:12 and 15:13–14, while success against them in Hebron as elsewhere is specifically attributed to Joshua in 11:21–22. Here in Judg. 1, a third claim is made—this time, that the success was Judah's. Verses 11–15 repeat Josh. 15:15–19 almost word for word, but give a different, and *Judean* impression. Indeed such are the quirks in these snatch memories of early times that the same Othniel they tell of will reappear in a very different role in Judg. 3:7–11, this time judging Israel!

Apart from the claim to an early capture of Jerusalem, the other striking boast is of supremacy over the Philistines (v. 18). Along with Gath and Ashdod, these cities of Gaza, Ashkelon and Ekron were the "home base" of the "five lords of the Philistines" (Judg. 3:3). Judah's claim here co-exists very uneasily with her craven attitude to the Philistines in the time of Samson (Judg. 15); and again represents an achievement of later times.

(iii)

In fact the record seems to be set straight in three deft verses (vv. 19–21). The first dutifully notes that Judah did enjoy divine assistance; but this had extended only to securing the hill country·

the Philistine plain (and historically it was that people who enjoyed the early monopoly of iron in the area) was denied to them. Secondly, Hebron is redesignated as Caleb's, and on nothing less than the authority of Moses himself. And finally (v. 21), not only is it pointed out that the taking of Jerusalem was less than completely successful, but the Israelite attackers are said to have been *Benjamin* (contrast Josh. 15:63).

These three footnotes surprisingly weaken the force of the main text. Verse 19 neutralizes verse 18; verse 20 contradicts verse 10; and verse 21 throws a very different light on verse 8.

THE SITUATION IN THE NORTH AND A DIVINE WARNING

Judges 1:22–2:5

²²The house of Joseph also went up against Bethel; and the Lord was with them. ²³And the house of Joseph sent to spy out Bethel. (Now the name of the city was formerly Luz.) ²⁴And the spies saw a man coming out of the city, and they said to him, "Pray, show us the way into the city, and we will deal kindly with you." ²⁵And he showed them the way into the city; and they smote the city with the edge of the sword, but they let the man and all his family go. ²⁶And the man went to the land of the Hittites and built a city, and called its name Luz; that is its name to this day.

²⁷Manasseh did not drive out the inhabitants of Beth-shean and its villages, or Taanach and its villages, or the inhabitants of Dor and its villages, or the inhabitants of Ible-am and its villages, or the inhabitants of Megiddo and its villages; but the Canaanites persisted in dwelling in that land. ²⁸When Israel grew strong, they put the Canaanites to forced labour, but did not utterly drive them out.

²⁹And Ephraim did not drive out the Canaanites who dwelt in Gezer; but the Canaanites dwelt in Gezer among them.

³⁰Zebulun did not drive out the inhabitants of Kitron, or the inhabitants of Nahalol; but the Canaanites dwelt among them, and became subject to forced labour.

³¹Asher did not drive out the inhabitants of Acco, or the inhabitants of Sidon, or of Ahlab, or of Achzib, or of Helbah, or of Aphik, or of

Rehob; [32]but the Asherites dwelt among the Canaanites, the inhabitants of the land; for they did not drive them out.

[33]Naphtali did not drive out the inhabitants of Beth-shemesh, or the inhabitants of Beth-anath, but dwelt among the Canaanites, the inhabitants of the land; nevertheless the inhabitants of Beth-shemesh and of Beth-anath became subject to forced labour for them.

[34]The Amorites pressed the Danites back into the hill country, for they did not allow them to come down to the plain; [35]the Amorites persisted in dwelling in Har-heres, in Aijalon, and in Sha-albim, but the hand of the house of Joseph rested heavily upon them, and they became subject to forced labour. [36]And the border of the Amorites ran from the ascent of Akrabbim, from Sela and upward.

[1]Now the angel of the Lord went up from Gilgal to Bochim. And he said, "I brought you up from Egypt, and brought you into the land which I swore to give to your fathers. I said, 'I will never break my covenant with you, [2]and you shall make no covenant with the inhabitants of this land; you shall break down their altars.' But you have not obeyed my command. What is this you have done? [3]So now I say, I will not drive them out before you; but they shall become adversaries to you, and their gods shall be a snare to you." [4]When the angel of the Lord spoke these words to all the people of Israel, the people lifted up their voices and wept. [5]And they called the name of that place Bochim; and they sacrificed there to the Lord.

(i)

The final three verses of the previous section, with their alternative tradition, make the whole piece much harder to interpret. To anyone ignorant about the other traditions of the settlement in the south in Josh. 10–11 and 14–15, Judg. 1:1–18 would occasion little surprise. After their official presentation of the case, verses 19–21 read like a rather impudent yet knowing aside: that's what they say in Judah, but I know better! So read, the opening eighteen verses represent the main stock of the chapter and the next three a supplement. The Biblical witness is seldom simple and straightforward. However, this should not disturb attentive Christian readers, given that the central figure of our faith is presented to us in four very different gospels. Polemic and discussion are represented in them too.

For our more immediate purposes, what I want to draw attention to is this. Since we are already a little confused as we leave
Benjamin putting pressure on a city Judah has already sacked, we
must be peculiarly sensitive to whatever hints the next verses
offer for an interpretation of the whole chapter.

(ii)

Much of the rest of the chapter is a series of notes about difficulties experienced by most of Israel's tribes in central and northern Palestine (vv. 27–36). However, a more positive note is
sounded first (vv. 22–26). The "house of Joseph" is the next main
Israelite force to "go up". The Lord was with them too (v. 22).
The move Joseph makes is against Bethel. Spies are dispatched.
Fortunately they are able to strike a deal with a man they see
leaving the city: they do not have to compromise themselves in
any harlot's house as in Josh. 2. Equally, when the city is captured, they do not have to accommodate their helpful alien
amongst themselves, like Rahab's family in Jericho. The infor-
mant is prepared to go with all his family to another country and
found another settlement to bear the name of Luz, the former
name of Bethel. And how many contemporary Israelis wish that
the Arab Palestinians, both the refugees and the many still in
their own homes in many parts of "Greater Israel", would simply
do likewise and go away! And how many Britons and western
Europeans wish that minority populations they encouraged to
immigrate, when their economies were booming, would render
their greatest service by simply disappearing!

The situation of the house of Joseph in Bethel was ideal. They
were alone in the area and beholden to no one. Just the opposite
was the case throughout the remainder of the chapter. Manasseh
and Ephraim failed to evict Canaanite inhabitants from the cities
in their territories (vv. 27–28 and 29—compare Josh. 17:11–13
and 16:10). A similar tale is told of Zebulun, Asher, and Naphtali
(vv. 30–33). In fact the situation is worse in the case of Galilean
Asher and Naphtali, for there it is quietly admitted not that
Canaanites managed to hold on amongst them but that they lived

on among the Canaanites! As for poor Dan (vv. 34–35), they were pushed into the hill country; and any pressure on the original Amorites in that area came not from them, but from the house of Joseph. Two different modes of dealing with the original inhabitants are set side by side. And it is fairly clear that both indeed do make the same point: an inadequate response to left-over alien minorities was responsible for a lot of future trouble in central and northern Israel, precisely the territory in which most of the Book of Judges is set.

As with verses 1–18 and 19–21, it is hard to believe that the two sections of this second main part of the chapter were drafted together. After all the house of Joseph, who are implicitly praised, are exactly the same people as the following Manasseh and Ephraim, who are implicitly blamed. We mentioned some of the evidence in our earlier handling of Josh. 16–17, which suggests that Joseph was added to these chapters about Ephraim and Manasseh. He is also mentioned in 18:1–10 as part of a later rewrite of the account of the division of Israel's land. That recasting of the tradition gave greater prominence than the earlier version to the two large groupings of Judah and Joseph. Somewhat similar motives may have been at work in Judg. 1.

(iii)

The speech of the divine messenger (2:1–5) serves to underscore just what message should be taken out of the rather confusing medley of traditional scraps of information that make up chapter 1. The Lord has observed faithfully all his covenanted promises to the people of Israel, in freeing them from Egypt and bringing them to Canaan. They have not been similarly faithful to him: in particular, alien altars and worship have been tolerated. That fact is used to explain a change in the divine plan for Israel. He will no longer drive out the former inhabitants before them, but will leave them as perennial enemies with their worship as a trap.

At the same time it is used for something much more matter-of-fact: to explain a place-name. Bochim literally means "Weepers"; and it bears that odd name because of the people's response to this announcement of the divine change of heart. Bochim is in fact yet another name for Bethel. This is confirmed by a short element in the Jacob traditions: "And Jacob came to Luz (that is, Bethel), which is in the land of Canaan, he and all the people who were with him, and there he built an altar, and called the place El-bethel, because there God had revealed himself to him when he fled from his brother. And Deborah, Rebekah's nurse, died, and she was buried under an oak below Bethel; so the name of it was called Allon-bacuth" (Gen. 35:6–8). We will meet her last resting place again in Judg. 4; let us simply note for the moment that its name means "Oak of Weeping".

Bethel occupies a very ambiguous position in the Old Testament. In the patriarchal traditions associated with Abraham and Jacob, it plays a positive role as one of their main centres and sanctuaries. On the other hand, in the writings associated with the Deuteronomic school, its name is associated with Jeroboam's breakaway from the Davidic rule and an alternative to the Jerusalem cult. In fact it becomes synonymous with apostasy. Though sharing a name with the Jacob story, Judg. 2:1–5 is part of the other tendency.

In their ultimate religious intention, this conclusion (2:1–5) and the opening section on the house of Joseph at Bethel (1:22–26) do agree with each other. And yet as historical record they can hardly co-exist. They agree that Israel would be a better place without the Canaanites and without their worship. But if everything had happened in Bethel as 1:22–26 describes, there would have been no problem for 2:1–5 to address.

THE JUDGES INTRODUCED

Judges 2:6–3:6

6When Joshua dismissed the people, the people of Israel went each to his inheritance to take possession of the land. 7And the people served the Lord all the days of Joshua, and all the days of the elders who outlived Joshua, who had seen all the great work which the Lord had done for Israel. [8]And Joshua the son of Nun, the servant of the Lord, died at the age of one hundred and ten years. [9]And they buried him within the bounds of his inheritance in Timnath-heres, in the hill country of Ephraim, north of the mountain of Gaash. [10]And all that generation also were gathered to their fathers; and there arose another generation after them, who did not know the Lord or the work which he had done for Israel.

[11]And the people of Israel did what was evil in the sight of the Lord and served the Baals; [12]and they forsook the Lord, the God of their fathers, who had brought them out of the land of Egypt; they went after other gods, from among the gods of the peoples who were round about them, and bowed down to them; and they provoked the Lord to anger. [13]They forsook the Lord, and served the Baals and the Ashtaroth. [14]So the anger of the Lord was kindled against Israel, and he gave them over to plunderers, who plundered them; and he sold them into the power of their enemies round about, so that they could no longer withstand their enemies. [15]Whenever they marched out, the hand of the Lord was against them for evil, as the Lord had warned, and as the Lord had sworn to them; and they were in sore straits.

[16]Then the Lord raised up judges, who saved them out of the power of those who plundered them. [17]And yet they did not listen to their judges; for they played the harlot after other gods and bowed down to them; they soon turned aside from the way in which their fathers had walked, who had obeyed the commandments of the Lord, and they did not do so. [18]Whenever the Lord raised up judges for them, the Lord was with the judge, and he saved them from the hand of their enemies all the days of the judge; for the Lord was moved to pity by their groaning because of those who afflicted and oppressed them. [19]But whenever the judge died, they turned back and behaved worse than their fathers, going after other gods, serving them and bowing down to them; they did not drop any of their practices or their stubborn ways. [20]So the anger of the Lord was kindled against Israel; and he said, "Because this people have transgressed my covenant which I commanded their fathers, and have not obeyed my voice, [21]I will not henceforth drive out before them any of the nations that Joshua left when he died, [22]that by them I may test Israel, whether they will take care to walk in the way of the Lord as their fathers did, or not." [23]So the Lord left those nations, not driving them out at once, and he did not give them into the power of Joshua.

¹Now these are the nations which the Lord left, to test Israel by them, that is, all in Israel who had no experience of any war in Canaan; ²it was only that the generations of the people of Israel might know war, that he might teach war to such at least as had not known it before. ³These are the nations: the five lords of the Philistines, and all the Canaanites, and the Sidonians, and the Hivites who dwelt on Mount Lebanon, from Mount Baal-hermon as far as the entrance of Hamath. ⁴They were for the testing of Israel, to know whether Israel would obey the commandments of the Lord, which he commanded their fathers by Moses. ⁵So the people of Israel dwelt among the Canaanites, the Hittites, the Amorites, the Perizzites, the Hivites, and the Jebusites; ⁶and they took their daughters to themselves for wives, and their own daughters they gave to their sons; and they served their gods.

After the fresh preface in the opening chapter to the *Book* of Judges, this section represents the Deuteronomistic introduction proper to the *period* of the judges. After a brief look backwards, it charts what we should expect from the following narratives.

(i)

Most of the opening paragraph (2:6–10) we met already as the tailpiece to the Book of Joshua (24:28–31). In the Deuteronomist's scheme of things the passage will have originally appeared only once, and probably in the shape we find it in Judg. 2. There is a great divide between the period of Joshua and the period that follows. Joshua's own death and burial are important enough. But the situation in Israel did not really change for the worse until the whole generation associated with him had gone the same way. The last two verses of the Book of Joshua (24:32–33) name just two names of former times, as they tell of the reburial of Joseph from an earlier great age and the passing of Eleazar, the priest who had been associated with Joshua just like Aaron with Moses.

As this transitional paragraph turns to look ahead, the RSV becomes less than precise, and it is important here to retrieve the original sense of the Hebrew: "and there arose another generation after them, who did not know the Lord, or *even* the work which he had done for Israel" (2:10*b*). What is achieved in these few words is a thumbnail sketch of an age very much like contemporary western Europe. Our period is often described as "post-Christian". It is not just that only a minority of people actually believe in God and promote the gospel and its standards—arguably that was always the case. This age is post-Christian because the great mass of people have little inkling what they are *not* part of. The Christian tradition is not familiar to them at all.

The age which followed Joshua did not just *not* "know the Lord", they were not even familiar with his reputation for decisive and beneficial action. Far from *knowing* him, in worship and love and obedience, they did not even know about him.

(ii)

Israel's lack of "knowledge of God" is spelled out with much repetition in several standard formulae, in verses 11–19. Religious nature, like any other nature, abhors a vacuum. Those who did not actively "know the Lord" must quite as actively serve and worship someone else. The opposition, the alternative to Yahweh, is labelled the Baals in verse 11 and, rather more fully, the Baals and Ashtaroth in verse 13. Baal and Ashtoreth, in the singular, are both familiar and important figures amongst the gods of the ancient Levant; but their own individual characteristics do not concern the Deuteronomists. They were not disinterested students of comparative religion! Together, and in the plural, these Baals and Ashtaroth (i.e. Astartes) are simply a shorthand reference to the sort of fuller list of divinities we shall meet in Judg. 10:6. Together they sum up all that was tragically and obnoxiously attractive as an alternative religion for Israel.

We will meet many times again in the Book of Judges several of the set expressions in these verses: "and the people of Israel did what was evil in the sight of the Lord" (v. 11); "so the anger of the Lord was kindled against Israel" (v. 14); "and he sold them into the power of their enemies" (v. 14). Yet this preface is not simply a preview; in fact that is offered very economically in narrative form in the first story of the next chapter (3:7–11). This introduction, both in its silences and in what it says, has its own independent point to make. I find it emphasizes the freedom and initiative of God; and it plays down any role of Israel in its own deliverance.

When Israel is "sorely distressed" in Judg. 10:9, they immediately and appropriately follow this by crying to the Lord in confession (10:10). In the Psalms too, distress is a frequent occasion for calling to God. Psalm 18:6 is typical:

> In my distress I called upon the Lord;
>   to my God I cried for help.
> From his temple he heard my voice,
>   and my cry to him reached his ears.

However, Judg. 2:16, with its talk of the Lord raising up "judges who saved them", bypasses the regular mention of the people's call for help. That this is not just chance is demonstrated in the second part of verse 18. Without any address to him, "the Lord was moved to pity by their groaning". "Groaning" is a rare word; and it is instructive that it is found also at the beginning of Exodus (6:5): "Moreover I have heard the groaning of the people of Israel whom the Egyptians hold in bondage". The situation the Lord faces now is as serious as the one he faced in Egypt: the impetus for its solution comes from him alone, as it had then.

We shall discuss later the meaning of "judge", especially in 10:1–5 and 12:7–14. Here it is important simply to note that for the Deuteronomists "judges" are "saviours" (v. 16); alternatively, "judges" are those through whom the Lord effects his own deliverance (v. 18).

(iii)

The final part of this introduction (2:20–3:6) is almost certainly an afterthought. It reflects the sort of thinking we discussed already in Josh. 1:7–9; 13:2–6; and 23 as a whole. The emphasis has subtly shifted from external "plunderers" and "enemies round about" (v. 14) to enemies within, left unconquered by Joshua at his death—left unconquered providentially, to test religious faithfulness (2:22), and provide experience of war (3:1–2).

A tragic contemporary reflex of this Biblical distinction between external and internal foes is to be seen in mighty Israel's readiness to strike militarily at the Palestinians, that "nation that remains", that nation without rights. Much bombing and shelling in Lebanon, a "nation round about", in the early 1980's has been justified by calling the targets "Palestinian", whether accurately or not.

Part of my concern here is to point out the *Biblical* dimension of one of today's intractable political issues. I should not want to suggest that Israel's Biblical heritage offers a *complete* explanation of her policies, that she is *trapped* in her history. *All* of us have our *own* ways of "demonizing" our opponents, depicting them as irretrievably wicked, wishing them away, denying their rights, and so seeking to excuse our treatment of them.

THREE SHORT STORIES

Judges 3:7–31

7And the people of Israel did what was evil in the sight of the Lord, forgetting the Lord their God, and serving the Baals and the Asheroth. 8Therefore the anger of the Lord was kindled against Israel, and he sold them into the hand of Cushan-rishathaim king of Mesopotamia; and the people of Israel served Cushan-rishathaim eight years. 9But when the people of Israel cried to the Lord, the Lord raised up a deliverer for the people of Israel, who delivered them, Othni-el the son of Kenaz, Caleb's younger brother. 10The Spirit of the Lord came upon him, and he judged Israel; he went out to war, and the Lord gave Cushan-rishathaim king of Mesopotamia into his hand; and his hand prevailed over Cushan-rishathaim. 11So the land had rest forty years. Then Othni-el the son of Kenaz died.

12And the people of Israel again did what was evil in the sight of the Lord; and the Lord strengthened Eglon the king of Moab against Israel, because they had done what was evil in the sight of the Lord. 13He gathered to himself the Ammonites and the Amalekites, and went and defeated Israel; and they took possession of the city of palms. 14And the people of Israel served Eglon the king of Moab eighteen years.

15But when the people of Israel cried to the Lord, the Lord raised up for them a deliverer, Ehud, the son of Gera, the Benjaminite, a left-handed man. The people of Israel sent tribute by him to Eglon the king of Moab. 16And Ehud made for himself a sword with two edges, a cubit in length; and he girded it on his right thigh under his clothes. 17And he presented the tribute to Eglon king of Moab. Now Eglon was a very fat man. 18And when Ehud had finished presenting the tribute, he sent away the people that carried the tribute. 19But he himself turned back at the sculptured stones near Gilgal, and said, "I have a secret message for you, O king." And he commanded, "Silence." And all his attendants went out from his presence. 20And Ehud came to him, as he was sitting alone in his cool roof chamber. And Ehud said, "I have a message from God for you." And he arose from his seat. 21And Ehud reached with his left hand, took the sword from his right thigh, and thrust it into his belly; 22and the hilt also went in after the blade, and the fat closed over the blade, for he did not draw the sword out of his belly; and the dirt came out. 23Then Ehud went out into the vestibule, and closed the doors of the roof chamber upon him, and locked them.

24When he had gone, the servants came; and when they saw that the doors of the roof chamber were locked, they thought, "He is only relieving himself in the closet of the cool chamber." 25And they waited till they were utterly at a loss; but when he still did not open the doors of the roof chamber, they took the key and opened them; and there lay their lord dead on the floor.

26Ehud escaped while they delayed, and passed beyond the sculptured stones, and escaped to Se-irah. 27When he arrived, he sounded the trumpet in the hill country of Ephraim; and the people of Israel went down with him from the hill country, having him at their head. 28And he said to them, "Follow after me; for the Lord has given your enemies the Moabites into your hand." So they went down after him, and seized the fords of the Jordan against the Moabites, and allowed not a man to pass over. 29And they killed at that time about ten thousand of the Moabites, all strong, able-bodied men; not a man escaped. 30So Moab was subdued that day under the hand of Israel. And the land had rest for eighty years.

31After him was Shamgar the son of Anath, who killed six hundred of the Philistines with an oxgoad; and he too delivered Israel.

This chapter is almost a miniature of the Book of Judges as a whole. It is made up of three accounts of very different lengths:

five verses, nineteen verses, and only one verse! And only the second and longest of these, the tale of Ehud, is a *proper* story.

(i)

The opening tale about Othniel tells us everything and tells us nothing. Let me stop speaking in riddles, and let me explain. To an extent even greater than the formal generalized introduction in chapter 2, these few verses gather up and anticipate significant elements in all the following stories. Most stories in Judges open with the note that Israel had been doing "evil in the sight of the Lord". Most stories describe their hero as a "deliverer" or "saviour" (although not the immediately following tale of Ehud). Many say that their hero "judged Israel". The Jephthah story too (10:7–10) talks of the kindling of the Lord's anger, of his "selling" his people into the hands of their enemies, and of his people's "cry". Israel cries also because of Midianite pressure in Judg. 6:6, and is sold into Canaanite hands in Judg. 4:2. Then again it is the "spirit of the Lord" which energizes Jephthah (11:29) and pre-eminently Samson (13:25; 14:6, 19; 15:14). But it is *only* this tale of Othniel that contains *all* of these features—and within five verses!

Some other facts deserve a mention before we try to evaluate all this. The second part of Cushan's double-barrelled name means "the doubly wicked". This twice-bad Cushan is king of Mesopotamia—and that takes us much further from Israel's territory than any of the following tales. The rest of Judges deals with a series of struggles on Israel's fringes. Finally of course we have met "Othniel, the son of Kenaz, Caleb's younger brother" already in Judg. 1 and in its doublet in Josh. 15.

In terms of introducing us to motifs scattered through the Book of Judges, this short story tells us everything. Yet this new tale about Othniel is so stereotyped, with an opponent fetched from so far and with so comical a name, that it can tell us nothing about Israel's ancient past—not even about her *early* story-telling.

Why such a story? Although it is very contrived, it does help to bind together the extremely diverse material that follows in the book. In fact it has already gathered into one rich chord the many notes that will be separately sounded later. Moreover, although Judah is not mentioned by name, Othniel who is related to Judah through Caleb claims a glorious place for the south which is otherwise lacking in the core of the Book of Judges.

(ii)

The story of Ehud (vv. 12–30) is more straightforward and more typical, if anything can be called typical in such a diverse book as Judges. It is not just a simple account of liberation by assassination of the overlord. We should note in passing that the story takes us back to the territory of Josh. 3–6: Jericho (the city of palms), Gilgal and its standing stones, and a fordable river Jordan.

This tale has several of the hallmarks of enthusiastic embroidery. The entry of Ehud's sword into Eglon's belly is described in loving detail. His cubit-length sword is little more than a long dagger (about a foot and a half); and Eglon is so fat that it can be driven in over its hilt. As he makes sport over the stupid fecklessness of the king of Moab's attendants, the narrator adds a delightfully macabre detail. They suppose their king has gone to relieve himself after Ehud's departure—little do they know that all the "dirt" has already oozed out of him (v. 22)!

Another delightful aspect of the story does not come out in translation at all. Our *left*-handed hero Ehud is a Benjaminite (v. 15), and that clan's name literally means "people of the *right*". They may originally have been called that because they were situated to the *south* of their relatives in Ephraim. The south is on the right hand, because you naturally *orientate* yourself by looking east for the sunrise. The southernmost Arab land, Yemen, bears a name related to Ben*jamin*. However, the pun involved in having a left-handed Benjaminite is there for any reader of the Hebrew text. What an improbable assailant for the Lord to use!

Yet if we do tumble into such a surprised assertion, we ought to remember just as quickly that improbable characters are almost the norm in the Bible, that God has a delightful sense of humour about those whom he uses and chooses. There are many more rascals among the saints than would be permitted if most of us were in charge of the recruiting. Most of his contemporaries, and multitudes since, doubted whether Jesus of Nazareth met the criteria for Messiahship.

In many societies, left-handed people have suffered great disadvantages. To be made to conform to the majority is bad enough. To be made to suffer as being "sinister" is much worse. However, for God, Ehud's "handicap" was a positive advantage: it gave him the benefit of surprise, like a left-handed tennis player.

Already in this early story we detect the smell of real action that pervades the Book of Judges. Many campaigns are recounted in Joshua—or at least enumerated. But in this book we see, hear, and smell much more blood actually being spilled in brief tales of action. Ehud is typical of the daring commando-style leadership that we find throughout. It is the stuff of a good yarn: and surely it must be part of the inspiration of modern Israel's most audacious military successes, like the fabled Entebbe raid.

(iii)

Finally Shamgar receives but the briefest mention, and may be an afterthought. The next chapter links with Ehud rather than with him; and some ancient versions of the Bible slip him in after Samson, rather than here. He makes one further appearance, in the Song of Deborah (5:6). There he seems more of a nuisance to Israel than a help. Here he has more than a walk-on part—he kills six hundred Philistines in a single verse! It is exactly that feat (whoever he was) which will have turned him into a "deliverer of Israel".

DEBORAH AND BARAK

Judges 4:1–24

[1]And the people of Israel again did what was evil in the sight of the Lord, after Ehud died. [2]And the Lord sold them into the hand of

Jabin king of Canaan, who reigned in Hazor; the commander of his army was Sisera, who dwelt in the Harosheth-ha-goiim. ³Then the people of Israel cried to the Lord for help; for he had nine hundred chariots of iron, and oppressed the people of Israel cruelly for twenty years.

⁴Now Deborah, a prophetess, the wife of Lappidoth, was judging Israel at that time. ⁵She used to sit under the palm of Deborah between Ramah and Bethel in the hill country of Ephraim; and the people of Israel came up to her for judgment. ⁶She sent and summoned Barak the son of Abino-am from Kedesh in Naphtali, and said to him, "The Lord, the God of Israel, commands you, 'Go, gather your men at Mount Tabor, taking ten thousand from the tribe of Naphtali and the tribe of Zebulun. ⁷And I will draw out Sisera, the general of Jabin's army, to meet you by the river Kishon with his chariots and his troops; and I will give him into your hand.'" ⁸Barak said to her, "If you will go with me, I will go; but if you will not go with me, I will not go." ⁹And she said, "I will surely go with you; nevertheless, the road on which you are going will not lead to your glory, for the Lord will sell Sisera into the hand of a woman." Then Deborah arose, and went with Barak to Kedesh. ¹⁰And Barak summoned Zebulun and Naphtali to Kedesh; and ten thousand men went up at his heels; and Deborah went up with him.

¹¹Now Heber the Kenite had separated from the Kenites, the descendants of Hobab the father-in-law of Moses, and had pitched his tent as far away as the oak in Za-anannim, which is near Kedesh.

¹²When Sisera was told that Barak the son of Abino-am had gone up to Mount Tabor, ¹³Sisera called out all his chariots, nine hundred chariots of iron, and all the men who were with him, from Harosheth-ha-goiim to the river Kishon. ¹⁴And Deborah said to Barak, "Up! For this is the day in which the Lord has given Sisera into your hand. Does not the Lord go out before you?" So Barak went down from Mount Tabor with ten thousand men following him. ¹⁵And the Lord routed Sisera and all his chariots and all his army before Barak at the edge of the sword; and Sisera alighted from his chariot and fled away on foot. ¹⁶And Barak pursued the chariots and the army to Harosheth-ha-goiim, and all the army of Sisera fell by the edge of the sword; not a man was left.

¹⁷But Sisera fled away on foot to the tent of Jael, the wife of Heber the Kenite; for there was peace between Jabin the king of Hazor and

the house of Heber the Kenite. ¹⁸And Jael came out to meet Sisera, and said to him, "Turn aside, my lord, turn aside to me; have no fear." So he turned aside to her into the tent, and she covered him with a rug. ¹⁹And he said to her, "Pray, give me a little water to drink; for I am thirsty." So she opened a skin of milk and gave him a drink and covered him. ²⁰And he said to her, "Stand at the door of the tent, and if any man comes and asks you, 'Is any one here?' say, No." ²¹But Jael the wife of Heber took a tent peg, and took a hammer in her hand, and went softly to him and drove the peg into his temple, till it went down into the ground, as he was lying fast asleep from weariness. So he died. ²²And behold, as Barak pursued Sisera, Jael went out to meet him, and said to him, "Come, and I will show you the man whom you are seeking." So he went in to her tent; and there lay Sisera dead, with the tent peg in his temple.

²³So on that day God subdued Jabin the king of Canaan before the people of Israel. ²⁴And the hand of the people of Israel bore harder and harder on Jabin the king of Canaan, until they destroyed Jabin king of Canaan.

In Judges 4 and 5 we have two different versions of the decisive show-down between the forces of Israel and of "Jabin king of Canaan, who reigned in Hazor" (4:2). The second of these in Judges 5 is widely regarded by scholars as the more interesting and important, as it seems to be perhaps the earliest *extended* piece of Israelite poetry, dating from early in the monarchy, or even before it. The prose version is very much later and contains several of the characteristics of a typical Judges story. It is no longer clear just how far Judg. 4 is dependent for some of its information on Judg. 5. Suffice it for the moment to say that as we read these chapters now in the Book of Judges, the basic record is given first (ch. 4), and is followed by a victory song dedicated to Yahweh (ch. 5).

(i)

The death of Ehud is not formally reported as such. Shamgar's period of activity had followed his (3:31). Israel's evil continued; but there was no more Ehud (4:1). Jabin of Hazor in northern Canaan represents the next menace.

Is this the same Jabin as we met in Josh. 11:1–15, with his
fortunes now restored? Or was Jabin perhaps the dynastic name
of the kings of Hazor? Certainly Scottish and English monarchic
history has known Edwards, Henrys, Jameses, and Georges in
plenty. No solution can be demonstrated with certainty, but my
own feeling is that the *one* decisive historic battle for the north
between Israel and Jabin of Canaan has been reported to us in
two quite separate traditions: one associated with Joshua, and the
other with Deborah and Barak. We have already noticed how
isolated geographically Hazor is from the rest of the action in the
Book of Joshua. We might add that there is a lot of repetition in
Josh. 10:40–43 and 11:16–23, which could well suggest that
Israel's action against the chariotry of the north was only secondarily associated with Joshua.

A decision about the relationship between these two traditions
is relevant to one of the issues we noted in our discussion of the
introduction to the judges in chapter 2. If Judg. 4–5 was drafted
without knowledge of Josh. 11, then Jabin of Hazor will still have
been one of Israel's *external* enemies. However, if his territory
had already figured in one of Israel's victories *in Canaan*, then he
was a remaining foe from within.

(ii)

Unlike many of the other heroes in this book, Deborah was a real
"judge": one to whom people came for judgment (4:4–5). Israel
resorted to her at the "palm of Deborah" near Bethel. When
commenting on 2:1–5, we noticed that Gen. 35:8 associates an
oak there with the only other Deborah in the Bible, nurse of
Rebekah.

She was a real judge for judgment; and it is interesting from the
point of view of social history that this first named judicial officer
in the Bible should have been a woman, and a married woman at
that. Two of her other "vital statistics" have caused rather more
comment. What is it about her that leads to her being termed a
"prophetess" (v. 4)? We have surprisingly little certain knowledge about the origins of prophecy in Israel, and a correspon-
dingly large amount of speculation. My own feeling is that it

is with the song in Judg. 5 in mind that Deborah is styled "prophetess". Just like Miriam before here (Exod. 15:20) she is a *prophetess* because she leads the *singing*. That was certainly one of the meanings of the word in the later books of Chronicles; and that sense fits well here too.

The other issue about her personal details is whether any play on words lurks behind the designation "wife of Lappidoth" in the same verse. *Lappidoth* could be an alternative plural of the Hebrew noun *lappid*, the word for the kind of torch which we shall meet in two later chapters of Judges: connected with Gideon (ch. 7), and Samson (ch. 15). However, its normal plural is sometimes used to express the flashing of lightning, as in Exod. 20:18. This line of speculation is encouraged here, because the name of Barak, the other hero of this piece, is the common Hebrew word for "lightning". We have no other knowledge of a proper name Lappidoth: are we dealing her with a husband-and-wife team? Is Lappidoth or "Flasher" a nickname for Barak or "Lightning"?

(iii)

Judges 4 is very much a story in which women take the lead; and this is the more striking because it is an episode from national life, not a more domestic narrative like the Book of Ruth. It is Deborah, the widely acknowledged judge, who issues a summons to Barak. When he appears before her, she gives him instructions in the name of God. When he responds cautiously, like Gideon, she agrees to accompany him—but with a warning that the praises to be sung will not be his, but a woman's. It might be thought she was referring to herself, as the more resolute of the two. In fact, Sisera was destined to be Jael's prize: her booty wrapped in a blanket in the recesses of the tent. The Hebrew in verse 20*b* hints at a fine contrast between the sexes, whose irony seems lost on Sisera as he briefs Jael. I should prefer to translate it: "Is there any *man* here?", to which the *correct* answer is "no". He who was once a commander of men has left his conspicuous leading chariot, and disguised himself by running on foot from the slaughter that has engulfed his men. He is hiding behind a woman's skirts. Jael is decidedly and decisively different, with her fatal mallet and tent peg at the ready. These contrasts in this chapter remind me of General Haig's "compliment" concerning Mrs Thatcher: that she was the best man in the British cabinet!

(iv)

The end of this military story corresponds perfectly to its beginning. It opens and closes with Jabin himself. It opens with him oppressing Israel cruelly, or "mightily", and closes with a contrast being realized: Israel is increasingly gaining the upper hand, to the point of Jabin's extinction. Good cause for a great celebration!

THE SONG OF DEBORAH

Judges 5:1–31

1Then sang Deborah and Barak the son of Abino-am on that day:
2"That the leaders took the lead in Israel,
    that the people offered themselves willingly,
    bless the Lord!
3"Hear, O kings; give ear, O princes;
    to the Lord I will sing,
    I will make melody to the Lord, the God of Israel.

4"Lord, when thou didst go forth from Seir,
    when thou didst march from the region of Edom,
 the earth trembled,
    and the heavens dropped,
    yea, the clouds dropped water.
5The mountains quaked before the Lord,
    yon Sinai before the Lord, the God of Israel.

6"In the days of Shamgar, son of Anath,
    in the days of Jael, caravans ceased
    and travellers kept to the byways.
7The peasantry ceased in Israel, they ceased
    until you arose, Deborah,
    arose as a mother in Israel.
8When new gods were chosen,
    then war was in the gates.

Was shield or spear to be seen
   among forty thousand in Israel?
9My heart goes out to the commanders of Israel
   who offered themselves willingly among the people.
   Bless the Lord.

10"Tell of it, you who ride on tawny asses,
   you who sit on rich carpets
   and you who walk by the way.
11To the sound of musicians at the watering places,
   there they repeat the triumphs of the Lord,
   the triumphs of his peasantry in Israel.

"Then down to the gates marched the people of the Lord.

12"Awake, awake, Deborah!
   Awake, awake, utter a song!
Arise, Barak, lead away your captives,
   O son of Abino-am.
13Then down marched the remnant of the noble;
   the people of the Lord marched down for him against the mighty.
14From Ephraim they set out thither into the valley,
   following you, Benjamin, with your kinsmen;
from Machir marched down the commanders,
   and from Zebulun those who bear the marshal's staff;
15the princes of Issachar came with Deborah,
   and Issachar faithful to Barak;
   into the valley they rushed forth at his heels.
Among the clans of Reuben
   there were great searchings of heart.
16Why did you tarry among the sheepfolds,
   to hear the piping for the flocks?
Among the clans of Reuben
   there were great searchings of heart.
17Gilead stayed beyond the Jordan;
   and Dan, why did he abide with the ships?
Asher sat still at the coast of the sea,
   settling down by his landings.
18Zebulun is a people that jeoparded their lives to the death;
   Naphtali too, on the heights of the field.

19"The kings came, they fought;
   then fought the kings of Canaan,

at Taanach, by the waters of Megiddo;
  they got no spoils of silver.
²⁰From heaven fought the stars,
  from their courses they fought against Sisera.
²¹The torrent Kishon swept them away,
  the onrushing torrent, the torrent Kishon.
  March on, my soul, with might!

²²"Then loud beat the horses' hoofs
  with the galloping, galloping of his steeds.

²³"Curse Meroz, says the angel of the Lord,
  curse bitterly its inhabitants,
because they came not to the help of the Lord,
  to the help of the Lord against the mighty.

²⁴"Most blessed of women be Jael,
  the wife of Heber the Kenite,
  of tent-dwelling women most blessed.
²⁵He asked water and she gave him milk,
  she brought him curds in a lordly bowl.
²⁶She put her hand to the tent peg
  and her right hand to the workmen's mallet;
she struck Sisera a blow,
  she crushed his head,
  she shattered and pierced his temple.
²⁷He sank, he fell,
  he lay still at her feet;
at her feet he sank, he fell;
  where he sank, there he fell dead.

²⁸"Out of the window she peered,
  the mother of Sisera gazed through the lattice:
'Why is his chariot so long in coming?
  Why tarry the hoofbeats of his chariots?'
²⁹Her wisest ladies make answer,
  nay, she gives answer to herself,
³⁰'Are they not finding and dividing the spoil?—
  A maiden or two for every man;
spoil of dyed stuffs for Sisera,
  spoil of dyed stuffs embroidered,
  two pieces of dyed work embroidered for my neck as spoil?'

[31]"So perish all thine enemies, O Lord!
But thy friends be like the sun as he rises in his might."

And the land had rest for forty years.

(i)

The Song of Deborah is a fascinating but very difficult poem. One recent commentator has remarked that "a catalogue of full-dress studies of the Song of Deborah would read like a *Who's Who* in Biblical research". An unusually large number of critical questions are open, and therefore disputed. In as many as seventy per cent of the verses the meaning of a key word is doubtful. This means that even those who do know some Hebrew are still surprised at the wide differences between the standard translations. Discussion of Judg. 5 must accordingly either be very detailed and also technical, or cursory and restricted to certain obvious features of the text. For a detailed treatment, I commend particularly Soggin's commentary (in the Old Testament Library, pp. 79–101). Following him, I suggest four alterations to the translation of the RSV above, all within verses 5–8:

v. 5:	for "yon Sinai"	read "him of Sinai" or "the Lord of Sinai" (with a comma following)
v. 6:	for "the days of Jael"	read "the days of the yoke"
v. 7:	for "the peasantry ceased"	read "the leading class was inactive"
v. 8:	for "when new gods were chosen"	read "God chose new men".

(ii)

The first point I should like to stress is that this song is religious but not cultic. It celebrates the work of God, but it does not belong in the sanctuary. There is an important Biblical tradition of praise which belongs in the place of worship; and it is massively represented in the Book of Psalms. But this song of triumph originated in what we often call the "market-place". The song is declaimed to a wide public (v. 3). The tale should be repeated wherever people gather in numbers with some time on their hands, as at the watering places where there may be musicians and bards (v. 11). Even more appropriately it should be the stuff of travellers' tales, whether riding or walking (v. 10), for part of the very problem that led to battle was interference with the highways.

It is the stuff of *sacred* ballad, for the protagonists are more than human. The opening is not just a ritual flashback:

"Lord, when thou didst go forth from Seir,
  when thou didst march from the region of Edom,
the earth trembled,
  and the heavens dropped,
  yea, the clouds dropped water.
The mountains quaked
  before the Lord, him of Sinai,
  before the Lord, the God of Israel."

(5:4–5)

Yahweh is God of the present and not just of the past. It is those early words that direct us to see the Lord's hand in verses 20–21:

"From heaven fought the stars,
  from their courses they fought against Sisera.
The torrent Kishon swept them away,
  the onrushing torrent, the torrent Kishon."

(There was an ancient belief that the stars were the source of the rain.)

(iii)

As far as the human combatants are concerned, the battle is between the *kings* of Canaan (v. 19) and the "*people* of the Lord" (vv. 11 and 13). At the very outset, the confident prelude to the song (v. 3) calls on kings and princes to pay attention. What Deborah will sing to Yahweh is for their ears too. And the contents of her song will deal almost exclusively with the efforts of Yahweh and his people. All mention of the opposition is tellingly brief:

"The kings came, they fought;
  then fought the kings of Canaan,
at Taanach, by the waters of Megiddo;
  they got no spoils of silver." (v. 19)

"Then loud beat the horses' hoofs
  with the galloping, galloping of his steeds." (v. 22)

"So perish all thine enemies, O Lord!" (v. 31*a*)

The kings of Canaan are of little account before the Lord. They should pay attention to the story; but they rate little place in it. This echoes a point we noticed more than once in the Book of Joshua.

Those who do rate more extended criticism are those within Israel who should have responded to the call, but did not: Reuben and Gilead, Dan and Asher (vv. 15*b*–17). Interestingly, those that did muster are more than Zebulun and Naphtali (v. 18), the only two listed in chapter 4. This Song pays tribute also to Ephraim and Benjamin, Machir and Issachar (vv. 13–15*a*). Ten Israelite "clans" are mentioned in all. These are mostly the familiar ones; but some are different from the standard lists of the twelve "tribes": Machir and Gilead, for Manasseh and Gad. Deborah's Song may be a precious historical source for our reconstruction of Israel's early development; but it is not easy to evaluate.

Meroz (v. 23) is particularly obscure. The name is nowhere repeated in the Bible. We do not even know whether they were Israelite. I tend to think not, since they are set apart from the enumeration of those in Israel who are praised or blamed, and appear immediately in front of the wife of Kenite Heber. Israelite or not, they should have come "to the help of the Lord, to the help of the Lord against the mighty." Like much of the Biblical tradition, this poem too sets Israel's God against the kings of the earth, ranges the Lord on the side of the weak against the mighty. When it comes to this struggle, it matters not one iota who you are, who your relatives are, which team you normally support, and whether you are a church member or not. But you merit a curse if you do not join the weak against the mighty. Heber's wife was non-Israelite, yet merits a generous blessing for not staying uncommitted and simply a good hostess.

(iv)

As in chapter 4, so too in the Song women have a vital role. Jael the Kenite is "most blessed of women" (v. 24) for her handwork with a mallet. Then we read in verse 7 that:

> The leading class was inactive,
>   it was inactive in Israel
>   until you arose, Deborah,
>   you arose, a mother in Israel.

Yet this poem most closely resembles the old Scottish Border Ballads as it lingers lovingly at the end over the growing worry of Sisera's noble mother back at home, clutching at proud reasons for his delay (vv. 29–30). It is a sensitive portrait of a woman by a woman. Yet, in the end, she is an enemy, and any sentiment is cut short in the final terse invocation (v. 31).

MIDIANITE MARAUDERS

Judges 6:1–10

[1]The people of Israel did what was evil in the sight of the Lord; and the Lord gave them into the hand of Midian seven years. [2]And the hand of Midian prevailed over Israel; and because of Midian the people of Israel made for themselves the dens which are in the mountains, and the caves and the strongholds. [3]For whenever the Israelites put in seed the Midianites and the Amalekites and the people of the East would come up and attack them; [4]they would encamp against them and destroy the produce of the land, as far as the neighbourhood of Gaza, and leave no sustenance in Israel, and no sheep or ox or ass. [5]For they would come up with their cattle and their tents, coming like locusts for number; both they and their camels could not be counted; so that they wasted the land as they came in. [6]And Israel was brought very low because of Midian; and the people of Israel cried for help to the Lord.

⁷When the people of Israel cried to the Lord on account of the Midianites, ⁸the Lord sent a prophet to the people of Israel; and he said to them, "Thus says the Lord, the God of Israel: I led you up from Egypt, and brought you out of the house of bondage; ⁹and I delivered you from the hand of the Egyptians, and from the hand of all who oppressed you, and drove them out before you, and gave you their land; ¹⁰and I said to you, 'I am the Lord your God; you shall not pay reverence to the gods of the Amorites, in whose land you dwell.' But you have not given heed to my voice."

The next main division of the Book of Judges comprises chapters 6 to 8, with chapter 9 on Abimelech as something of an appendix. This opening section is in two parts: vv. 1–6, and vv. 7–10.

(i)

The opening six verses of the Gideon story begin and end in an almost formulaic way. In verse 1 after the standard mention of the evil done by Israel in the Lord's eyes we read that he *gave* them into the power of Midian. Apart from Midian which is a new peril in the Book of Judges, the only change to the formula is that God "gives" rather than "sells" (4:2) Israel into their power. Then verse 6 ends with Israel crying to the Lord—a response we find also in 3:9, 15; 10:10.

Inside this framework of clichés we find a freshly written introduction (verses 2 to 6a). Its beginning and end are in fine balance and together they are quite unique in the Bible. Verse 2 introduces the power (*'oz* in Hebrew) of Midian, while verse 6a notes the corresponding weak and perilous situation of Israel. The Hebrew word *dal* is a significant one in several Biblical contexts and is differently translated. The adjective is translated "needy" in Isaiah 10:2 and "poor" in Isaiah 11:4 and Amos 2:7; 5:11. In short it describes those to whom Israel's Proverbs, Prophets and Pentateuch combine to promise God's protection in their need. This is the fundamentally correct Biblical insight of today's "liberation" theologians in Latin America and elsewhere.

The threat is graphically described in the intervening verses— scavenging Midianites, like an oversized plague of locusts. Many of us who do not live there have a very romantic notion of the desert areas and fringes of the Middle East. We think of the desert as pure, if stark; and inhabited by noble Bedouin. It is not my business here to decry a culture which I do not fully understand and whose hospitality I have occasionally enjoyed; and feuding neighbours are seldom best judges of each other. What is true is that the settled farmers and townspeople of the Levant do not share our idealized notions of the Bedouin. We have a classic description here of a period of years in which the desert marauders could not be kept out of Israel's settled territory. They entered from the east and scavenged as far as Gaza which then, as now, marked the south-west corner of Palestine where Egypt begins. Israel's only hope of protection was to hide themselves and their goods in the caves which were plentiful in many parts of that land. Anyone who has visited the Israel Museum in Jerusalem will need no reminder that several of its most fascinating displays from ancient times have been recovered in recent decades from caves in which they had been stored for safety in time of trouble. Particularly famous are the Dead Sea Scrolls from Qumran and the more varied materials from the so-called "Cave of Letters" a little further south. These and many other finds well illustrate the predicament of Israel under Midianite pressure.

One last point. We meet for the first time in verse 3 a puzzling feature of this whole Gideon story. Mostly the enemy is simply Midian. In a few places we read about Midian, Amalek and "the people of the East". The latter two are almost certainly a secondary addition to the tale to give a generalized impression of all the menacing desert forces that were ever ranged against Israel.

(ii)

Before the story of deliverance begins in verse 11, verses 7 to 10 point out that Israel's distress is Israel's fault. The message itself is a standard one—it reads like a short digest of the lengthy warnings of Moses in Deuteronomy 7–8. Israel had been given her new land and everything in it by her God with the exception of the right to worship the gods of that land; yet she had done exactly that. The message is familiar but the method of delivering it is more surprising than at first appears.

This is one of only two mentions of "prophet" in the Book of Judges—and prophets are nowhere mentioned in the whole Book of Joshua (although we did note when discussing Josh. 1:7–9 that the summons to Joshua shared some features of the call of Jeremiah and Ezekiel). We have already seen that Deborah was styled "prophetess" in Judg. 4:4; but that may well be because she sang a famous song. The introduction of this prophet here rather interrupts the development of the narrative. It seems to me to be designed to answer in advance two problems that arise in the following section. (a) It attempts to suggest that the "messenger of the Lord", whose dealings with Gideon are the stuff of the next part of the chapter, was in fact a prophet. (b) It offers a proper orthodox response to Gideon's otherwise unanswered comment: "If the Lord is with us, why then has all this befallen us?" (verse 13).

Everything points to these four verses being a late insert into the chapter, drafted from the standpoint of developed prophetic orthodoxy. It was interests like these which led later synagogue tradition to label the books from Joshua to Kings "The Former Prophets".

GIDEON CALLED TO ARMS

Judges 6:11–24

[11]Now the angel of the Lord came and sat under the oak at Ophrah, which belonged to Joash the Abiezrite, as his son Gideon was beating out wheat in the wine press, to hide it from the Midianites. [12]And the angel of the Lord appeared to him and said to him, "The Lord is with you, you mighty man of valour." [13]And Gideon said to him, "Pray, sir, if the Lord is with us, why then has all this befallen us? And where are all his wonderful deeds which our fathers recounted to us, saying, 'Did not the Lord bring us up from Egypt?' But now the Lord has cast us off, and given us into the hand of Midian." [14]And the Lord turned to him and said, "Go in this might of yours and deliver Israel from the hand of Midian; do not I send you?" [15]And he said to him, "Pray, Lord, how can I deliver Israel? Behold, my clan is the weakest in Manasseh, and I am the least in my family." [16]And the Lord said to him, "But I will be

with you, and you shall smite the Midianites as one man." [17]And he said to him, "If now I have found favour with thee, then show me a sign that it is thou who speakest with me. [18]Do not depart from here, I pray thee, until I come to thee, and bring out my present, and set it before thee." And he said, "I will stay till you return."

[19]So Gideon went into his house and prepared a kid, and unleavened cakes from an ephah of flour; the meat he put in a basket, and the broth he put in a pot, and brought them to him under the oak and presented them. [20]And the angel of God said to him, "Take the meat and the unleavened cakes, and put them on this rock, and pour the broth over them." And he did so. [21]Then the angel of the Lord reached out the tip of the staff that was in his hand, and touched the meat and the unleavened cakes; and there sprang up fire from the rock and consumed the flesh and the unleavened cakes; and the angel of the Lord vanished from his sight. [22]Then Gideon perceived that he was the angel of the Lord; and Gideon said, "Alas, O Lord God! For now I have seen the angel of the Lord face to face." [23]But the Lord said to him, "Peace be to you; do not fear, you shall not die." [24]Then Gideon built an altar there to the Lord, and called it, The Lord is peace. To this day it still stands at Ophrah, which belongs to the Abiezrites.

(i)

Before we go any further, we have to clear away an entirely natural misconception. It influences the very translation of this passage. English and many other modern languages have several specialized words for messenger. A messenger from government we call an "envoy" or "ambassador"; and a messenger from God on high is an "angel". However "angel" is simply the common Greek word for messenger—*angelos*. And that Greek word, like the one common Hebrew word for messenger, is used to describe everyone from the menial errand boy to the royal and even divine plenipotentiary. Hebrew too has no special word for "angel" or "ambassador".

There is another issue at stake too. When we talk of an "angel", we mean not only that the messenger's *master* is God, but that the *messenger too* is non-human. That assumption distances us still further from Biblical messenger stories, and their way of thinking. What is important in them is simply the *relation-*

ship between the messenger and the divine master. The important thing in international law about an ambassador is not who he is in himself, but whom he represents. Some of God's "messengers" in the Old Testament are clearly members of the heavenly court. Others are quite as obviously human. The difference may *interest* us; but it is fundamentally *irrelevant* to our understanding of the function of the envoy. When a new ambassador arrives in London, the gossip columns in the press may tell us how noble or common he or she is; yet the status of envoys depends rather on the status of those who send them.

In the three prophetic books that close the Old Testament, Haggai and Malachi are designated "messenger of Yahweh"; in fact Malachi's very name means "my [i.e. the Lord's] messenger". Yet in the intervening Book of Zechariah, the visionary intermediary spoken of in the first six chapters is clearly an "angelic" being from above. Given such an alternative, we are left to speculate over what sort of being it was who supplied food to Elijah (1 Kings 19:5, 7) or sent him to King Ahaziah (2 Kings 1:3, 15). Some medieval Jewish commentators understood Exodus to be talking of Moses in the words, "Behold, I send an angel before you, to guard you on the way and to bring you to the place which I have prepared" (23:20). Just who was it, we might ask, who "went up from Gilgal to Bochim" in Judg. 2:1? But it is not a question to which we *need* an answer.

(ii)

The Lord's messenger got Gideon on a bad day. The confined secrecy of a wine press was not a very convenient situation for beating out wheat! His visitor interrupts him with a standard pleasantry, "The Lord is with you". Boaz greets his harvesters in exactly the same terms when he goes to the fields (Ruth 2:4). And our English "goodbye" is simply a telescoped version of something very similar—"God-be-with-you". Perhaps it was the envoy's addition of "you mighty man of valour" which touched Gideon on the raw. It is not very heroic to attend to your wheat while skulking in a wine press.

Yet Gideon's very name alerts the Hebrew reader to expect something of him: it means "Chopper" or "Hacker". Our sullen young hero quibbles over the greeting—how can we be in such a mess if the Lord is with us? How often do *we* object to being greeted with a "*good* morning"? In another typical move, young Chopper distances himself from his fathers' religion. The Lord's reputation is bound up with the story of the deliverance from Egypt. Gideon at least *knows* the story of the past (contrast 2:10). How can the Lord be with us, if wonderful things like that are no longer happening?

Quite uncomfortably, the young man is told that *he* could be the one to do what had to be done: "Go in this might of yours and deliver Israel from the hand of Midian; do not I send you?" (v. 14). How often do we say that there are no longer great men like there used to be? Every generation says the same. Yet men and women were not different then—we have simply idealized them, and perhaps idolized them as well. Of course there is a measure of self-protection involved, because we believe it is not in us to emulate them. Gideon has two standard excuses: (a) His family is to Midian what Midian is to Israel ("weak" in verse 15 translates *dal*, which is rendered "very low" in verse 6). And (b) he is himself the youngest in his family.

(iii)

However, at least Gideon knows now with whom he is dealing. When you speak to an envoy, you are effectively speaking to his master. He recognizes the divine imperative ringing through the words "do not *I* send you?" And so, when he replies, he addresses his visitor as "Lord" and not simply "sir" (compare verses 13 and 15).

Having achieved this recognition, Gideon is now addressed in terms that remind us of Moses' encounter with God before the burning bush (Exod. 3). Another way of translating verse 16 is: "But I AM is with you, and you shall smite the Midianites..."; just as Moses is told, "Say this to the people of Israel, 'I AM has sent me to you'"(Exod. 3:14). It is not simply that God will be with Gideon; but the God who will be with Gideon is the great I

AM: he who is who he is, who has mercy on whom he has mercy; he whose grace is free, yet who can also keep himself to himself. Gideon like Moses is hearing too much, and is afraid, and must have a sign to be sure that he *is* hearing what he is hearing.

Rather strangely our text now offers us a second recognition scene (N.B. v. 22). Gideon goes to prepare food, apparently as an act of hospitality. But when it arrives, the messenger touches it with his staff, and it is burned as befits a sacrifice. The visitor then *proceeds* from his sight—"vanished" is almost too magical or theatrical. Gideon now realizes that the offering was for God and not for a man, and he fears for his life, for he has seen God. On that score God says him neither yea nor nay; but rather bids him "peace"—*shalom, salaam*. This is another conventional greeting, but rich in its overtones: so rich and so comforting, that Gideon gives the name "The Lord is peace" to the altar which he builds to commemorate the location of his involuntary sacrifice.

ACTION BEGINS

Judges 6:25–40

[25]That night the Lord said to him, "Take your father's bull, the second bull seven years old, and pull down the altar of Baal which your father has, and cut down the Asherah that is beside it; [26]and build an altar to the Lord your God on the top of the stronghold here, with stones laid in due order; then take the second bull, and offer it as a burnt offering with the wood of the Asherah which you shall cut down." [27]So Gideon took ten men of his servants, and did as the Lord had told him; but because he was too afraid of his family and the men of the town to do it by day, he did it by night.

[28]When the men of the town rose early in the morning, behold, the altar of Baal was broken down, and the Asherah beside it was cut down, and the second bull was offered upon the altar which had been built. [29]And they said to one another, "Who has done this thing?" And after they had made search and inquired, they said, "Gideon the son of Joash has done this thing." [30]Then the men of the town said to Joash, "Bring out your son, that he may die, for he has pulled down the altar of Baal and cut down the Asherah beside it." [31]But Joash said to all

who were arrayed against him, "Will you contend for Baal? Or will you defend his cause? Whoever contends for him shall be put to death by morning. If he is a god, let him contend for himself, because his altar has been pulled down." ³²Therefore on that day he was called Jerubbaal, that is to say, "Let Baal contend against him," because he pulled down his altar.

³³Then all the Midianites and the Amalekites and the people of the East came together, and crossing the Jordan they encamped in the Valley of Jezreel. ³⁴But the Spirit of the Lord took possession of Gideon; and he sounded the trumpet, and the Abiezrites were called out to follow him. ³⁵And he sent messengers throughout all Manasseh; and they too were called out to follow him. And he sent messengers to Asher, Zebulun, and Naphtali; and they went up to meet them.

³⁶Then Gideon said to God, "If thou wilt deliver Israel by my hand, as thou hast said, ³⁷behold, I am laying a fleece of wool on the threshing floor; if there is dew on the fleece alone, and it is dry on all the ground, then I shall know that thou wilt deliver Israel by my hand, as thou hast said." ³⁸And it was so. When he rose early next morning and squeezed the fleece, he wrung enough dew from the fleece to fill a bowl with water. ³⁹Then Gideon said to God, "Let not thy anger burn against me, let me speak but this once, pray, let me make trial only this once with the fleece; pray, let it be dry only on the fleece, and on all the ground let there be dew." ⁴⁴And God did so that night; for it was dry on the fleece only, and on all the ground there was dew.

In this passage of Judges 6 we see action begun on two fronts: against Baal and against Midian.

(i)

The action against Baal leads to Gideon being renamed. However, it is attractive to see in the first part of our text a good reason for Gideon's first name too. I have already noted that it means "Chopper". That is exactly what God tells Gideon to do to Baal's altar and to the wooden cultic object erected beside it. A new altar in favour of Yahweh is to be built. The wooden Asherah will serve to burn the sacrifice and the inaugurating sacrificial victim will be supplied from Gideon's father's herd. (We are told it should be his father's *second* bull, perhaps to show that the offering would not be too much of an imposition!) Fearful Gideon does all this—but at night.

Joash is in a situation many fathers with grown-up but still dependent sons have to face. The townspeople are baying for the blood of the headstrong revolutionary in his household; and he himself has lost his seven-year-old bull to his son's new-found principles. Family solidarity drives him to a successful ploy. Desperation often works quite as well as inspiration! He insists that Baal not Gideon is on trial. An angry god who is worthy to be called a god can take his own measures against those who slight him. Let Baal be a god and stand up for himself! And this very jibe against Baal, "Let Baal plead the cause (RSV contend)", attaches itself as a nickname to Chopper or Hacker.

One last point should be made before we leave verses 25–32. This story of Gideon's new altar to the Lord in place of one to Baal reads a little oddly after verses 19–24 which have already culminated in the building of a new altar. That passage also surprised us with its second scene (v. 22) after the first in verses 14–18. Such doublets are regular features of popular oral tradition. However, what interests me about these two *separate* altar stories is that *together* they anticipate significant features of that great later contest between Yahweh and Baal. The contest which involves Elijah and the prophets of Baal on Mount Carmel (1 Kings 18) is precisely over which god is *God*: over which god can really stand up for himself. And that contest is also settled in practice by the god who is able to send down fire to burn up the sacrifice.

(ii)

The eastern marauders cross the river Jordan some miles south of the Sea of Galilee near the ancient and modern town of Beth-Shean and encamp in that fertile valley which runs north-east from there to the modern Haifa on the Mediterranean coast, a valley whose richness is reflected in its name (Jezreel), which means that God sows it. The valley separates the hill country of Galilee to the north from the heartland hill country of Israel in central Palestine. This force is answered by divine force. The very Hebrew word translated "spirit" is the common word also for "wind"—and wind is something forceful rather than quiet. The

Hebrew verse 34 is more striking than the RSV with its standard formula "took possession"—it says literally "the wind/spirit of the Lord *clothed* Gideon". The trumpet is sounded for muster, and the triple force of Midianites, Amalekites and people of the East is matched by a triple appeal to Gideon's own clan (v. 34), to the rest of Manasseh (all based south of the valley), and to the three immediately neighbouring tribes in the Galilee hills to the north (v. 35). The introductory formula (6:1) may have talked about "Israel", but the conflict when it happens involves a fairly local muster. The same was the case with Ehud who "sounded the trumpet in the hill country of Ephraim" (3:27); and we drew attention to the tribal situation in the Song of Deborah (chapter 5).

(iii)

One of Gideon's names may sound as resolute as "Hacker" while the other is as bold as a taunt against a god. He has had favoured dealings with the Lord, he has desecrated Baal's sanctuary with apparent impunity. He has successfully mustered a force out of four tribes of Israel. And he is racked with doubt (vv. 36–40)! I was tempted to write, "and *yet* he is racked with doubt"; but it is the experience of many leading figures to feel much less resolute inside than they appear to be outside. Only some of them admit that it is a force from beyond them that drives them on. However, the reality of their private sufferings and doubts is no less—and may even be greater—for not being admitted. This should perhaps be a matter of comfort to many weaker souls.

It is not easy to bring any system to the many Old Testament passages that talk about testing God. The Exodus generation is blamed repeatedly for putting God to the test in the desert, and Aaron (Num. 20) and Moses (Num. 27 and Deut. 32) finally pay the supreme penalty for involvement in such faithlessness. On the other hand Isaiah actually *offers* King Ahaz a sign from the Lord and offers him free choice of any sign from the underworld to highest heaven. That opportunity is too great for him, and he turns down the offer, whether piously or faithlessly: "I will not put the Lord to the test" (Isa. 7:12). Here God seems extraordinarily patient with Gideon. Perhaps our young hero's state of mind is best captured in the response to Jesus of the father of a sick lad who said, "I believe: help my unbelief" (Mark 9:24).

"THE DAY OF MIDIAN"

Judges 7:1–8:3

[1]Then Jerubbaal (that is, Gideon) and all the people who were with him rose early and encamped beside the spring of Harod; and the camp of Midian was north of them, by the hill of Moreh, in the valley.

[2]The Lord said to Gideon, "The people with you are too many for me to give the Midianites into their hand, lest Israel vaunt themselves against me, saying, 'My own hand has delivered me.' [3]Now therefore proclaim in the ears of the people, saying, 'Whoever is fearful and trembling, let him return home.'" And Gideon tested them; twenty-two thousand returned, and ten thousand remained.

[4]And the Lord said to Gideon, "The people are still too many; take them down to the water and I will test them for you there; and he of whom I say to you, 'This man shall go with you,' shall go with you; and any of whom I say to you, 'This man shall not go with you,' shall not go." [5]So he brought the people down to the water; and the Lord said to Gideon, "Every one that laps the water with his tongue, as a dog laps, you shall set by himself; likewise every one that kneels down to drink." [6]And the number of those that lapped, putting their hands to their mouths, was three hundred men; but all the rest of the people knelt down to drink water. [7]And the Lord said to Gideon, "With the three hundred men that lapped I will deliver you, and give the Midianites into your hand; and let all the others go every man to his home." [8]So he took the jars of the people from their hands, and their trumpets; and he sent all the rest of Israel every man to his tent, but retained the three hundred men; and the camp of Midian was below him in the valley.

[9]That same night the Lord said to him, "Arise, go down against the camp; for I have given it into your hand. [10]But if you fear to go down, go down to the camp with Purah your servant; [11]and you shall hear what they say, and afterward your hands shall be strengthened to go down against the camp." Then he went down to the outposts of the armed men that were in the camp. [12]And the Midianites and the Amalekites and all the people of the East lay along the valley like

locusts for multitude; and their camels were without number, as the sand which is upon the seashore for multitude. [13]When Gideon came, behold, a man was telling a dream to his comrade; and he said, "Behold, I dreamed a dream; and lo, a cake of barley bread tumbled into the camp of Midian, and came to the tent, and struck it so that it fell, and turned it upside down, so that the tent lay flat." [14]And his comrade answered, "This is no other than the sword of Gideon the son of Joash, a man of Israel; into his hand God has given Midian and all the host."

[15]When Gideon heard the telling of the dream and its interpretation, he worshipped; and he returned to the camp of Israel, and said, "Arise; for the Lord has given the host of Midian into your hand." [16]And he divided the three hundred men into three companies, and put trumpets into the hands of all of them and empty jars, with torches inside the jars. [17]And he said to them, "Look at me, and do likewise; when I come to the outskirts of the camp, do as I do. [18]When I blow the trumpet, I and all who are with me, then blow the trumpets also on every side of all the camp, and shout, 'For the Lord and for Gideon.'"

[19]So Gideon and the hundred men who were with him came to the outskirts of the camp at the beginning of the middle watch, when they had just set the watch; and they blew the trumpets and smashed the jars that were in their hands. [20]And the three companies blew the trumpets and broke the jars, holding in their left hands the torches, and in their right hands the trumpets to blow; and they cried, "A sword for the Lord and for Gideon!" [21]They stood every man in his place round about the camp, and all the army ran; they cried out and fled. [22]When they blew the three hundred trumpets, the Lord set every man's sword against his fellow and against all the army; and the army fled as far as Beth-shittah toward Zererah, as far as the border of Abel-meholah, by Tabbath. [23]And the men of Israel were called out from Naphtali and from Asher and from all Manasseh, and they pursued after Midian.

[24]And Gideon sent messengers throughout all the hill country of Ephraim, saying, "Come down against the Midianites and seize the waters against them, as far as Beth-barah, and also the Jordan." So all the men of Ephraim were called out, and they seized the waters as far as Beth-barah, and also the Jordan. [25]And they took the two princes of Midian, Oreb and Zeeb; they killed Oreb at the rock of Oreb, and Zeeb they killed at the wine press of Zeeb, as they pursued Midian; and they brought the heads of Oreb and Zeeb to Gideon beyond the Jordan.

¹And the men of Ephraim said to him, "What is this that you have done to us, not to call us when you went to fight with Midian?" And they upbraided him violently. ²And he said to them, "What have I done now in comparison with you? Is not the gleaning of the grapes of Ephraim better than the vintage of Abi-ezer? ³God has given into your hands the princes of Midian, Oreb and Zeeb; what have I been able to do in comparison with you?" Then their anger against him was abated, when he had said this.

Like the story of Jericho where the walls fell down, this chapter records one of the great routs in Biblical narrative. The two-stage selection of the small band of three hundred and the simple equipment for the ruse of trumpets, pitchers and torches, are well known to many readers from childhood. The affair seems to have achieved almost proverbial status: Isaiah makes two references to it in a couple of words talking of "the day of Midian" (9:4) and "the smiting of Midian" (10:26). Yet this is also one of these Biblical narratives where familiarity and understanding do not appear to progress in step with each other. The closer we look, the more puzzling some of its aspects become. We can hardly hope to solve these problems in the few paragraphs that follow. At least we can try to bring some of the issues into clearer focus.

(i)

Israel's human leader is the first to be mentioned in the chapter and lest there be any doubt over his identification he is given both his names, Gideon and Jerubbaal. Gideon is in fact the name which is used throughout chapter 7 and in most of chapter 8 until the very end. Jerubbaal is used alone in the story of his son Abimelech (Judg. 9) and in the remaining two Old Testament references (1 Sam. 12:11; 2 Sam. 11:21) (in the latter case *besheth* "shame" is substituted for Baal), while Gideon has pride of place in Hebrews 11:32, where he actually heads the worthies there listed: Gideon, Barak, Samson, Jephthah, David and Samuel.

"Hacker" may be mentioned first but the decisive initiative comes from his God: "The people with you are too many for *me* to give the Midianites into their hand, lest Israel vaunt themselves against me" (v. 2). The success will be Yahweh's not Israel's; and, rather neatly, Gideon does not rate a mention. The point is reinforced in v. 7 where the Lord declares himself Israel's deliverer. Gideon appropriately schools his troops with the war cry, "*For the Lord* and for Gideon" (v. 18—contrast Henry V: "*God for Harry*, England and St. George!").

(ii)

Perhaps the biggest puzzle in the chapter is the nature and rationale of the selection process. The first reduction from thirty-two thousand to ten thousand men on the basis of those admitting to fear is easy enough to understand; yet this very criterion might have excluded the Gideon of chapter 6 who was very backward at coming forward (6:15) and had to press God for assurance (6:36–40). Even in the midst of the battle preparations in this chapter God has to coax him forward (vv. 10–11) by letting him overhear a worrying dream and its interpretation within the Midianite camp.

The water drinking scene has baffled readers since very ancient times and possibly even since it was first told. Even the details of the scene are obscure, let alone its interpretation; for verses 4–6 have come down to us in several competing versions. I suspect that the two problems go hand in hand: that the precise definition of the details is closely allied to pinning down the nature of the test. It is not even easy to *visualize* the contrast; for one way of understanding a human kneeling by water to drink is to suppose it *is* like the action of a four-footed animal.

There is always a danger about simply shrugging off intractable questions, about simply wishing problems away. However, in this case I am persuaded that a mountain is being made out of a molehill. All the argument about which way a good soldier will drink water from a river to avoid being surprised quite misses the point. God certainly speaks of a "test" in v. 4. The relevant Hebrew word regularly has to do with the refining process for metals. It is not an examination which some will succeed in and others fail. It is rather a process all are put through—a process for separation, a process which usually results in much refuse and little usable metal.

God retains control until the very end of the surprise attack as v. 22 makes clear. Instructed to use the battle cry "For the Lord and for Gideon" (v. 18), what the three hundred in fact roar amid the trumpets blasting, torches flaring and pots crashing is "*A sword* for the Lord and for Gideon!" This in no sense describes what they have in their own hand. Whether an appeal or an expression of confidence, it is answered by God's setting "every man's sword against his fellow and against all the army". Confusion wins the day. Indeed this whole story can be read as a powerful corrective to our all-too-frequent preoccupation with what *we* can do to save a situation and with the *reasons* for God's choice of this one, rather than that, to do a particular job.

(iii)

The sequel to the midnight surprise is almost as confusing in our text. (a) First of all "Israel" is called out (v. 23) and that means much the same grouping as 6:35 listed (here without Zebulun). (b) The next brief passage (7:24–8:3) concerns a special appeal to Ephraim, Manasseh's immediate Israelite neighbour to the south, to help by holding water crossings. This they achieved successfully, killing two Midianite princes into the bargain. They protest they have not seen enough of the action. Their anger (the Hebrew says "their spirit") has to be averted by good diplomacy on Gideon's part. (c) Finally the remainder of chapter 8 envisages the pursuit being carried out only by Gideon and his small band of three hundred now exhausted men (8:4). Perhaps as the story was repeated in later times, different clans made different claims to a share of that fateful ancient action.

It is easy to understand how a few tribes can come to represent "all Israel". Not many highland families were represented at the Battle on Culloden Moor which sealed the fate of the Stuart claim to the British throne in 1746; it was a claim indeed that few Scots at the time were keen to see succeed. Yet in the mythology of Scottish sentiment and nationalism that battle is now a national disaster at the hands of a brutal English foe with Bonnie Prince Charlie a young martyr of the nationalist cause—and all our forbears were there!

MIDIAN AND KINGSHIP

Judges 8:4–35

⁴And Gideon came to the Jordan and passed over, he and the three hundred men who were with him, faint yet pursuing. ⁵So he said to the men of Succoth, "Pray, give loaves of bread to the people who follow me; for they are faint, and I am pursuing after Zebah and Zalmunna, the kings of Midian." ⁶And the officials of Succoth said, "Are Zebah and Zalmunna already in your hand, that we should give bread to your army?" ⁷And Gideon said, "Well then, when the Lord has given Zebah and Zalmunna into my hand, I will flail your flesh with the thorns of the wilderness and with briers." ⁸And from there he went up to Penuel, and spoke to them in the same way; and the men of Penuel answered him as the men of Succoth had answered. ⁹And he said to the men of Penuel, "When I come again in peace, I will break down this tower."

¹⁰Now Zebah and Zalmunna were in Karkor with their army, about fifteen thousand men, all who were left of all the army of the people of the East; for there had fallen a hundred and twenty thousand men who drew the sword. ¹¹And Gideon went up by the caravan route east of Nobah and Jogbehah, and attacked the army; for the army was off its guard. ¹²And Zebah and Zalmunna fled; and he pursued them and took the two kings of Midian, Zebah and Zalmunna, and he threw all the army into a panic.

¹³Then Gideon the son of Joash returned from the battle by the ascent of Heres. ¹⁴And he caught a young man of Succoth, and questioned him; and he wrote down for him the officials and elders of Succoth, seventy-seven men. ¹⁵And he came to the men of Succoth, and said, "Behold Zebah and Zalmunna, about whom you taunted me, saying, 'Are Zebah and Zalmunna already in your hand, that we should give bread to your men who are faint?'" ¹⁶And he took the elders of the city and he took thorns of the wilderness and briers and with them taught the men of Succoth. ¹⁷And he broke down the tower of Penuel and slew the men of the city.

¹⁸Then he said to Zebah and Zalmunna, "Where are the men whom you slew at Tabor?" They answered, "As you are, so were they, every one of them; they resembled the sons of a king." ¹⁹And he said, "They were my brothers, the sons of my mother; as the Lord lives, if you had saved them alive, I would not slay you." ²⁰And he said to Jether his

first-born, "Rise, and slay them." But the youth did not draw his sword; for he was afraid, because he was still a youth. ²¹Then Zebah and Zalmunna said, "Rise yourself, and fall upon us; for as the man is, so is his strength." And Gideon arose and slew Zebah and Zalmunna; and he took the crescents that were on the necks of their camels.

²²Then the men of Israel said to Gideon, "Rule over us, you and your son and your grandson also; for you have delivered us out of the hand of Midian." ²³Gideon said to them, "I will not rule over you, and my son will not rule over you; the Lord will rule over you." ²⁴And Gideon said to them, "Let me make a request of you; give me every man of you the earrings of his spoil." (For they had golden earrings, because they were Ishmaelites.) ²⁵And they answered, "We will willingly give them." And they spread a garment, and every man cast in it the earrings of his spoil. ²⁶And the weight of the golden earrings that he requested was one thousand seven hundred shekels of gold; besides the crescents and the pendants and the purple garments worn by the kings of Midian, and besides the collars that were about the necks of their camels. ²⁷And Gideon made an ephod of it and put it in his city, in Ophrah; and all Israel played the harlot after it there, and it became a snare to Gideon and to his family. ²⁸So Midian was subdued before the people of Israel, and they lifted up their heads no more. And the land had rest forty years in the days of Gideon.

²⁹Jerubbaal the son of Joash went and dwelt in his own house. ³⁰Now Gideon had seventy sons, his own offspring, for he had many wives. ³¹And his concubine who was in Shechem also bore him a son, and he called his name Abimelech. ³²And Gideon the son of Joash died in a good old age, and was buried in the tomb of Joash his father, at Ophrah of the Abiezrites.

³³As soon as Gideon died, the people of Israel turned again and played the harlot after the Baals, and made Baal-berith their god. ³⁴And the people of Israel did not remember the Lord their God, who had rescued them from the hand of all their enemies on every side; ³⁵and they did not show kindness to the family of Jerubbaal (that is, Gideon) in return for all the good that he had done to Israel.

(i)

Gideon's pursuit of the fleeing Midianites eastwards into Trans-jordan is doubly remarkable. First of all, as we have already noted at the end of the previous section, this is the *third* report of pursuit since the midnight ruse. Then secondly, Zebah and

Zalmunna are the *second* pair of Midianite rulers to be so pursued. We appear to be dealing with originally alternative traditions, both of which have ended up in Judg. 7–8. The book of Isaiah appears to know the Ephraimite version, for it mentions smiting "Midian at the rock of Oreb" (10:26). The only other Biblical record of this tradition is Psalm 83, which at first sight is hostile to my case. The relevant verses read as follows:

> Do to them as thou didst to Midian,
>> as to Sisera and Jabin at the river Kishon,
> who were destroyed at Endor,
>> who became dung for the ground.
> Make their nobles like Oreb and Zeeb,
>> all their princes like Zebah and Zalmunna,
> who said, "Let us take possession for ourselves
>> of the pastures of God." (vv. 9–12)

The Hebrew of the third verse quoted is longer than the verses round about, and has probably been overloaded. A more literal translation would be, "Make their nobles like Oreb and like Zeeb /and like Zebah and Zalmunna/all their princes". We may reconstruct the "original" briefer line as follows:

> Make their nobles like Oreb
>> and like Zeeb all their princes.

The words marked off as intruders had been added to adjust the text of the Psalm to the information in the Book of Judges (in the form we know it).

We should note in passing that Psalm 83 localizes the rout at Endor, a name we encounter elsewhere in the Bible. The opening of Judg. 7 speaks of En-harod (RSV "the spring of Harod"). This latter may not be a real place-name at all, but rather contrived for effect: *harod* is probably related to the word rendered "trembling" in 7:3. Our Judges story-teller will have set his version of the tale at "Trembling Spring".

(ii)

It appears that the people of the Transjordanian towns like Succoth and Penuel had had even more cause to fear the roving Midianites on their camels than Gideon's folk in the west. They are in no mood to humour a young upstart and his exhausted band, flushed with only one success. As names, both Succoth and Penuel or Peniel have caught the imagination of certain Christian communities who have tended to use them as names for their own houses or settlements. Yet they appear very rarely in the Bible. Links between the few relevant passages seem more than co-incidental, and easily lead to speculation about stock themes in Biblical narrative.

1 Kings 12:25 reports building operations by Jeroboam, northern Israel's first king, in Shechem and Penuel. That reminds me of Penuel's tower in verses 9 and 17 here—and a Tower of Shechem appears in 9:46–49. Scholars have often noted the closeness in name between *Jerob*oam and *Jerub*baal. The only other scene at Penuel is Jacob's epic struggle with the divine stranger at the Jabbok ford (Gen. 32:22–32). Jacob, like Gideon (Judg. 6:22), was terrified at having seen God face to face. Again like Gideon (Judg. 6:32), the episode leads to a new name for Jacob— "Israel". As for Succoth, its very origins are attributed to Jacob in Gen. 33:17, who had made "booths" (the meaning of the name) there.

(iii)

In its classic brevity, the closing scene between Gideon and the Midianite chiefs is very powerful. It is in fact only from this conclusion to the story that we learn there has been an element of personal vendetta in Gideon's campaign: "What about [rather than "Where are"] the men you slew at Tabor?" (v. 18) Zebah and Zalmunna must already know their fate; yet they reply with a well-turned compliment. Their king-like victims had been Gideon's full brothers. Gideon seeks to make the feud even more of a family business by involving his young son; but Jether is not able to face the task of hacking them down. Again the Midianites observe gracefully that Gideon will be man enough for the strong task of cutting them down. Vendetta is no grubby episode, but has its own savage code of honour. I am reminded of "family" feuds in the Mafia of Sicily; and also a recurring theme of great Turkish films.

(iv)

We shall find that kingship, or at least the want of it, is an important theme in the last five chapters of this Book of Judges. However, we find it first in chapters 8–9, strategically placed at the very heart of the traditions of the judges themselves. Grateful Israel offers kingship, hereditary kingship, to Gideon: "Rule over us, you and your son and your grandson also; for you have delivered us out of the hand of Midian" (v. 22).

Gideon's words apparently reject the offer out of loyalty to Yahweh: "I will not rule over you, and my son will not rule over you; the Lord will rule over you" (v. 23). Yet these are merely the words *on the line*; there are several different signals *between the lines* in this chapter. (a) Zebah and Zalmunna, who are designated "kings" in verse 5 (unlike Oreb and Zeeb who are called "princes" in 7:25), remember Gideon's brothers as resembling the sons of a king (v. 18). (b) Gideon expects a lot of Jether, his first born (v. 20), as if he were a valiant crown prince. (c) His seventy sons of many wives (v. 30) are an almost royal household. And (d) the very name Abimelech which he himself gives to his concubine's son in Shechem means "my father is a king"! If actions speak louder than words, what then of Gideon's refusal of kingship?

One further action deserves special mention. This Gideon, whose other name Jerubbaal reminds us of Jeroboam, takes a freewill offering (gold only!) from the booty and makes a cultic object which traps Israel into apostasy (v. 27). We shall have more to say about "ephod" in discussing chapter 18. It is not simply the hinted anticipation of King Jeroboam which suggests this is a further royal action; cultic oversight in general was a royal responsibility—like the role of the English monarch as head of the Church of England.

ABIMELECH AND JOTHAM

Judges 9:1–22

¹Now Abimelech the son of Jerubbaal went to Shechem to his mother's kinsmen and said to them and to the whole clan of his mother's family,

²"Say in the ears of all the citizens of Shechem, 'Which is better for you, that all seventy of the sons of Jerubbaal rule over you, or that one rule over you?' Remember also that I am your bone and your flesh ." ³And his mother's kinsmen spoke all these words on his behalf in the ears of all the men of Shechem; and their hearts inclined to follow Abimelech, for they said, "He is our brother." ⁴And they gave him seventy pieces of silver out of the house of Baal-berith with which Abimelech hired worthless and reckless fellows, who followed him. ⁵And he went to his father's house at Ophrah, and slew his brothers the sons of Jerubbaal, seventy men, upon one stone; but Jotham the youngest son of Jerubbaal was left, for he hid himself. ⁶And all the citizens of Shechem came together, and all Beth-millo, and they went and made Abimelech king, by the oak of the pillar at Shechem.

⁷When it was told to Jotham, he went and stood on the top of Mount Gerizim, and cried aloud and said to them, "Listen to me, you men of Shechem, that God may listen to you. ⁸The trees once went forth to anoint a king over them; and they said to the olive tree, 'Reign over us.' ⁹But the olive tree said to them, 'Shall I leave my fatness, by which gods and men are honoured, and go to sway over the trees?' ¹⁰And the trees said to the fig tree, 'Come you, and reign over us.' ¹¹But the fig tree said to them, 'Shall I leave my sweetness and my good fruit, and go to sway over the trees?' ¹²And the trees said to the vine, 'Come you, and reign over us.' ¹³But the vine said to them, 'Shall I leave my wine which cheers gods and men, and go to sway over the trees?' ¹⁴Then all the trees said to the bramble, 'Come you, and reign over us.' ¹⁵And the bramble said to the trees, 'If in good faith you are anointing me king over you, then come and take refuge in my shade; but if not, let fire come out of the bramble and devour the cedars of Lebanon.'

¹⁶"Now therefore, if you acted in good faith and honour when you made Abimelech king, and if you have dealt well with Jerubbaal and his house, and have done to him as his deeds deserved— ¹⁷for my father fought for you, and risked his life, and rescued you from the hand of Midian; ¹⁸and you have risen up against my father's house this day, and have slain his sons, seventy men on one stone, and have made Abimelech, the son of his maidservant, king over the citizens of Shechem, because he is your kinsman— ¹⁹if you then have acted in good faith and honour with Jerubbaal and with his house this day, then rejoice in Abimelech, and let him also rejoice in you; ²⁰but if not, let fire come out from Abimelech, and devour the citizens of Shechem, and Beth-millo; and let fire come out from the citizens of Shechem,

and from Beth-millo, and devour Abimelech." 21And Jotham ran away and fled, and went to Beer and dwelt there, for fear of Abimelech his brother.

22Abimelech ruled over Israel three years.

(i)

Any suspicion that not enough has been said about kingship in our discussion of Judg. 8 is amply confirmed as we turn to the opening verses of this next chapter. The alternative proposed by Abimelech (v. 2) more or less assumes that Gideon had wielded sole rule throughout his long life. His proposal was merely about the succession to Gideon. No new principle was involved.

This must force us back to another brief scrutiny of vv. 22–23 of the previous chapter. Readers familiar with 1 Sam. 7–12 will remember that the introduction of kingship in Israel was a contentious matter, probably at the time itself, and certainly in later reflection on it. Israel's proposal to Gideon, like Abimelech's alternative to Shechem, talks neutrally in terms of "rule" whether by accident or studied choice. The loaded terms "king" and "reign" are absent. Non-use of the technical term need not blind us to the real situation; in fact this neutral word "rule" is to be found even in the David and Solomon stories (2 Sam. 23:3; 1 Kings 4:21). A rose by any other name . . . ! Gideon's response to the proposal made him is carefully open. Ascribing rule to God alone is both religiously orthodox, and at the same time side-steps the issue of who will interpret God and act for him on earth. Whatever the import of his words, it is his actions that will have been the background to his son Abimelech's move.

The affair of Abimelech and the seventy sons of Gideon or Jerubbaal is almost a mirror image of Jehu's revolt against the house of Ahab described at the beginning of 2 Kings 10. We should not suppose that Gideon's sons were functioning as an organized council of seventy; however, the strength of Abimelech's proposal for their assassination may derive from strife among Gideon's offspring over which of them should rule. Better one than confusion among many, especially when that one is also a Shechemite on his mother's side. The seventy are eliminated "upon one stone" (was it on the local altar?) with the assistance of a force of ruffians dignified only by the source of their payment—the temple treasury of Baal-berith. That done, and with no lingering hesitation over using the term "king", the leaders of Shechem in full assembly make king the man whose very name means "my father is king". The "oak of the pillar" (v. 6) takes us back to the oak and the great stone in Josh. 24:26, and to the oak near Shechem under which Jacob hid the evidence of foreign worship (Gen. 35:1–4); and even to Abram's first goal on reaching the land of Canaan: "the place at Shechem, the oak of Moreh" (Gen. 12:6).

(ii)

The tension in this finely crafted narrative is provided by Jotham's survival of the slaughter at Ophrah. Jotham is not just the youngest son of a youngest son (9:5 and 6:15), but his very name reminds us of the Hebrew word for orphan. It can hardly have been as a mere child that he escaped notice; for he takes himself to the top of Mount Gerizim, the mount of blessing (Deut. 27:12), and delivers himself of a finely barbed fable in the hearing of Shechem's leaders, a fable which adds up to a curse (v. 57). All our Biblical evidence, though admittedly scanty, suggests that tree fables like Jotham's in vv. 8–15 were a part of royal wisdom and diplomacy. The note about Solomon's amazing wisdom in 1 Kings 4:29–34 tells us that "He also uttered three thousand proverbs; and his songs were a thousand and five. He spoke of trees, from the cedar that is in Lebanon to the hyssop that grows out of the wall" (vv. 32–33). Then when a king of Israel wants to side-step an arrogant military challenge from his neighbour in Jerusalem, his contemptuous reply begins: "A thistle on Lebanon sent to a cedar on Lebanon saying, 'Give your daughter to my son for a wife'; and a wild beast of Lebanon passed by and trampled down the thistle" (2 Kings 14:9).

Jotham's speech is fuller and thoroughly appropriate to the context. It encapsulates beautifully the widespread human judgment that those who seem the best potential leaders are already happy doing what they do well, while those who take the job are without the best qualifications. Olive, fig, and vine delight gods and men alike. Their noble credentials are beyond question. Only on their refusal of sway over the other trees would one think of approaching the bramble! Yet the bramble is not without its own shrewd insight; indeed I wonder whether in verse 15 Jotham does not intend a contrast with Abimelech's seeking the kingdom for himself. The Hebrew phrase "in truth" here is ambiguous. The RSV takes it to mean "in good faith", which is certainly appropriate in the following verse. I wonder whether the point is not better got by translating "truly" or "really". The bramble is surprised at the approach; he knows he is unsuitable, and a last resort. By choosing him, they will involve themselves in a double bind: heads they lose, and tails they do not win! He knows he cannot hold *sway* over the other trees. They are welcome to his shade: but they will be prostrate and prickled. Should they play him false, they should be in no doubt about his power to harm them: fire to destroy even the noblest cedar is readily kindled in his thorns.

This uneasy alternative is spelled out in verses 16–21. They propose in still other terms a no-win alternative. (a) *If* they have dealt well and honourably with Jerubbaal's house, then let them enjoy (v. 19) Abimelech's rule (but of course the clear implication is that they have played false with the family of their one-time saviour, and so will "enjoy" very painful "pleasure" under his bastard son). (b) If they have *not* acted honourably, then they and Abimelech will be destroyed in mutual conflagration. Whether mistakenly wrong or openly wrong, they cannot win. I cannot be sure, but I suspect that this unstable situation is perfectly expressed in a deliberate word-play in the following verse 22. When we read there that Abimelech "ruled" over Israel three years, we are dealing with a different word from the one we discussed in 8:22–23 and 9:2. It is a relatively rare verb in the Bible. Hosea uses it once in criticism of monarchy:

They made kings, but not through me.
They *set up princes*, but without my knowledge.   (8:4)

Then in Hos. 12:3–4 it is used again in the same sense in which it appears in Gen. 32:28, of Jacob *striving* or contending successfully with God's strange messenger. The word has in it an element of both rule and struggle. Perhaps the best way of catching the sense of verse 22 would be to translate in English "Abimelech mastered Israel three years."

THE FATE OF ABIMELECH AND SHECHEM

Judges 9:23–57

23And God sent an evil spirit between Abimelech and the men of Shechem; and the men of Shechem dealt treacherously with Abimelech; 24that the violence done to the seventy sons of Jerubbaal might come and their blood be laid upon Abimelech their brother, who slew them, and upon the men of Shechem, who strengthened his hands to slay his brothers. 25And the men of Shechem put men in ambush against him on the mountain tops, and they robbed all who passed by them along that way; and it was told Abimelech.

26And Gaal the son of Ebed moved into Shechem with his kinsmen; and the men of Shechem put confidence in him. 27And they went out into the field, and gathered the grapes from their vineyards and trod them, and held festival, and went into the house of their god, and ate and drank and reviled Abimelech. 28And Gaal the son of Ebed said, "Who is Abimelech, and who are we of Shechem, that we should serve him? Did not the son of Jerubbaal and Zebul his officer serve the men of Hamor the father of Shechem? Why then should we serve him? 29Would that this people were under my hand! then I would remove Abimelech. I would say to Abimelech, 'Increase your army, and come out.'"

30When Zebul the ruler of the city heard the words of Gaal the son of Ebed, his anger was kindled. 31And he sent messengers to Abimelech at Arumah, saying, "Behold, Gaal the son of Ebed and his kinsmen have come to Shechem, and they are stirring up the city against you. 32Now therefore, go by night, you and the men that are with you, and lie in wait in the fields. 33Then in the morning, as soon as the sun is up, rise early and rush upon the city; and when he and the men that are with him come out against you, you may do to them as occasion offers."

34And Abimelech and all the men that were with him rose up by night, and laid wait against Shechem in four companies. 35And Gaal the son of Ebed went out and stood in the entrance of the gate of the city; and Abimelech and the men that were with him rose from the ambush. 36And when Gaal saw the men, he said to Zebul, "Look, men are coming down from the mountain tops!" And Zebul said to him, "You see the shadow of the mountains as if they were men." 37Gaal spoke again and said, "Look, men are coming down from the centre of the land, and one company is coming from the direction of the Diviners' Oak." 38Then Zebul said to him, "Where is your mouth now, you who said, 'Who is Abimelech, that we should serve him?' Are not these the men whom you despised? Go out now and fight with them." 39And Gaal went out at the head of the men of Shechem, and fought with Abimelech. 40And Abimelech chased him, and he fled before him; and many fell wounded, up to the entrance of the gate. 41And Abimelech dwelt at Arumah; and Zebul drove out Gaal and his kinsmen, so that they could not live on at Shechem.

42On the following day the men went out into the fields. And Abimelech was told. 43He took his men and divided them into three companies, and laid wait in the fields; and he looked and saw the men coming out of the city, and he rose against them and slew them. 44Abimelech and the company that was with him rushed forward and stood at the entrance of the gate of the city, while the two companies rushed upon all who were in the fields and slew them. 45And Abimelech fought against the city all that day; he took the city, and killed the people that were in it; and he razed the city and sowed it with salt.

46When all the people of the Tower of Shechem heard of it, they entered the stronghold of the house of El-berith. 47Abimelech was told that all the people of the Tower of Shechem were gathered together. 48And Abimelech went up to Mount Zalmon, he and all the men that were with him; and Abimelech took an axe in his hand, and cut down a bundle of brushwood, and took it up and laid it on his shoulder. And he said to the men that were with him, "What you have seen me do, make haste to do, as I have done." 49So every one of the people cut down his bundle and following Abimelech put it against the stronghold, and they set the stronghold on fire over them, so that all the people of the Tower of Shechem also died, about a thousand men and women.

50Then Abimelech went to Thebez, and encamped against Thebez, and took it. 51But there was a strong tower within the city, and all the people of the city fled to it, all the men and women, and shut themselves in; and they went to the roof of the tower. [52] And Abimelech came to the tower, and fought against it, and drew near to the door of the tower to burn it with fire. [53] And a certain woman threw an upper millstone upon Abimelech's head, and crushed his skull. [54] Then he called hastily to the young man his armour-bearer, and said to him, "Draw your sword and kill me, lest men say of me, 'A woman killed him.'" And his young man thrust him through, and he died. [55] And when the men of Israel saw that Abimelech was dead, they departed every man to his home. [56] Thus God requited the crime of Abimelech, which he committed against his father in killing his seventy brothers; [57] and God also made all the wickedness of the men of Shechem fall back upon their heads, and upon them came the curse of Jotham the son of Jerubbaal.

At one level, the reader of this unfolding of the come-uppance experienced jointly by Abimelech and Shechem can be content that here at least are thirty-five verses of straightforward Biblical narrative. At beginning (vv. 23–24) and end (vv. 56–57) the wider moral context is signalled. In between is a straightforward, knockabout plot about a local conflict, worthy of any Wild West movie. The narrative even includes the standard scene of the interloper Gaal "shooting off his mouth" with his band after a little too much to drink (vv. 27–29). It is interesting that the local temple should have doubled in function as the local bar! (Amos 2:8 gives further evidence of this phenomenon.)

Critical readers have sometimes argued that the whole Gaal episode in vv. 26–41 has been secondarily inserted into the story, in order to supply a straightforward human motivation for the strife between Abimelech and his original supporters in Shechem. We can readily agree with them that the situation described in verse 25, of Abimelech being tipped off about an ambush, is precisely mirrored in verse 42. The point at issue is whether we ought to go one stage further and deduce that the Gaal story is secondary because it changes nothing, or whether we take the chapter at face value as a report of shifting but not dissimilar scenes of strife. Yet two matters call for rather fuller comment.

(i)

The story is peopled with a whole series of fascinating and singular, and presumably significant, names. (a) Abimelech's lieutenant is called Zebul, and in the language of Canaan that means "prince" or "royal one". This may produce a more accurate translation of Solomon's claim in 1 Kings 8:13—

I have built a *royal* house for thee,
  an established place for thy throne for ever.

(b) The "men of Hamor" (v. 28) are apparently the traditional aristocracy of Shechem. This same Hamor appears in other Biblical texts that chart Israel's relationships with Shechem. Josh. 24:32 records the reburial of Joseph's bones in a plot his father Jacob had purchased near Shechem from Hamor. (The tomb is still venerated close to Jacob's Well.) That purchase is reported in Gen. 33:18-20, which tells of Jacob stopping at Shechem on arrival from Paddan-aram, just as we earlier noted Abram did (12:6-7). Like Abram too, he erected an altar there celebrating the name "El is God of Israel". The immediately following narrative that takes up all of Genesis 34 is a delightfully scandalous story of sour and indeed sore relationships between Jacob's family and the people of Hamor in Shechem. (We should remind ourselves in passing just how many links we have now spotted between Judges 6-9 and Genesis 31-34.)

(c) If the "people of Hamor" are the traditional leading group in the city they are one and the same as the group which the RSV wrongly translates sometimes "citizens of Shechem" (vv. 6, 18, 20) and sometimes "men of Shechem". In fact the Hebrew uses the plural of *ba'al*, which means "master" or "owner" (just as, as a divine name, it means "Master"). These will be the land-owning, chief families, whose representatives presumably constitute a council in the city. The same word is used of the leaders of Jericho (Josh. 24:11); Keilah (1 Sam. 23:11-12); and Jabesh (2 Sam. 21:12)—all of which may have had a certain independence from mainstream Israelite influence. (d) Mention of *ba'al* reminds us of the sanctuary and treasury of the divine *Baal*-berith in Shechem (9:4), and the corresponding temple of *El*-berith in the

Tower of Shechem (9:46), which may well be a locality distinct from Shechem itself. (El-berith is reminiscent of "El (is) God of Israel" in Gen. 33:20).

All in all, the names are rather too exalted for this to be the report of any local skirmish. The Diviners' Oak too in verse 37 reminds us of the references we noted when discussing 9:6; and the "centre of the land", which would be better rendered "navel of the earth", is another important cultic term. The same expression is used in Ezek. 38:12. The great Greek sanctuary at Delphi was also considered to be at the world's navel. And ancient Christian tradition locates the centre of the world in Jerusalem, and precisely within the Church of the Holy Sepulchre. Either these rare names are a priceless historical source, or a story-teller has dressed up his tale in very pretentious terms: perhaps in mockery of this would-be king and successor to Gideon.

(ii)

Some comment is also appropriate about the "evil spirit" God sends between Abimelech and the "masters" of Shechem (9:23). Elsewhere in the Book of Judges, the divine "spirit" or power invigorates one of Israel's judges or deliverers (see 3:10; 6:34; 11:29; 13:25; 14:6,19; 15:14). We should not draw any false contrast between the spirit of *Yahweh* in all these passages and the spirit of *God* here. "God" so often refers to Yahweh that we should not assume a distinction is intended.

In any case Yahweh is quite regularly the agent or author of disaster in the Old Testament. Amos asks, "Does evil befall a city, unless the Lord has done it?" (3:6). Isaiah has him say, "I form light and create darkness, I make weal and create woe, I am the Lord, who do all these things" (45:7). Similarly readers can consult at greater length the story of the "lying spirit" in 1 Kings 22:1–40.

What Biblical scholars do argue about is the theological significance of these claims about Yahweh. Was it inevitable that in a *poly*theistic setting, where contradictory influences on the world were attributed to different divine beings, the attempt of the Biblical writers to be consistently *mono*theistic resulted in contradictory things being said about Yahweh?

Perhaps. Yet it is arguable here in Judges 9, and elsewhere, that God does simply preside consistently over a world in which people reap what they sow. Abimelech had eliminated his half-brothers, and assumed their position. The notables of Shechem had fallen in with his plans, whether in feckless innocence or culpable guilt. Verse 23 says no more and no less than the concluding verses 56–57.

A LIST OF JUDGES

Judges 10:1–5 and 12:7–14

¹After Abimelech there arose to deliver Israel Tola the son of Puah, son of Dodo, a man of Issachar; and he lived at Shamir in the hill country of Ephraim. ²And he judged Israel twenty-three years. Then he died, and was buried at Shamir.

³After him arose Jair the Gileadite, who judged Israel twenty-two years. ⁴And he had thirty sons who rode on thirty asses; and they had thirty cities, called Havvoth-jair to this day, which are in the land of Gilead. ⁵And Jair died, and was buried in Kamon.

12 ⁷Jephthah judged Israel six years. Then Jephthah the Gileadite died, and was buried in his city in Gilead.

⁸After him Ibzan of Bethlehem judged Israel. ⁹He had thirty sons; and thirty daughters he gave in marriage outside his clan, and thirty daughters he brought in from outside for his sons. And he judged Israel seven years. ¹⁰Then Ibzan died, and was buried at Bethlehem.

¹¹After him Elon the Zebulunite judged Israel; and he judged Israel ten years. ¹²Then Elon the Zebulunite died, and was buried at Aijalon in the land of Zebulun.

¹³After him Abdon the son of Hillel the Pirathonite judged Israel. ¹⁴He had forty sons and thirty grandsons, who rode on seventy asses; and he judged Israel eight years. ¹⁵Then Abdon the son of Hillel the Pirathonite died, and was buried at Pirathon in the land of Ephraim, in the hill country of the Amalekites.

The next main narrative in the Book of Judges concerns Jephthah (11:1–12:7). However, Jephthah's name apparently belongs also to a short list of judges, found now in two parts (10:1–5 and 12:7–14), separated by the main Jephthah tradition. This is also more immediately prefaced by a full account (10:6–18) of Israel's religious mischief against Yahweh and her resultant subjection to the people of Ammon. In this section, by way of preface to our study of Jephthah, we shall consider first the judges associated with him.

(i)

The list of five "minor" judges has fascinated scholars in recent generations. It is clear first of all that it is a list. Information about each judge is given in a fixed, almost stereotyped way. Sometimes more information is given, sometimes less. Yet for everyone we are given at least his name, his local or family connection, the period for which he judged Israel, and a notice of his death and the place of his burial (cf. 12:11–12, which is the briefest and most schematic of the notes). What is disputed is how to evaluate the list. One fact above all has persuaded many critics to pay close attention to it; and that is that the length of each judgeship is expressed in *real* figures: twenty-three years for Tola, twenty-two for Jair, seven for Ibzan, ten for Elon, and eight for Abdon. These numbers, like the three years of Abimelech's rule (9:22), are in noticeable contrast to the rounded figures of twenty, forty and eighty years which punctuate and structure so much of the narrative of the Book of Judges (e.g. 3:11; 3:30; 4:3; 5:31; 8:28; 13:1; 15:20). If the round figures derive from the editors of the material, so the argument goes, the real figures will belong to their sources.

The next step we might take down the road of contrasting this list with the rest of the Book of Judges would be to note that it is precisely here that the very term "judge" is most at home. In fact it is arguable that almost every other occurrence of the word in the whole book is in secondary editorial constructions. Judg. 2:16–19 is certainly one of these—the main Deuteronomistic introduction. We have already noted that the story of Othniel (see especially 3:10) is a hotch-potch of representative standard terms. A repeated conclusion (15:20; 16:31) talks of Samson as a "judge" over twenty years. And that leaves us with just two passages which *might* offer us some leverage over this issue. We saw already that Judg. 4:5 introduces Deborah as someone who "used to sit under the palm of Deborah . . . in the hill country of Ephraim; and the people of Israel came up to her for judgment." Then the message taken by Jephthah's embassy to the king of Ammon concludes with the words: "the Lord, the *Judge*, decide this day between the people of Israel and the people of Ammon" (11:27). Both Deborah and God are apparently "judges" in the sense of arbitrators, giving a verdict.

If the judges listed in 10:1–5 and 12:7–14 are of the same sort, their function may be clarified in the rather similar note in 1 Sam. 7:15–18 about Samuel's role:

> Samuel judged Israel all the days of his life. And he went on a circuit year by year to Bethel, Gilgal, and Mizpah; and he judged Israel in all these places. Then he would come back to Ramah, for his home was there, and there also he administered justice to Israel.

Samuel's own role is also illustrated by his error in appointing his sons judges in his place in his old age, especially since they "did not walk in his ways, but turned aside after gain; they took bribes and perverted justice" (1 Sam. 8:1–3).

In the absence of other information, we may presume that such "judges" had a basically peaceful role; and that respect for their wisdom in arbitration made them a natural focus for common Israelite aspirations. When external trouble menaced Israel, some of them were clearly available as leaders: at least Deborah, Jephthah and Samuel. To say any more would go dangerously beyond our evidence.

(ii)

If the actual length of office of the five "minor" judges is stated in real numbers, the other details reported of them are in round figures. About Jair, Ibzan, and Abdon, we learn of large numbers of sons, daughters, and asses. They were apparently men of substance like Gideon: not necessarily supreme rulers, but rather perhaps substantial *sheikhs*, figures of weight and presence in the community.

At two rather significant points, the list is less regular. The first concerns the introduction of Tola (10:1). His predecessor is given as Abimelech who of course has not been presented as a judge of Israel. Of Tola it is said not that he *judged* Israel, but that he *delivered* Israel. It is not easy to decide whether we have here just an editorial device to link this list of judges with the wider collection of deliverer stories, or whether, and possibly at the same time, the editor is intending a "dig" at Abimelech's ill-fated struggle for mastery over Israel (9:22), after which Israel now deserved restoration. So much in this book is achieved by hint and innuendo, that it is dangerous to be sure.

The other irregularity is over the handling of Jephthah (12:7). There are those who claim that this verse has been created by the writer of the main Jephthah story to provide a tail-piece that resembles the fixed form of the list. I prefer to suppose that an originally standard note on Jephthah has been distorted when some of it became unnecessary, through the availability of the longer tradition we must now turn to study. Why else, if Jephthah had no original connection with this list, should the list have been broken in two pieces to accommodate him?

Whatever the precise details of the literary history of chapters 10 to 12 of the Book of Judges, they reflect in their given form the way that reminiscing memory often actually works. It is only *after* we have begun to associate similar details in sketchy form that a much larger memory is triggered of the more striking career of one of the personalities remembered.

SETTING THE RECORD STRAIGHT

Judges 10:6–11:28

⁶And the people of Israel again did what was evil in the sight of the Lord, and served the Baals and the Ashtaroth, the gods of Syria, the gods of Sidon, the gods of Moab, the gods of the Ammonites, and the gods of the Philistines; and they forsook the Lord, and did not serve him. ⁷And the anger of the Lord was kindled against Israel, and he sold them into the hand of the Philistines and into the hand of the Am-

monites, [8]and they crushed and oppressed the children of Israel that year. For eighteen years they oppressed all the people of Israel that were beyond the Jordan in the land of the Amorites, which is in Gilead. [9]And the Ammonites crossed the Jordan to fight also against Judah and against Benjamin and against the house of Ephraim; so that Israel was sorely distressed.

[10]And the people of Israel cried to the Lord, saying, "We have sinned against thee, because we have forsaken our God and have served the Baals." [11]And the Lord said to the people of Israel, "Did I not deliver you from the Egyptians and from the Amorites, from the Ammonites and from the Philistines? [12]The Sidonians also, and the Amalekites, and the Maonites, oppressed you; and you cried to me, and I delivered you out of their hand. [13]Yet you have forsaken me and served other gods; therefore I will deliver you no more. [14]Go and cry to the gods whom you have chosen; let them deliver you in the time of your distress." [15]And the people of Israel said to the Lord, "We have sinned; do to us whatever seems good to thee; only deliver us, we pray thee, this day." [16]So they put away the foreign gods from among them and served the Lord; and he became indignant over the misery of Israel.

[17]Then the Ammonites were called to arms, and they encamped in Gilead; and the people of Israel came together, and they encamped at Mizpah. [18]And the people, the leaders of Gilead, said one to another, "Who is the man that will begin to fight against the Ammonites? He shall be head over all the inhabitants of Gilead."

[1]Now Jephthah the Gileadite was a mighty warrior, but he was the son of a harlot. Gilead was the father of Jephthah. [2]And Gilead's wife also bore him sons; and when his wife's sons grew up, they thrust Jephthah out, and said to him, "You shall not inherit in our father's house; for you are the son of another woman." [3]Then Jephthah fled from his brothers, and dwelt in the land of Tob; and worthless fellows collected round Jephthah, and went raiding with him.

[4]After a time the Ammonites made war against Israel. [5]And when the Ammonites made war against Israel, the elders of Gilead went to bring Jephthah from the land of Tob; [6]and they said to Jephthah, "Come and be our leader, that we may fight with the Ammonites." [7]But Jephthah said to the elders of Gilead, "Did you not hate me, and drive me out of my father's house? Why have you come to me now when you are in trouble?" [8]And the elders of Gilead said to Jephthah, "That is why we have turned to you now, that you may go with us and

fight with the Ammonites, and be our head over all the inhabitants of Gilead." ⁹Jephthah said to the elders of Gilead, "If you bring me home again to fight with the Ammonites, and the Lord gives them over to me, I will be your head." ¹⁰And the elders of Gilead said to Jephthah, "The Lord will be witness between us; we will surely do as you say." ¹¹So Jephthah went with the elders of Gilead, and the people made him head and leader over them; and Jephthah spoke all his words before the Lord at Mizpah.

¹²Then Jephthah sent messengers to the king of the Ammonites and said, "What have you against me, that you have come to me to fight against my land?" ¹³And the king of the Ammonites answered the messengers of Jephthah, "Because Israel on coming from Egypt took away my land, from the Arnon to the Jabbok and to the Jordan; now therefore restore it peaceably." ¹⁴And Jephthah sent messengers again to the king of the Ammonites ¹⁵and said to him, "Thus says Jephthah: Israel did not take away the land of Moab or the land of the Ammonites, ¹⁶but when they came up from Egypt, Israel went through the wilderness to the Red Sea and came to Kadesh. ¹⁷Israel then sent messengers to the king of Edom, saying, 'Let us pass, we pray, through your land'; but the king of Edom would not listen. And they sent also to the king of Moab, but he would not consent. So Israel remained at Kadesh. ¹⁸Then they journeyed through the wilderness, and went around the land of Edom and the land of Moab, and arrived on the east side of the land of Moab, and camped on the other side of the Arnon; but they did not enter the territory of Moab, for the Arnon was the boundary of Moab. ¹⁹Israel then sent messengers to Sihon king of the Amorites, king of Heshbon; and Israel said to him, 'Let us pass, we pray, through your land to our country.' ²⁰But Sihon did not trust Israel to pass through his territory; so Sihon gathered all his people together, and encamped at Jahaz, and fought with Israel. ²¹And the Lord, the God of Israel, gave Sihon and all his people into the hand of Israel, and they defeated them; so Israel took possession of all the land of the Amorites, who inhabited that country. ²²And they took possession of all the territory of the Amorites from the Arnon to the Jabbok and from the wilderness to the Jordan. ²³So then the Lord, the God of Israel, dispossessed the Amorites from before his people Israel; and are you to take possession of them? ²⁴Will you not possess what Chemosh your god gives you to possess? And all that the Lord our God has dispossessed before us, we will possess. ²⁵Now are you any better than Balak the son of Zippor, king of Moab? Did he ever strive against Israel, or did he ever go to war with them? ²⁶While Israel dwelt in

Heshbon and its villages, and in Aroer and its villages, and in all the cities that are on the banks of Arnon, three hundred years, why did you not recover them within that time? 27I therefore have not sinned against you, and you do me wrong by making war on me; the Lord, the Judge, decide this day between the people of Israel and the people of Ammon." 28But the king of the Ammonites did not heed the message of Jephthah which he sent to him.

Anyone who believes that the conduct of public affairs might be improved by a move to greater honesty and more plain speaking and a lessened use of cynical half-truths might take some enlightenment from this passage. In fact three records are explored and set "straight": between Israel and her God; between Gilead and Jephthah; and between Israel and Ammon.

(i)

The first issue, between Israel and her God, is handled in 10:6– 16. This section opens in stock general terms. Different gods and peoples are listed in verses 6–7, and at the same time these verses have their full share of standard Judges expressions: "And the people of Israel did what was evil in the sight of the Lord . . . and the anger of the Lord was kindled against Israel, and he sold them into the hand . . ." Verses 8–9 are more specific, and apparently have only Ammonite pressure in mind: verse 8 is located in the territory of Gilead in Transjordan, while verse 9 sees the Ammonites carrying their success westwards, into the central highlands of Ephraim, Benjamin and Judah.

The distress provokes a general lament and confession; and at first a rather indignant response from the Lord (vv. 11–14). They are beyond excuse: his care for them has been shown, not only in the deliverance from Egypt, but in repeated deliverances since. They have not only left him in the lurch, but have deliberately chosen other gods for themselves: let them test *their* efficiency!

The implied analysis of the situation is very like Jeremiah's:

"Has a nation changed its gods,
  even though they are no gods?
But my people have changed their glory
  for that which does not profit."   (2:11)

"For they have turned their back to me,
    and not their face.
But in the time of their trouble they say,
    'Arise and save us!'
But where are your gods
    that you made for yourself?
Let them arise, if they can save you,
    in your time of trouble;
for as many as your cities
    are your gods, O Judah."

(2:27–28)

Faced with this response, they quietly return to Yahweh's service and throw themselves on his mercy. In time "he became indignant over the misery of Israel" (v. 16*b*)

(ii)

Gilead needed a leader against Ammon. Doubtless they had traditional and properly validated leaders; but they were of no use. In the Ammonite crisis military success was the only relevant criterion (10:17–18). The narrative at this point flashes back to sketch the new hero's past (11:1–3). Like Abimelech he had been born on the wrong side of the blanket, had bad dealings with his legitimate brothers, and gathered a motley gang in exile. King David's power would later grow from a similar base. In fact it is only in the context of David's dealings with Ammon (2 Sam. 10:6–8) that we meet again in the Bible the land of Tob, place of Jephthah's exile.

Invited home to help, Jephthah deals with Gilead exactly as Yahweh has: "Did you not hate me, and drive me out of my father's house? Why have you come to me now when you are in trouble?" (11:7). With delightful candour, Gilead's elders admit their trouble is exactly what has brought them to him. He agrees to put his fighting skills at their disposal, against a solemn promise that he will be sole leader thereafter. He is careful to issue his terms in a sacred setting: "before the Lord at Mizpah" (11:11).

More than a common attitude links Yahweh and Jephthah in these first two scenes. There is a delightful pun in the Hebrew text too. Israel has said to God (10:15): "You do to us exactly what is good [*tob*] in your eyes"; and it is from *Tob* that their deliverance comes! Nathanael asked scornfully concerning Jesus: "Can anything *good* come out of Nazareth?" (John 1:46). Any similar detractor of Jephthah in Gilead would have choked on his words!

(iii)

The third section of our text (11:12–28) represents a rather different sort of exercise. Jephthah's attempt at a historical refutation of Ammon's claim is hardly likely to have impressed the king of Ammon. (That name lives on in Amman, the capital of the Hashemite Kingdom of Jordan.) It is often said that Jephthah's message is not real diplomacy, but a legal argument based on speculative history and presented as diplomacy. I suspect that the same judgment could be passed on many of the claims and counter-claims of dubious historical worth traded between present-day Israel and her neighbours, including King Hussein in Amman.

The story of the passage through Transjordan on the way from Egypt is rehearsed from Num. 21 and Deut. 2–3. Jephthah's case is clever, but has elements of special pleading. (a) The Amorites were their foe in those days. They were rightfully dispossessed. To Ammon's claim to the land (v. 13) Jephthah responds, implicitly at least, that Ammon was not yet on the scene. We now have no independent record. (b) The next clever move he makes is to suggest that each side settle now for what its own god has managed to achieve (v. 24). There is of course a scornful threat implied, as the comparison with Balak (v. 25) makes clear. He knew better than to try to square accounts with Israel! (c) Anyway (v. 26), why have they not made this move at any time in the last three hundred years? This rather gives away any strength in the earlier suggestion that Ammon was not originally a partner in Israel's dealings in Tranjordan. Jephthah's conclusion (v. 27) drops the earlier pretence at even-handedness between Chemosh and Yahweh: "Yahweh, the Judge, decide this day between the people of Israel and people of Ammon."

If he was acting on the merits of the argument, I have some sympathy with the king of the Ammonites who "did not heed the message of Jephthah which he sent to him" (v. 28). Perhaps it was not *just* because he was a bastard that his brothers had forced him into exile—other Biblical heroes before him, like Jacob and Joseph, were too ready with their tongues for the good of family relationships!

A FATAL VOW AND A PASSWORD

Judges 11:29–12:6

²⁹Then the Spirit of the Lord came upon Jephthah, and he passed through Gilead and Manasseh, and passed on to Mizpah of Gilead, and from Mizpah of Gilead he passed on to the Ammonites. ³⁰And Jephthah made a vow to the Lord, and said, "If thou wilt give the Ammonites into my hand, ³¹then whoever comes forth from the doors of my house to meet me, when I return victorious from the Ammonites, shall be the Lord's, and I will offer him up for a burnt offering." ³²So Jephthah crossed over to the Ammonites to fight against them; and the Lord gave them into his hand. ³³And he smote them from Aroer to the neighbourhood of Minnith, twenty cities, and as far as Abel-keramim, with a very great slaughter. So the Ammonites were subdued before the people of Israel.

³⁴Then Jephthah came to his home at Mizpah; and behold, his daughter came out to meet him with timbrels and with dances; she was his only child; beside her he had neither son nor daughter. ³⁵And when he saw her, he rent his clothes, and said, "Alas, my daughter! you have brought me very low, and you have become the cause of great trouble to me; for I have opened my mouth to the Lord, and I cannot take back my vow." ³⁶And she said to him, "My father, if you have opened your mouth to the Lord, do to me according to what has gone forth from your mouth, now that the Lord has avenged you on your enemies, on the Ammonites." ³⁷And she said to her father, "Let this thing be done for me; let me alone two months, that I may go and wander on the mountains, and bewail my virginity, I and my companions." ³⁸And he said, "Go." And he sent her away for two months; and she departed, she and her companions, and bewailed her virginity upon the mountains. ³⁹And at the end of two months, she returned to her father, who did with her according to his vow which he had made. She had never

known a man. And it became a custom in Israel ⁴⁰that the daughters of Israel went year by year to lament the daughter of Jephthah the Gileadite four days in the year.

¹The men of Ephraim were called to arms, and they crossed to Zaphon and said to Jephthah, "Why did you cross over to fight against the Ammonites, and did not call us to go with you? We will burn your house over you with fire." ²And Jephthah said to them, "I and my people had a great feud with the Ammonites; and when I called you, you did not deliver me from their hand. ³And when I saw that you would not deliver me, I took my life in my hand, and crossed over against the Ammonites, and the Lord gave them into my hand; why then have you come up to me this day, to fight against me?" ⁴Then Jephthah gathered all the men of Gilead and fought with Ephraim; and the men of Gilead smote Ephraim, because they said, "You are fugitives of Ephraim, you Gileadites, in the midst of Ephraim and Manasseh." ⁵And the Gileadites took the fords of the Jordan against the Ephraimites. And when any of the fugitives of Ephraim said, "Let me go over," the men of Gilead said to him, "Are you an Ephraimite?" When he said, "No," ⁶they said to him, "Then say Shibboleth," and he said, "Sibboleth," for he could not pronounce it right; then they seized him and slew him at the fords of the Jordan. And there fell at that time forty-two thousand of the Ephraimites.

(i)

There are parallels enough in the story-telling and drama of other cultures to the sacrifice of Jephthah's daughter. One thinks automatically of Iphigenia, daughter of Agamemnon, on the altar because her father's fleet is long becalmed on its way to Troy—and of all the tragedy that flowed from that situation. There are parallels enough: but this brief awesome story loses none of its force thereby. It is yet another triumph of terse Hebrew story-telling. I suppose one could argue that the telling can be so brief because this sort of story was well known. Only the essentials needed to be told. Be that as it may, the terse economical stripped-down telling conveys to me the numbness and shock of the narrator at what he must narrate.

Two other Biblical stories pinpoint the particular horror at sacrificing one's own child. 2 Kings 3 tells of a joint campaign by

Israel, Judah and Edom against Moab. A dirty, destructive campaign was waged; and its culmination is told as follows:

> And they overthrew the cities, and on every good piece of land every man threw a stone, until it was covered; they stopped every spring of water, and felled all the good trees; till only its stones were left in Kir-hareseth, and the slingers surrounded and conquered it. When the king of Moab saw that the battle was going against him, he took with him seven hundred swordsmen to break through, opposite the king of Edom; but they could not. Then he took his eldest son who was to reign in his stead, and offered him for a burnt offering upon the wall. And there came great wrath on Israel; and they withdrew from him and returned to their own land.
>
> (vv. 25–27)

This king is not just sacrificing his child; he is publicly imperilling the destiny of his dynasty. Whether fearful of divine retribution for having pushed Moab too hard, or whether faced by a Moabite force stiffened by their king's lead, Israel melts away stunned.

The other great story in the Bible which has figured prominently in Jewish commentary on Jephthah's sacrifice is of course the near-sacrifice of Isaac by Abraham in Genesis 22. Despite the brevity which characterizes them both, each story lingers over the same significant detail: "Take your son, your only son Isaac, whom you love, . . ." (Gen. 22:2) and "she was his only child; beside her he had neither son nor daughter" (Judg. 11:34).

The story-teller does not dissociate himself from Jephthah's action, although he is certainly restrained in face of it. "The Spirit of the Lord" has come upon Jephthah (v. 29); and his solemn vow seeks assurance from the Lord, just like Gideon's double fleece test in 6:34–40. There is of course a particular poignancy that the victim was his only daughter; but we cannot seek to absolve Jephthah of full responsibility by any suggestion that he simply blurted out a rash vow. The vow was "to the Lord"; and it surely implies a *human* sacrifice: "whoever comes forth from the doors of my house to meet me" hardly has his favourite dog in mind! The awful personal cost to him of this operation against Ammon gives an added dimension to the stock phrase he uses in rejecting the Ephraimites' criticism (12:3): "I took my life in my hand". In most of the Old Testament there is no apparent hope for life after death. A good life is a full life, which is in a sense ended by burial with your fathers and is in another sense continued in your family and in their memory of you. In this latter sense Jephthah certainly took his life in his hands.

One last word. His daughter knew the code of honour, just like Zebah and Zalmunna before Gideon (8:21). She not only accepted what had to be done but in fact confirmed it: "Not only have *you* made a vow, but *Yahweh* has kept his part of the bargain." The poignant end of the story is bound up in some age-old custom, presumably a women's fertility rite.

(ii)

Many people must use the word "shibboleth" without knowing the background to it. The people of Ephraim (who were briefly noted in 10:9) make another late entrance as they did in the Gideon story (7:24–8:3). Jephthah has less diplomatic patience with their bluster than had Gideon; and external conflict becomes civil war. The Jordan fords are again the front line, as in 3:28; 7:24; and 10:9—but this time for Israelite *against* Israelite.

The core of the story is provided by two different plays on words. The first does not come across very easily in the RSV translation. The western Ephraimites charge the eastern Gileadites with being refugees from themselves. Better translated, verse 4*b* reads: "You are fugitives of Ephraim; Gilead is in the midst of Ephraim and Manasseh." Our story-teller finds a grim humour in Ephraim being faster with their mouths than with their swords. Having made this charge about their fellow-citizens, Ephraimite survivors have now to make their way westwards through Gilead's lines. But the tables are turned! Who is an Ephraimite fugitive now?

It is the other fateful word-play which has gone into our language. "Shibboleth" means a "stream" or "current" of water. Any stranger trying to cross was directed to a section of the river and asked what *that* was; and if he was from Ephraim he said "Sibboleth", and did not live much longer. So it is that in English the word has come to mean a catch-word or a custom that helps you distinguish members of one movement or party from another or, more accurately, that helps them to betray themselves.

Every people takes delight in elements of its own language or dialect which strangers find difficult to pronounce. Scots enjoy trying place-names like Auchtermuchty on their visitors. In peace time this is acceptable as a game or a tease. In conflict and under interrogation it can mean life or death.

(On 12:7–14 see the commentary on 10:1–5.)

SAMSON'S BIRTH

Judges 13:1–25

[1]And the people of Israel again did what was evil in the sight of the Lord; and the Lord gave them into the hand of the Philistines for forty years.

[2]And there was a certain man of Zorah, of the tribe of the Danites, whose name was Manoah; and his wife was barren and had no children. [3]And the angel of the Lord appeared to the woman and said to her, "Behold, you are barren and have no children; but you shall conceive and bear a son. [4]Therefore beware, and drink no wine or strong drink, and eat nothing unclean, [5]for lo, you shall conceive and bear a son. No razor shall come upon his head, for the boy shall be a Nazirite to God from birth; and he shall begin to deliver Israel from the hand of the Philistines." [6]Then the woman came and told her husband, "A man of God came to me, and his countenance was like the countenance of the angel of God, very terrible; I did not ask him whence he was, and he did not tell me his name; [7]but he said to me, 'Behold, you shall conceive and bear a son; so then drink no wine or strong drink, and eat nothing unclean, for the boy shall be a Nazirite to God from birth to the day of his death.'"

[8]Then Manoah entreated the Lord, and said, "O, Lord, I pray thee, let the man of God whom thou didst send come again to us, and teach us what we are to do with the boy that will be born." [9]And God listened to the voice of Manoah, and the angel of God came again to the woman as she sat in the field; but Manoah her husband was not with her. [10]And the woman ran in haste and told her husband, "Behold, the man who came to me the other day has appeared to me." [11]And Manoah arose and went after his wife, and came to the man and said to

him, "Are you the man who spoke to this woman?" And he said, "I am." [12]And Manoah said, "Now when your words come true, what is to be the boy's manner of life, and what is he to do?" [13]And the angel of the Lord said to Manoah, "Of all that I said to the woman let her beware. [14]She may not eat of anything that comes from the vine, neither let her drink wine or strong drink, or eat any unclean thing; all that I commanded her let her observe."

[15]Manoah said to the angel of the Lord, "Pray, let us detain you, and prepare a kid for you." [16]And the angel of the Lord said to Manoah, "If you detain me, I will not eat of your food; but if you make ready a burnt offering, then offer it to the Lord." (For Manoah did not know that he was the angel of the Lord.) [17]And Manoah said to the angel of the Lord, "What is your name, so that, when your words come true, we may honour you?" [18]And the angel of the Lord said to him, "Why do you ask my name, seeing it is wonderful?" [19]So Manoah took the kid with the cereal offering, and offered it upon the rock to the Lord, to him who works wonders. [20]And when the flame went up toward heaven from the altar, the angel of the Lord ascended in the flame of the altar while Manoah and his wife looked on; and they fell on their faces to the ground.

[21]The angel of the Lord appeared no more to Manoah and to his wife. Then Manoah knew that he was the angel of the Lord. [22]And Manoah said to his wife, "We shall surely die, for we have seen God." [23]But his wife said to him, "If the Lord had meant to kill us, he would not have accepted a burnt offering and a cereal offering at our hands, or shown us all these things, or now announced to us such things as these." [24]And the woman bore a son, and called his name Samson; and the boy grew, and the Lord blessed him. [25]And the Spirit of the Lord began to stir him in Mahanehdan, between Zorah and Eshtaol.

(i)

The foreshadowing of Jesus' birth and naming by a messenger of the Lord is the best known but not the only annunciation in the Bible. Even there Matthew and Luke provide us with two rather different versions of the tradition: in the one, an unnamed messenger appears to Joseph in a dream; in the other, Mary is addressed directly by a messenger named Gabriel. Within the Old Testament, this promise of Samson's birth has close links with two other passages: with Hagar's meeting with the Lord's messenger in Gen. 16:7–13, and with Isaiah's Immanuel sign (7:10–17).

It is very often said that Samson is the most unlikely figure in the Book of Judges. How suitable are his rowdy pranks for the leadership of Israel? Does he not devalue the notion of charismatic leadership? People have also noted that the boisterous Samson is a useful foil to the more sober Samuel, both born to long-barren mothers. And it is arguable that the four chapters on Samson have been rather loosely linked with the rest of the book by means of the opening typical note (13:1) about the people of Israel again doing evil in the sight of the Lord and being given into the hand of the Philistines, and the repeated conclusion (15:20; 16:31) about his activity of judging lasting twenty years.

There is some force to all these points. But it should not be thought that they add up to a convincing case for the Samson stories being merely a loose appendix to the main traditions in chapters 2–12. We are told more about Samson than about any other figure in the book. There is no denying that he is a larger-than-life hero typical of popular story-telling, with a list of exploits like a Hercules. More, but not different! After Deborah and Barak and Jael, after Gideon the "Hacker", the questionable Abimelech, and impulsive, violent Jephthah, Samson is not out of character. If he does not fit our criteria for charismatic leadership, if he is not a suitable leader for Israel, then we must change our notions of charisma, and ask a much wider question about whether the traditions of the judges as a whole enshrine "suitable" models for leadership. The extended introduction to the Samson cycle (Judg. 13) at least indicates to us that here is someone of whom much was expected.

(ii)

As so often with skilful narratives out of stock tradition, the interesting and significant features of this chapter are the points at which it *diverges* from the pattern. Usually what immediately follows the words "you shall conceive and bear a son" is an indication of the name of the child and the reason for this name: Ishmael, Immanuel, or Jesus. In Samson's case, however, the stress is on his Nazirite status. There may be different reasons for this. One may be the concealment of a religious skeleton in the cupboard. Samson's name—in Hebrew *Shimshon*—means "Sunny". It is related to the word for "sun": *shemesh*. Then Zorah and Eshtaol (13:25) are both in the close vicinity of Beth-*shemesh*, which means "house (or temple) of the Sun". It may well be that when Samson's prodigious feats were first in circulation they were ascribed to the Sun-god and not to Yahweh. Perhaps there was no way to explain his name without causing religious embarrassment.

However, an interesting positive point is made as well. In place of naming him, the messenger of the Lord stressed his Nazirite status (vv. 4–5). And the chapter underscores its importance by repeating twice this vow laid upon his mother on his behalf (vv. 7 and 13–14). I say "vow" deliberately, because Nazirite is from the Hebrew "root" *nzr*, which is just an alternative form of *ndr*, the word for "vow". In contrast to Jephthah's reckless vow which cost him his daughter (Judg. 11), we now have a special *form* of vow—and one which originates from the Lord himself. To repeat: Samson is someone of whom much is expected.

(iii)

Another interesting aspect of this annunciation scene is the way in which Manoah and his wife interact with the Lord's messenger. The envoy himself is portrayed very like the one who deals with Gideon in chapter 6. Their growing appreciation of his role and identity is rather nicely sketched. Manoah's wife first describes him as a "man of God" (v. 6), a term often used in the Old Testament in what can loosely be called "prophetic" contexts. She had taken him for a human emissary of God, but one with a difference: his *appearance* was like that of a divine envoy; and this made her sufficiently uneasy that she did not indulge in the usual small talk with a stranger: "I did not ask him whence he was, and he did not tell me his name".

Although we talk typically of "Manoah and his wife", the woman—like so many we know simply as Mrs X after her husband—comes across as the much stronger and more interesting character. Manoah cautiously asks for a return visit of the emissary (v. 8). Is he perhaps quietly checking the credentials of his wife's visitor who has made her talk about childbirth? When the request is granted Manoah *follows* his wife (v. 11); and when he puts his own question for supplementary information (v. 12) the messenger politely suggests (vv. 13–14) that he has already told Mrs Manoah *all* they need to know. Only after his attempt at entertainment is turned into a sacrifice in whose flame the messenger disappears (vv. 15–21, compare Judges 6:19–21) does *Manoah* realize who he was dealing with. We are left to suppose that his wife, like so many wives, had already got to the point in verse 6! This reading of the chapter seems confirmed in the cold douche of common sense with which she calms his agitation lest having seen God they die (v. 22): "If the Lord had meant to kill us, he would not have accepted a burnt offering and a cereal offering at our hands, or shown us all these things, or now announced to us such things as these" (v. 23). What a sensible mother for a boy that the Lord would bless and move with his spirit!

SAMSON'S RIDDLE OF THE LION

Judges 14:1–20

[1]Samson went down to Timnah, and at Timnah he saw one of the daughters of the Philistines. [2]Then he came up, and told his father and mother, "I saw one of the daughters of the Philistines at Timnah; now get her for me as my wife." [3]But his father and mother said to him, "Is there not a woman among the daughters of your kinsmen, or among all our people, that you must go to take a wife from the uncircumcised Philistines?" But Samson said to his father, "Get her for me; for she pleases me well."

[4]His father and mother did not know that it was from the Lord; for he was seeking an occasion against the Philistines. At that time the Philistines had dominion over Israel.

[5]Then Samson went down with his father and mother to Timnah, and he came to the vineyards of Timnah. And behold, a young lion

roared against him; [6]and the Spirit of the Lord came mightily upon him, and he tore the lion asunder as one tears a kid; and he had nothing in his hand. But he did not tell his father or his mother what he had done. [7]Then he went down and talked with the woman; and she pleased Samson well. [8]And after a while he returned to take her; and he turned aside to see the carcass of the lion, and behold, there was a swarm of bees in the body of the lion, and honey. [9]He scraped it out into his hands, and went on, eating as he went; and he came to his father and mother, and gave some to them, and they ate. But he did not tell them that he had taken the honey from the carcass of the lion.

[10]And his father went down to the woman, and Samson made a feast there; for so the young men used to do. [11]And when the people saw him, they brought thirty companions to be with him. [12]And Samson said to them, "Let me now put a riddle to you; if you can tell me what it is, within the seven days of the feast, and find it out, then I will give you thirty linen garments and thirty festal garments; [13]but if you cannot tell me what it is, then you shall give me thirty linen garments and thirty festal garments." And they said to him, "Put your riddle, that we may hear it." [14]And he said to them,

"Out of the eater came something to eat.

Out of the strong came something sweet."

And they could not in three days tell what the riddle was.

[15]On the fourth day they said to Samson's wife, "Entice your husband to tell us what the riddle is, lest we burn you and your father's house with fire. Have you invited us here to impoverish us?" [16]And Samson's wife wept before him, and said, "You only hate me, you do not love me; you have put a riddle to my countrymen, and you have not told me what it is." And he said to her, "Behold, I have not told my father nor my mother, and shall I tell you?" [17]She wept before him the seven days that their feast lasted; and on the seventh day he told her, because she pressed him hard. Then she told the riddle to her countrymen. [18]And the men of the city said to him on the seventh day before the sun went down,

"What is sweeter than honey?

What is stronger than a lion?"

And he said to them,

"If you had not ploughed with my heifer,

you would not have found out my riddle."

[19]And the Spirit of the Lord came mightily upon him, and he went

down to Ashkelon and killed thirty men of the town, and took their spoil and gave the festal garments to those who had told the riddle. In hot anger he went back to his father's house. [20]And Samson's wife was given to his companion, who had been his best man.

(i)

Before embarking on the next scene, another word or two about the closing couple of verses of chapter 13 may be appropriate. "And the Spirit of the Lord began to stir him" is the RSV translation of a rare and interesting Hebrew phrase. The Jerusalem Bible has "move him"; while the New English Bible offers "drive him hard". The ancient Greek translation of the Book of Judges used a verb meaning "accompany". The rare Hebrew verb in question is found in just three other Biblical passages, all relating to "spirit", yet always our own spirit. In two of these (Gen. 41:8; Dan. 2:1, 3) the expression relates to the agitation caused by a dream so aggravating that Pharaoh requires Joseph, and Nebuchadnezzar requires Daniel, to unlock the secret that is communicated from God. Psalm 77 reflects similar nightly distress and anguish about the future:

> Thou dost hold my eyelids from closing;
>> I am so *troubled* that I cannot speak.
> I consider the days of old,
>> I remember the years long ago.
> I commune with my heart in the night;
>> I meditate and search *my spirit*:
> "Will the Lord spurn for ever,
>> and never again be favourable?"

(vv. 4–7)

Here as so often in poetry a normal word-pair has been broken up for effect.

In the light of these other passages I find unsatisfactory *all* the translations I mentioned above. "Move" and "stir" and "accompany" are all too neutral and conventional; "press hard" is better. But "afflict" or "trouble" would be closer to the few other Biblical passages, and thoroughly appropriate as the introduction to a career as chequered as the one we shall read about in chapters 14–16. No Christian should ever suppose that God's blessing (v. 24) implies a life of tranquillity and repose.

The New Testament never suggests clearly that Jesus was a Nazirite, although some commentators have thought that "Nazarene" in passages like Matt. 2:23 puns on both Nazareth and Nazirite. There is certainly a faint echo of the end of Judg. 13 in Luke 2 where we read that Jesus' parents "returned into Galilee, to their own city, Nazareth. And the child grew and became strong, filled with wisdom; and the favour of God was upon him" (vv. 39*b*–40).

(ii)

There is a delightful heroic gusto and larger-than-life enthusiasm about Samson's career which are deftly captured in these opening scenes. He sees a beautiful woman, and immediately he must marry her, no matter that she comes (v. 3) from these foreigners with their barbarous practices who were his people's competitors for mastery over Canaan. (Remember our discussion of circumcision in connection with Josh. 5:2–9.) A young lion roars at him, and he deals with it as a normal man might break the neck of a kid, and butchers it with his bare hands. This prodigy is explicitly attributed to the divine spirit (v. 6), perhaps remembering the received wisdom noted by Amos: "The lion has roared; who will not fear?" (3:8). When he makes a wager with his companions, it is for high stakes (vv. 12, 13); and when called to honour his bond, thirty dead Philistines and a deserted wife pay the price (vv. 19–20). This unprovoked slaughter in Ashkelon is again attributed to divine power, just like the disposal of the lion who chose to roar. However, it appears from verse 4 that Samson's *God* is responsible for his *choice* of activities and not just the superhuman strength to carry them out. Many may disapprove of Samson as little more than a lusty Philistine-basher, with an appetite that would be his downfall, and lamentable proclivity for fomenting intercommunal strife. Even Samson's "father and mother did not know that it was from the Lord; for he was seeking an occasion against the Philistines." With models like this in what is Scripture to Jews and Christians alike, on what basis do we disapprove of Israeli or Palestinian murderous terror?

(iii)

Of course we can easily moralize about the mess his appetites landed him in. If he hadn't gorged on illicit honey from the (ritually unclean) corpse of his lion, the fateful riddle would never have occurred to him. If he hadn't fallen so heavily for a Philistine lass, however pleasing, he would not have been tricked out of his secret by pillow talk on his honeymoon!

(iv)

There are several ancient near eastern parallels to Samson's impossible riddle. Part of its delight is its ambiguity, and the several answers possible. After all it was intended to keep his companions guessing and thinking over the seven days of the feast. After three days of failure, they decided to put pressure on his bride. She herself had apparently wanted to be let into the secret at the very beginning of the week (v. 17). The most obvious interpretation is a bawdy one, about sexual prowess—quite in keeping with the humour at a stag party! To arrive at the "proper" answer, members of the wedding party would have had to have knowledge of Samson's encounter with the lion. (One of the Arabic nicknames for the lion is the "eater".) But that he had kept secret even from his parents (vv. 9, 16).

Samson may have had an eye for attractive women, yet little success with them. Perhaps his handling of them was partly to blame. His reply to his bride that she should not expect to learn from him anything not yet divulged to his parents appears insensitive and gauche. Even if true, it might better have remained unsaid!

The insult with which he replies to his deceivers is also finely turned poetry (v. 18b). Some suppose that he uses "heifer" as a term of abuse for his young wife, rather as "cow" is used in modern English. I suspect that his rage leads him further than that—and that he is charging his wife and his companions with sexual misbehaviour. Like too many of us, he judges others by his own standards. What had been extracted from him in bed must have been passed on by her in the same way. Does the closing verse simply confirm these suspicions when it tells us that "Samson's wife was given to his companion who had been his best man"?

FOXES' TAILS AND AN ASS'S JAWBONE

Judges 15:1–20

¹After a while, at the time of wheat harvest, Samson went to visit his wife with a kid; and he said, "I will go in to my wife in the chamber." But her father would not allow him to go in. ²And her father said, "I really thought that you utterly hated her; so I gave her to your companion. Is not her younger sister fairer than she? Pray take her instead." ³And Samson said to them, "This time I shall be blameless in regard to the Philistines, when I do them mischief." ⁴So Samson went and caught three hundred foxes, and took torches; and he turned them tail to tail, and put a torch between each pair of tails. ⁵And when he had set fire to the torches, he let the foxes go into the standing grain of the Philistines, and burned up the shocks and the standing grain, as well as the olive orchards. ⁶Then the Philistines said, "Who has done this?" And they said, "Samson, the son-in-law of the Timnite, because he has taken his wife and given her to his companion." And the Philistines came up, and burned her and her father with fire. ⁷And Samson said to them, "If this is what you do, I swear I will be avenged upon you, and after that I will quit." ⁸And he smote them hip and thigh with great slaughter; and he went down and stayed in the cleft of the rock of Etam.

⁹Then the Philistines came up and encamped in Judah, and made a raid on Lehi. ¹⁰And the men of Judah said, "Why have you come up against us?" They said, "We have come up to bind Samson, to do to him as he did to us." ¹¹Then three thousand men of Judah went down to the cleft of the rock of Etam, and said to Samson, "Do you not know that the Philistines are rulers over us? What then is this that you have done to us?" And he said to them, "As they did to me, so have I done to them." ¹²And they said to him, "We have come down to bind you, that we may give you into the hands of the Philistines." And Samson said to them, "Swear to me that you will not fall upon me yourselves."

¹³They said to him, "No; we will only bind you and give you into their hands; we will not kill you." So they bound him with new ropes, and brought him up from the rock.

¹⁴When he came to Lehi, the Philistines came shouting to meet him; and the Spirit of the Lord came mightily upon him, and the ropes which were on his arms became as flax that has caught fire, and his bonds melted off his hands. ¹⁵And he found a fresh jawbone of an ass, and put out his hand and seized it, and with it he slew a thousand men. ¹⁶And Samson said,

"With the jawbone of an ass,
  heaps upon heaps,
with the jawbone of an ass
  have I slain a thousand men."

¹⁷When he had finished speaking, he threw away the jawbone out of his hand; and that place was called Ramath-lehi.

¹⁸And he was very thirsty, and he called on the Lord and said, "Thou hast granted this great deliverance by the hand of thy servant; and shall I now die of thirst, and fall into the hands of the uncircumcised?" ¹⁹And God split open the hollow place that is at Lehi, and there came water from it; and when he drank, his spirit returned, and he revived. Therefore the name of it was called En-hakkore; it is at Lehi to this day. ²⁰And he judged Israel in the days of the Philistines twenty years.

There are three more or less discrete scenes in this chapter, which we may conveniently discuss in turn: verses 1–8, 9–13 and 14–20.

(i)

Samson and his father-in-law offer different interpretations of what had happened during the week of his wedding celebrations. Samson certainly recalls that he had returned to his own father's house in hot anger; and that he had killed thirty of his in-laws' people. Accordingly, when he seeks to return to his wife's bed-chamber, he brings a practical token of contrition, in the form of a young goat. Her father, however, whether honestly or not, presents Samson with a very different understanding of the business. We have to remember that he is defending a fait accompli, for his daughter is already remarried to the best man.

His case is expressed in a nutshell in verse 2: "I really thought that you utterly hated her". Given the woman's deceit, that statement makes perfect sense even at face value. But when the father's next words are "so I gave her to your companion", we have a clue that something more is being stated. We know from marital legislation in the Book of Deuteronomy that the Hebrew verb "to hate" was used in a technical sense in divorce proceedings. (In Deut. 22:13, 16 the RSV quite appropriately renders it "spurns"; although oddly in 24:3 it appears to miss the point by translating "dislikes".) The father-in-law's case appears to be that public repudiation was implicit in Samson's behaviour: behaviour so obvious that a bill of divorce, such as Deut. 24 also requires, would have been an unnecessary formality.

Perhaps recognizing by Samson's very return that he had in fact misjudged the nature of his earlier hot-tempered withdrawal, perhaps just intimidated by Samson's powerful presence, he seeks to make the best of a bad job. He offers him his younger daughter, making her out to be even more beautiful than the woman Samson loved at first sight. However, like many men, Samson preferred to take his own initiatives with women.

One more word may be useful about the formal legal sense of "hate" in the Old Testament. It helps to put in context those words from the beginning of Malachi, "I have loved Jacob, but I have hated Esau" (1:2–3), which are quoted by Paul in Romans 9:13. I am not seeking here to eliminate the theological problems implicit in the doctrine of election. I want simply to suggest that the term "hate" is used by Malachi in its formal sense of "repudiate", and not in its literal sense of passionate loathing.

There is careful ambiguity about Samson's response to his father-in-law, which I should prefer to translate: "This time *I am clear* of the Philistines, if I do them mischief" (v. 3). The word in question is used both of innocence or freedom from guilt and of freedom from an obligation or burden (both ideas being of course closely related). Samson wants both to be finished with the Philistines, and to be deemed innocent in respect of them. His Philistine father-in-law has given him an opportunity; but it is not directly against his in-laws that he makes his move.

There are guerrilla parallels in plenty to his stratagem with the tails of the unfortunate animals. Some scholars believe them to have been not foxes but jackals, which are both more social and commoner in Palestine. Typical of all such reprisal and vendetta situations, each side claims only to be responding in kind to what the other has done (vv. 6–7). Again typically Samson repeats his claim (vv. 3 and 7) that this is his *last* campaign. After a further slaughter he takes off to a cave.

(ii)

The cave he chose was in a prominent rock near Etam which, from the evidence in 2 Chron. 11:6, was a little south of Beth-lehem. That means he went right up to the mountains, removing himself by about fifteen miles from the last episode. It is uncertain whether or not this second episode deliberately portrays the people of Judah as particularly craven. They certainly jump to attention when the Philistines exert some military pressure. But that may just be how things were, and why Israel as a whole needed deliverance. Both parties protest to Judah that the other started the quarrel.

The Judeans seek to impress both their Philistine masters and Samson by their firm resolve: committing three thousand men to capture one! Like many a hero who has hoped to fight another day, if he can only live through today, Samson extracts an under-taking from Judah's police force that they will do no worse to him than hand him over bound to the occupying military authorities. He is duly tied and brought out of his cave.

(iii)

With God nothing is impossible. The hostility of the Philistines is even more obvious in the Hebrew text than RSV suggests. They came to meet him not just "shouting", but "with a war cry"—"whooping" might be a better rendering. They were to be finished with him once and for all, just as he had hoped to be clear of them. However a greater power came to his aid (v. 14), and he snapped his bonds like cord in flame. An ass's jawbone (Hebrew *lehi*—hence the naming of the place in v. 17), that was fresh and so not yet brittle, came to hand; and with it he disposed of a full company of Philistines. His victory song is another typical pun. The Hebrew *hmr* can mean both "ass" and "heap" or "pile". The result is effective in Hebrew, but barely translatable in English.

I suspect that the closing verses of this chapter once concluded a first version of the Samson story. Samson has not uttered a word to God in chapters 14 or 15. Exhausted by his effort, he now does address Yahweh (v. 18). He opens with a tribute to the deliverance whose instrument he has been; but then observes in a quite matter-of-fact way that he will be of no further use if he dies of thirst. His words are not couched in normal prayer form, but they are not untrue! God responds by creating a new spring. If Lehi and Etam are in the same vicinity, south of Bethlehem, then this spring may well be the one which feeds the ancient reservoirs called Solomon's Pools.

Samson's mention of a "great deliverance" (v. 18) recalls to mind the divine promise to his mother: "He shall begin to deliver Israel from the hand of the Philistines" (13:5). The Philistine menace would last much longer. Samson's violent and erratic career was only a beginning. That may explain the unique qualification that is made in the final formal note about him (15:20): "And he judged Israel *in the days of the Philistines* twenty years." It was Samson's role to harry the Philistines, but not to make an end of their rule over Israel (14:4; 15:11).

THE END OF SAMSON

Judges 16:1–31

[1]Samson went to Gaza, and there he saw a harlot, and he went in to her. [2]The Gazites were told, "Samson has come here," and they surrounded the place and lay in wait for him all night at the gate of the city. They kept quiet all night, saying, "Let us wait till the light of the morning; then we will kill him." [3]But Samson lay till midnight, and at midnight he arose and took hold of the doors of the gate of the city and the two posts, and pulled them up, bar and all, and put them on his shoulders and carried them to the top of the hill that is before Hebron.

⁴After this he loved a woman in the valley of Sorek, whose name was Delilah. ⁵And the lords of the Philistines came to her and said to her, "Entice him, and see wherein his great strength lies, and by what means we may overpower him, that we may bind him to subdue him; and we will each give you eleven hundred pieces of silver." ⁶And Delilah said to Samson, "Please tell me wherein your great strength lies, and how you might be bound, that one could subdue you." ⁷And Samson said to her, "If they bind me with seven fresh bowstrings which have not been dried, then I shall become weak, and be like any other man." ⁸Then the lords of the Philistines brought her seven fresh bowstrings which had not been dried, and she bound him with them. ⁹Now she had men lying in wait in an inner chamber. And she said to him, "The Philistines are upon you, Samson!" But he snapped the bowstrings, as a string of tow snaps when it touches the fire. So the secret of his strength was not known.

¹⁰And Delilah said to Samson, "Behold, you have mocked me, and told me lies; please tell me how you might be bound." ¹¹And he said to her, "If they bind me with new ropes that have not been used, then I shall become weak, and be like any other man." ¹²So Delilah took new ropes and bound him with them, and said to him, "The Philistines are upon you, Samson!" And the men lying in wait were in an inner chamber. But he snapped the ropes off his arms like a thread.

¹³And Delilah said to Samson, "Until now you have mocked me, and told me lies; tell me how you might be bound." And he said to her, "If you weave the seven locks of my head with the web and make it tight with the pin, then I shall become weak, and be like any other man." ¹⁴So while he slept, Delilah took the seven locks of his head and wove them into the web. And she made them tight with the pin, and said to him, "The Philistines are upon you, Samson!" But he awoke from his sleep, and pulled away the pin, the loom, and the web.

¹⁵And she said to him, "How can you say, 'I love you,' when your heart is not with me? You have mocked me these three times, and you have not told me wherein your great strength lies." ¹⁶And when she pressed him hard with her words day after day, and urged him, his soul was vexed to death. ¹⁷And he told her all his mind, and said to her, "A razor has never come upon my head; for I have been a Nazirite to God from my mother's womb. If I be shaved, then my strength will leave me, and I shall become weak, and be like any other man."

¹⁸When Delilah saw that he had told her all his mind, she sent and called the lords of the Philistines, saying, "Come up this once, for he

has told me all his mind." Then the lords of the Philistines came up to her, and brought the money in their hands. [19]She made him sleep upon her knees; and she called a man, and had him shave off the seven locks of his head. Then she began to torment him, and his strength left him. [20]And she said, "The Philistines are upon you, Samson!" And he awoke from his sleep, and said, "I will go out as at other times, and shake myself free." And he did not know that the Lord had left him. [21]And the Philistines seized him and gouged out his eyes, and brought him down to Gaza, and bound him with bronze fetters; and he ground at the mill in the prison. [22]But the hair of his head began to grow again after it had been shaved.

[23]Now the lords of the Philistines gathered to offer a great sacrifice to Dagon their god, and to rejoice; for they said, "Our god has given Samson our enemy into our hand." [24]And when the people saw him, they praised their god; for they said, "Our god has given our enemy into our hand, the ravager of our country, who has slain many of us." [25]And when their hearts were merry, they said, "Call Samson, that he may make sport for us." So they called Samson out of the prison, and he made sport before them. They made him stand between the pillars; [26]and Samson said to the lad who held him by the hand, "Let me feel the pillars on which the house rests, that I may lean against them." [27]Now the house was full of men and women; all the lords of the Philistines were there, and on the roof there were about three thousand men and women, who looked on while Samson made sport.

[28]Then Samson called to the Lord and said, "O Lord God, remember me, I pray thee, and strengthen me, I pray thee, only this once, O God, that I may be avenged upon the Philistines for one of my two eyes." [29]And Samson grasped the two middle pillars upon which the house rested, and he leaned his weight upon them, his right hand on the one and his left hand on the other. [30]And Samson said, "Let me die with the Philistines." Then he bowed with all his might; and the house fell upon the lords and upon all the people that were in it. So the dead whom he slew at his death were more than those whom he had slain during his life. [31]Then his brothers and all his family came down and took him and brought him up and buried him between Zorah and Eshtaol in the tomb of Manoah his father. He had judged Israel twenty years.

The last chapter of the present version of the Samson cycle may be a supplement to an earlier draft, but it is no mere appendix.

Indeed it contains many of the scenes which writers, painters, musicians and dramatists have found most memorable.

(i)

Every chapter begins with our hero's eye on a woman. Our opening verse is almost as taciturn as Caesar's famous *veni, vidi, vici*: "Samson *went* to Gaza, and there he *saw* a harlot, and he *went in* to her." Presumably he expected an ambush, for he roused himself in the middle of the night and showed his scorn for Gaza's defences by carrying its gates as far as Hebron in the heart of Judah's hill country—this time a walk of some forty miles!

One wonders just how significant it may be that this brief "professional" encounter does not land Samson in as deep water as his other longer entanglements. Perhaps of course the woman was a foreigner in Gaza like himself. At any rate, and even if the point of his visit to her was only as a backdrop to yet another tale of superhuman power, this arrival in Gaza introduces the scene of his fatal triumph.

(ii)

Delilah is Samson's most famous woman: indeed hers is the only name the Bible gives us. We are not told she was a Philistine. Yet, since in so many ways she replays the role of Samson's wife (chapter 14), and since like her she is susceptible to Philistine pressure, we may suppose that she too was one of them. In fact she is the perfect embodiment of the "stranger" who is regularly contrasted with Wisdom in Proverbs 1–9. The following is a rendering by the Jerusalem Bible of a typical passage:

> My son, keep my words,
>   and treasure my principles,
> keep my principles and you will live,
>   keep my teaching as the apple of your eye.
> Bind these to your fingers,
>   write them on the tablet of your heart.
> To Wisdom say, "My sister!"
>   Call Perception your dearest friend,
> to preserve you from the alien woman,

from the stranger, with her wheedling words.
From the window of her house
  she looked out on the street,
to see if among the men, young, and callow,
  there was one young man who had no sense at all.

(7:1–7)

"Callow" or "simple" renders the Hebrew adjective related to the verb which is usually translated "entice" or "seduce". The connection in ideas can perhaps be caught in English by using the word "dupe". This is exactly what the lords of the Philistines want of Delilah (v. 5): to dupe Samson, to make a fool of him, so that he betrays the secret of his strength.

We may not like this low estimate of foreign women. We know well enough that when someone says of another people, "They are all right, I suppose, but you wouldn't want to marry one", this may be covert racialism. Indeed we shall see in our handling of the Book of Ruth that one of its purposes may have been to rehabilitate the reputation of a "foreign woman".

Delilah was Samson's most famous woman; she was also the only woman whom the story-teller informs us that he really loved (v. 4). His wife had pleased him at first acquaintance (14:3 and 7), and both she and Delilah chided him with not loving them enough (14:16 and 16:15). Poor Samson's love was to prove fatal. His love was sadly misplaced; and words achieved more against him than brute force had ever managed. He was a great bear of a man, but he was also a sensual dupe.

(iii)

His end, like all the rest of his life, has been variously assessed. Martin Luther assessed him negatively, while John Milton saw in him elements of the tragic hero. I do not want to take sides; but I mention again my opening suggestion (in discussing chapter 13) that it may involve unfair pleading to detach Samson from his predecessors in the Book of Judges.

His career in the mill, harnessed to usefulness like a blind-folded ox, has often been illustrated. No less familiar is the scene in the temple of Dagon where he is baited like a bear for the delight of the crowd. However, a few words might be added to the scene of his last and greatest slaughter (v. 30).

Ironically it is in a hostile place of foreign worship that Samson utters his first *formal* prayer to God (contrast 15:18). Equally it is only after he has been brought low that he needs to ask for help. He had not himself asked for the gift of great strength. It had been granted to him, and the accompanying Nazirite vow had been laid upon his mother, not himself. (Many adults who have been baptized as youngsters wonder quite what their parents have let them in for!) God's spirit had always come to him unasked when necessary. But now, humbled and blinded, the butt of cruel sport like many a later victim in the arena, he knew he was in need. We do not require to know we are in need for God to come to our aid. But we need to know that, whenever and wherever we are in need, we may ask for help. That brings its own death-defying dignity to Samson "eyeless in Gaza".

It is the knowledge that Samson too is vulnerable which increases the fascination he has exerted on people of action, people who normally reckon that nimble footwork and an experienced arm will keep them out of trouble. His blindness has been a recurring theme of painters, for whom that state is the end of their activity. "Samson Agonistes" is the work of a poet blind half his life; yet the closing lines of Milton's ode on his own blindness point us in a direction very different from Samson's end:

> God doth not need
> Either man's work, or His own gifts: who best
>   Bear His mild yoke, they serve Him best: His State
> Is Kingly; thousands at His bidding speed
>   And post o'er Land and Ocean without rest:
>   They also serve who only stand and wait.

Samson's final concern is for revenge—he of course had not just lost his sight, but had had it taken away. Incidentally the RSV's notion of vengeance "for one of my two eyes" (v. 28) misconstrues the Hebrew, which calls rather for *one* act of revenge for *both* eyes. Such bloody personal "satisfaction" separates the heroes of the Old Testament and our own natural instincts by a great chasm from the ethics of Jesus, who called for his Father's forgiveness for those who had inflicted on him sufferings much less merited than Samson's.

MICAH AND THE LEVITE FROM BETHLEHEM

Judges 17:1–13

¹There was a man of the hill country of Ephraim, whose name was Micah. ²And he said to his mother, "The eleven hundred pieces of silver which were taken from you, about which you uttered a curse, and also spoke it in my ears, behold, the silver is with me; I took it." And his mother said, "Blessed be my son by the Lord." ³And he restored the eleven hundred pieces of silver to his mother; and his mother said, "I consecrate the silver to the Lord from my hand for my son, to make a graven image and a molten image; now therefore I will restore it to you." ⁴So when he restored the money to his mother, his mother took two hundred pieces of silver, and gave it to the silversmith, who made it into a graven image and a molten image; and it was in the house of Micah. ⁵And the man Micah had a shrine, and he made an ephod and teraphim, and installed one of his sons, who became his priest. ⁶In those days there was no king in Israel; every man did what was right in his own eyes.

⁷Now there was a young man of Bethlehem in Judah, of the family of Judah, who was a Levite; and he sojourned there. ⁸And the man departed from the town of Bethlehem in Judah, to live where he could find a place; and as he journeyed, he came to the hill country of Ephraim to the house of Micah. ⁹And Micah said to him, "From where do you come?" And he said to him, "I am a Levite of Bethlehem in Judah, and I am going to sojourn where I may find a place." ¹⁰And Micah said to him, "Stay with me, and be to me a father and a priest, and I will give you ten pieces of silver a year, and a suit of apparel, and your living." ¹¹And the Levite was content to dwell with the man; and the young man became to him like one of his sons. ¹²And Micah installed the Levite, and the young man became his priest, and was in the house of Micah. ¹³Then Micah said, "Now I know that the Lord will prosper me, because I have a Levite as priest."

(i)

With this short chapter we move into the final section of the Book of Judges. Chapters 17–21 are not in themselves a literary unity. There are two groups of narratives: chapters 17–18 and 19–21. These have certain common themes, and are given at least a semblance of organization by the recurring comment that "in those days there was no king in Israel" (17:6; 18:1; 19:1; 21:25).

There are common motifs and topics, and there are a number of significant links with the fresh introduction to the *Book* of Judges, some of which we noted in our discussion of chapter 1. However, the most important bond between chapter 1 and chapters 17–21 is an invisible one. Neither "judge" nor "deliverer", nor indeed any external foe, is to be found within these pages.

It is often held that the materials in these final chapters are ancient, like many of the materials within the stories of the judges themselves (chapters 2–16), and that for some reason or other they escaped re-edition at the hands of the Deuteronomistic historians. The compilers of the Book of Judges as we know it simply filed these traditions of a time when there was no king in Israel alongside the traditions of the judges which equally preceded the development of kingship in Israel. It was similar orderly filing that would lead later compilers of the Old Testament (in the shape that Christianity knows it) to insert the Book of Ruth between Judges and Samuel (compare our discussion in the Introduction to this volume).

I have already suggested in connection with chapter 1 that these outer chapters are more deliberately relevant to the whole book as we know it than would be likely if their position was simply the result of mechanical though relevant filing. Indeed some recent scholars have attempted each in a different way to argue that the hand of the Deuteronomists is in these chapters too. One of these studies leans heavily on the fact that "every man did what was right in his own eyes" (the note which follows the observation in 17:6 and 21:25 that there was no king then in Israel) is thoroughly Deuteronomic. We shall return to this point shortly. For this scholar, judges had their proper role in combating *external* foes: they had no place in the *internal* altercations which are the stuff of Judges 17–21. We should note immediately that our discussion both of Deborah (4:4–5) and of the list of judges (10:1–5 and 12:7–14) make his approach unlikely. I want now to offer an approach to these chapters rather different from most of those sketched above.

(ii)

There is humour in Judges 17 from the very beginning. The story-teller mocks Micah at almost every opportunity. How can anyone set up his own shrine? And as for installing one of his own sons as priest (v. 5), that was doubly absurd: (a) there was a God-given special priestly clan; and (b) how anyway could your son be a proper "father" to you (v. 10)? What a stupid northerner! What a muddle-headed Ephraimite! There are no prizes for guessing the original audience for this story that saw at least a measure of sanity restored when a proper Levite, originating from "David's royal city", happened on him; and in his state of youthful unemployment consented to be his priest. (Admittedly, the young Levite's employment could also be construed as making the situation worse; if he was a non-priestly Levite, he should have been content with a subservient role in any sanctuary.)

It is possible that the opening four verses are a fragment of an earlier story on which the present one has been built. The "graven image" and "molten image" of v. 4 may simply be given new names in the "ephod" and "teraphim" of verse 5. Then Micah's name in the Hebrew of verses 1 and 4 is written in the longer older form; and that has the effect of drawing attention to its original meaning: "Who-is-like-Yahweh?" In the present form of the story that is a mischievous name for a character who presides over such a doubtful cult.

Like any fond parent, indeed like the father in Jesus' parable of the prodigal son, Micah's mother is overwhelmed by her son's confession of his guilt, and immediately seeks to replace her curse on the thief with a blessing (v. 2). It seems from the following chapter that she was less than successful!

(iii)

There are humour and mockery in plenty in this chapter. But the pleasures are like those enjoyed in gossiping about a real scandal. Aided and abetted by his mother's example, and money, Micah goes from bad to worse. The terms used for the various cultic objects in verses 4 and 5 would send a frisson of horror tingling up the spine of any pious reader of the Hebrew Bible.

I suspect that this story is quite late within the writings of the Old Testament; and that it actually quotes two or three key passages which would have been familiar to its readers. Making a "graven image" is vetoed in the Ten Commandments (Exod. 20:4; Deut. 5:8), while "molten gods" are prohibited in the related Exod. 34:17. The fact it is a "molten god" is no small part of what is wrong with the golden calf (Exod. 32 and Deut. 9).

However, it is in only two other Biblical passages that graven and molten images are paired. One of these is the powerful climax of the opening chapter of Nahum's diatribe against the Assyrian city of Nineveh, a city for which the Bible tends to reserve its bitterest venom:

> "No more shall your name be perpetuated;
> from the house of your gods I will cut off
>   the graven image and the molten image.
> I will make your grave, for you are vile."

(1:14)

The other passage is even closer to home. It heads the curses listed towards the end of the Book of Deuteronomy as first called down on any covert sinner by the whole company of the twelve tribes of Israel in solemn assembly on mounts Ebal and Gerizim, which are in "the hill country of Ephraim" (Judg. 17:1,8):

> "Cursed be the man who makes a graven or a molten image, an abomination to the Lord, a thing made by the hands of a craftsman, and sets it up in secret."

(Deut. 27:15)

Judg. 17:4 reports behaviour which in public in Nineveh had led to divine condemnation, and in secret in Israel was subject to solemn curse. And all this at the hands of a woman, who would curse a secret thief and seek divine blessing on her son!

The situation with ephod and teraphim is similar. This is not the commoner sort of ephod, which was part of priestly dress, but a plated statue. Teraphim (a plural) appear to have been domestic household gods, which are mocked in some Biblical stories. David's wife Michal stuffs one into his bed to fool assassins from her father Saul (1 Sam. 19:13, 16). Then when Laban tries to recover his teraphim, purloined by Jacob and his daughters, Rachel conceals them (Gen. 31:34–35) by sitting on them and claiming "the way of women is upon me".

However, again there is one close Biblical parallel, which casts a shaft of light across our chapter:

> For the children of Israel shall dwell many days without king or prince, without sacrifice or pillar, without ephod or teraphim. Afterward the children of Israel shall return and seek the Lord their God, and David their king; and they shall come in fear to the Lord and to his goodness in the latter days.
>
> (Hosea 3:4–5)

Only here and in Judg. 17:5 are ephod and teraphim paired. Ephod and teraphim are for Hosea among the evils Israel must learn to do without, before a return is conceivable to the true God and to true kingship.

In the light of these Biblical passages, the central verse 6 takes on a richer meaning: "In those days there was no king in Israel; every man did what was right in his own eyes." This may well be reminiscent of language in Deuteronomy (12:8–14). But that does not mean this chapter is a Deuteronomistic creation. It simply quotes Deuteronomy, like it quotes Hosea and Nahum.

MICAH'S LEVITE AND MIGRATING DAN

Judges 18:1–31

[1]In those days there was no king in Israel. And in those days the tribe of the Danites was seeking for itself an inheritance to dwell in; for until then no inheritance among the tribes of Israel had fallen to them. [2]So the Danites sent five able men from the whole number of their tribe, from Zorah and from Eshta-ol, to spy out the land and to explore it;

and they said to them, "Go and explore the land." And they came to the hill country of Ephraim, to the house of Micah, and lodged there. ³When they were by the house of Micah, they recognised the voice of the young Levite; and they turned aside and said to him, "Who brought you here? What are you doing in this place? What is your business here?" ⁴And he said to them, "Thus and thus has Micah dealt with me: he has hired me, and I have become his priest." ⁵And they said to him, "Inquire of God, we pray thee, that we may know whether the journey on which we are setting out will succeed." ⁶And the priest said to them, "Go in peace. The journey on which you go is under the eye of the Lord."

⁷Then the five men departed, and came to Laish, and saw the people who were there, how they dwelt in security, after the manner of the Sidonians, quiet and unsuspecting, lacking nothing that is in the earth, and possessing wealth, and how they were far from the Sidonians and had no dealings with any one. ⁸And when they came to their brethren at Zorah and Eshta-ol, their brethren said to them, "What do you report?" ⁹They said, "Arise, and let us go up against them; for we have seen the land, and behold, it is very fertile. And will you do nothing? Do not be slow to go, and enter in and possess the land. ¹⁰When you go, you will come to an unsuspecting people. The land is broad; yea, God has given it into your hands, a place where there is no lack of anything that is in the earth."

¹¹And six hundred men of the tribe of Dan, armed with weapons of war, set forth from Zorah and Eshta-ol, ¹²and went up and encamped at Kiriath-jearim in Judah. On this account that place is called Mahaneh-dan to this day; behold, it is west of Kiriath-jearim. ¹³And they passed on from there to the hill country of Ephraim, and came to the house of Micah.

¹⁴Then the five men who had gone to spy out the country of Laish said to their brethren, "Do you know that in these houses there are an ephod, teraphim, a graven image, and a molten image? Now therefore consider what you will do." ¹⁵And they turned aside thither, and came to the house of the young Levite, at the home of Micah, and asked him of his welfare. ¹⁶Now the six hundred men of the Danites, armed with their weapons of war, stood by the entrance of the gate; ¹⁷and the five men who had gone to spy out the land went up, and entered and took the graven image, the ephod, the teraphim, and the molten image, while the priest stood by the entrance of the gate with the six hundred men armed with weapons of war. ¹⁸And when these went into Micah's

house and took the graven image, the ephod, the teraphim, and the molten image, the priest said to them, "What are you doing?" [19]And they said to him, "Keep quiet, put your hand upon your mouth, and come with us, and be to us a father and a priest. Is it better for you to be priest to the house of one man, or to be priest to a tribe and family in Israel?" [20]And the priest's heart was glad; he took the ephod, and the teraphim, and the graven image, and went in the midst of the people.

[21]So they turned and departed, putting the little ones and the cattle and the goods in front of them. [22]When they were a good way from the home of Micah, the men who were in the houses near Micah's house were called out, and they overtook the Danites. [23]And they shouted to the Danites, who turned round and said to Micah, "What ails you that you come with such a company?" [24]And he said, "You take my gods which I made, and the priest, and go away, and what have I left? How then do you ask me, 'What ails you?'" [25]And the Danites said to him, "Do not let your voice be heard among us, lest angry fellows fall upon you, and you lose your life with the lives of your household." [26]Then the Danites went their way; and when Micah saw that they were too strong for him, he turned and went back to his home.

[27]And taking what Micah had made, and the priest who belonged to him, the Danites came to Laish, to a people quiet and unsuspecting, and smote them with the edge of the sword, and burned the city with fire. [28]And there was no deliverer because it was far from Sidon, and they had no dealings with any one. It was in the valley which belongs to Beth-rehob. And they rebuilt the city, and dwelt in it. [29]And they named the city Dan, after the name of Dan their ancestor, who was born to Israel; but the name of the city was Laish at the first. [30]And the Danites set up the graven image for themselves; and Jonathan the son of Gershom, son of Moses, and his sons were priests to the tribe of the Danites until the day of the captivity of the land. [31]So they set up Micah's graven image which he made, as long as the house of God was at Shiloh.

Fat rich Micah is a goose ripe for plucking! There is layer upon layer of meaning in this chapter. At one of these levels it is surely intended as appropriate, in a postscript in a book about "judges", that the agents of Micah's undoing should be a people called Dan, when another *dan* is but a different Hebrew word for "judge". One could easily imagine that Judg. 17 was originally a story complete in itself, and indeed that the repeated (sad?) comment in the first part of 18:1, "In those days there was no king in Israel", was its tailpiece. Now, however, that note is simply the backdrop or the occasion for the narrative in Judg. 18. Something else was wrong in those days: Dan was without territory.

(i)

One function of Judg. 18 is to build a link between two separate pieces of information about Dan in the Old Testament. Some traditions know Dan as a small tribal territory to the north-west of Judah, or in contemporary terms in the south-eastern hinterland of Tel Aviv. Josh. 19:40–46 outlines its extent. However, Josh. 19:47 and Judg. 1:34–35 partly neutralize this tradition by talking of serious local difficulties, and already sketch the tradition found in Judg. 18. The Song of Deborah, which links Dan with ships (5:17), obviously has this southern location in mind. For the other historical traditions of the Old Testament, Dan is in the far north, nestling under Mount Hermon, near the sources of the Jordan, and later Caesarea Philippi. Dan and Beersheba mark the northern and southern limits of the promised land (Judg. 20:1), while Dan and Bethel are chosen as Jeroboam's sanctuaries (1 Kings 12:29–30) as the northern and southern points of the separate northern kingdom of Israel. Judg. 18 (anticipated in Josh. 19:47 and Judg. 1) links the two localities by an account of a migration.

This migration has been helpfully styled a miniature of Israel's great exodus and settlement. Spies are sent out and bring back a report. In Dan's case this is entirely favourable, as in Josh. 2:24— but not like the extended traditions in Numbers 13–14 and Deut. 1. In mountain territory, of Ephraim instead of Sinai, they acquire cultic apparatus and a priesthood. They are too strong for Micah when he seeks to block their progress. And when they come to Laish, it is an easy prey for them: they put the people to the sword, and burn the city before rebuilding it and giving it their own name.

If a miniature, it is also a mockery. The success of these late arrivals comes easily to them. They do it all in their *own* strength. They behave reprehensibly to Micah, and are equalled in their behaviour only by the cheek of the Levite who is enough of an opportunist to welcome their offer of a bigger job. His lack of scruple over stealing the secrets of his former employer makes him a familiar figure in our own contemporary society.

(ii)

This helps to bring into focus another aspect of the chapter's purpose. The issue will become clearer if we start at the end. Verses 30–31 sum up the whole episode in rather different style. The idols hijacked by the migrating Danites are described in a varying cluster of terms in the main body of the story (vv. 14, 17, 18, and 20). However, the matter is summed up (v. 30) in the words: "the Danites set up the *graven image* for themselves". When brevity is called for, the writer chooses the term which falls foul of Israel's basic charter in the Ten Commandments. Ironically it is only at this point that the Levite is finally named, Jonathan, son of Gershom, son of Moses. A grandson of Moses, who could have stayed safely at home in Bethlehem, presiding over worship by a graven image! That was what Israel had come to—at least northern Israel at Dan! Talk of a "molten image" earlier in the chapter already reminded us of the tradition of the golden calf. And of course that story in Exod. 32 and Deut. 9 is closely related to Jeroboam's cultic "reforms" described in 1 Kings 12—that re-ordering of religion in northern Israel which the Deuteronomistic historians consistently and tersely damn as "the sin which Jeroboam made Israel to sin".

The issue is expressed perfectly in Hosea's poetry:

When Ephraim spoke, men trembled;
    he was exalted in Israel;
    but he incurred guilt through Baal and died.
And now they sin more and more,
    and make for themselves molten images,
idols skilfully made of their silver,
    all of them the work of craftsmen.
Sacrifice to these, they say.
    Men kiss calves! (13:1–2)

The author of Judg. 18 has a similar point to make. He shares the Judean Deuteronomistic critique; yet like Hosea, though in a quite different medium, he makes his point more artistically, and perhaps more effectively. He does not simply brand northern religion as "sinful". He offers an explanation of its worthlessness: it had been stolen by easy-going louts from an effete and heretical founder. In commenting on the end of Judg. 8, we noted another possible disparaging reference to the northern cult: that it had resulted from an individual's personal whim, and that its focus had been manufactured from Ishmaelite earrings!

Such witty barbs penetrate far deeper than carefully prepared and oft repeated theological probes. And the Bible's poet-prophets of the eighth and seventh centuries B.C. are masters of the art. Amos devastates the easy optimism which we sum up in our proverb that *every* cloud has a silver lining:

> Woe to you who desire the day of the Lord!
>   Why would you have the day of the Lord?
> It is darkness and not light;
>   as if a man fled from a lion,
>   and a bear met him;
> or went into the house and leaned with his hand against the wall,
>   and a serpent bit him.
> Is not the day of the Lord darkness, and not light,
>   and gloom with no brightness in it?
>
>   (5:18–20)

Jeremiah develops the manifest contrast between fresh and stored water to expose the double absurdity of Israel in exchanging Yahweh for Baal:

> for my people have committed two evils:
>   they have forsaken me,
> the fountain of living waters,
>   and hewed out cisterns for themselves,
> broken cisterns,
>   that can hold no water.   (2:13)

And no one ever portrayed the agony of God's unrequited love more poignantly than Hosea:

When Israel was a child, I loved him,
    and out of Egypt I called my son.
The more I called them,
    the more they went from me;
they kept sacrificing to the Baals,
    and burning incense to idols.

Yet it was I who taught Ephraim to walk,
    I took them up in my arms;
    but they did not know that I healed them.
I led them with cords of compassion,
    with the bands of love,
and I became to them as one
    who eases the yoke on their jaws,
    and I bent down to them and fed them.   (11:1–4)

or earlier:

Like grapes in the wilderness,
    I found Israel.
Like the first fruit on the fig tree,
    in its first season,
    I saw your fathers.
But they came to Baal-peor,
    and consecrated themselves to Shame,
    and became detestable like the thing they loved.   (9:10)

With artists and preachers like these, who would prefer the developed argument of a theological editor? It is to similar effect that the several scandals that fill Judg. 17–21 are crisply and humorously retailed.

MODELS OF HOSPITALITY

Judges 19:1–30

¹In those days, when there was no king in Israel, a certain Levite was sojourning in the remote parts of the hill country of Ephraim, who took to himself a concubine from Bethlehem in Judah. ²And his concubine became angry with him, and she went away from him to her

father's house at Bethlehem in Judah, and was there some four months. ³Then her husband arose and went after her, to speak kindly to her and bring her back. He had with him his servant and a couple of asses. And he came to her father's house; and when the girl's father saw him, he came with joy to meet him. ⁴And his father-in-law, the girl's father, made him stay, and he remained with him three days; so they ate and drank, and lodged there. ⁵And on the fourth day they arose early in the morning, and he prepared to go; but the girl's father said to his son-in-law, "Strengthen your heart with a morsel of bread, and after that you may go." ⁶So the two men sat and ate and drank together; and the girl's father said to the man, "Be pleased to spend the night, and let your heart be merry." ⁷And when the man rose up to go, his father-in-law urged him, till he lodged there again. ⁸And on the fifth day he arose early in the morning to depart: and the girl's father said, "Strengthen your heart, and tarry until the day declines." So they ate, both of them. ⁹And when the man and his concubine and his servant rose up to depart, his father-in-law, the girl's father, said to him, "Behold, now the day has waned toward evening; pray tarry all night. Behold, the day draws to its close; lodge here and let your heart be merry; and tomorrow you shall arise early in the morning for your journey, and go home."

¹⁰But the man would not spend the night; he rose up and departed, and arrived opposite Jebus (that is, Jerusalem). He had with him a couple of saddled asses, and his concubine was with him. ¹¹When they were near Jebus, the day was far spent, and the servant said to his master, "Come now, let us turn aside to this city of the Jebusites, and spend the night in it." ¹²And his master said to him, "We will not turn aside into the city of foreigners, who do not belong to the people of Israel; but we will pass on to Gibe-ah." ¹³And he said to his servant, "Come and let us draw near to one of these places, and spend the night at Gibe-ah or at Ramah." ¹⁴So they passed on and went their way; and the sun went down on them near Gibe-ah, which belongs to Benjamin, ¹⁵and they turned aside there to go in and spend the night at Gibe-ah. And he went in and sat down in the open square of the city; for no man took them into his house to spend the night.

¹⁶And behold, an old man was coming from his work in the field at evening; the man was from the hill country of Ephraim, and he was sojourning in Gibe-ah; the men of the place were Benjaminites. ¹⁷And

he lifted up his eyes, and saw the wayfarer in the open square of the city; and the old man said, "Where are you going? and whence do you come?" 18And he said to him, "We are passing from Bethlehem in Judah to the remote parts of the hill country of Ephraim, from which I come. I went to Bethlehem in Judah; and I am going to my home; and nobody takes me into his house. 19We have straw and provender for our asses, with bread and wine for me and your maidservant and the young man with your servants; there is no lack of anything." 20And the old man said, "Peace be to you; I will care for all your wants; only, do not spend the night in the square." 21So he brought him into his house, and gave the asses provender; and they washed their feet, and ate and drank.

22As they were making their hearts merry, behold, the men of the city, base fellows, beset the house round about, beating on the door; and they said to the old man, the master of the house, "Bring out the man who came into your house, that we may know him." 23And the man, the master of the house, went out to them and said to them, "No, my brethren, do not act so wickedly; seeing that this man has come into my house, do not do this vile thing. 24Behold, here are my virgin daughter and his concubine; let me bring them out now. Ravish them and do with them what seems good to you; but against this man do not do so vile a thing." 25But the men would not listen to him. So the man seized his concubine, and put her out to them; and they knew her, and abused her all night until the morning. And as the dawn began to break, they let her go. 26And as morning appeared, the woman came and fell down at the floor of the man's house where her master was, till it was light.

27And her master rose up in the morning, and when he opened the doors of the house and went out to go on his way, behold, there was his concubine lying at the door of the house, with her hands on the threshold. 28He said to her, "Get up, let us be going." But there was no answer. Then he put her upon the ass; and the man rose up and went away to his home. 29And when he entered his house, he took a knife, and laying hold of his concubine he divided her, limb by limb, into twelve pieces, and sent her throughout all the territory of Israel. 30And all who saw it said, "Such a thing has never happened or been seen from the day that the people of Israel came up out of the land of Egypt until this day; consider it, take counsel, and speak."

(i)

In a number of respects this story is a variation on a theme. The key signature is closely related to that of the preceding two chapters. Like Micah its main character is from the hill country of Ephraim, although from one of its remote areas. As with Micah, an important member of his household comes from Bethlehem in Judah. Again we are dealing with a story about a Levite. And the opening words of the chapter remind us that this is still the period when there was no king in Israel. All in all, the transition from chapters 17–18 to 19–21 is made very easy. In similar manner chapter 18 links easily with the Samson cycle; for its repeated mention of Zorah and Eshtaol, and even Mahaneh-dan (vv. 2, 8, 11) remind us of that other Danite's locale (13:25 and 16:31). Indeed the later attachment of the Book of Ruth to the end of the Book of Judges must have been assisted by the fact that it too begins and ends in Bethlehem of Judah.

However, those details are simply matters of presentation. The actual stuff of the story reminds us of a scandal associated with the wicked city of Sodom, which Genesis relates in 19:1–11. The whole male population of that city threaten to assault sexually two divine emissaries whom Lot is entertaining. Lot's offer of his own virgin daughters is rejected; and the rascals begin to abuse him instead. At this point his guests afflict them with blindness, as a prelude to the divine destruction of the city.

(ii)

At one important level this story is about different expectations and different experiences of hospitality. The Levite's second-rank wife had left him in the lurch, and returned to her father in Bethlehem. After four months the man sought to rectify the situation, travelled to Bethlehem with a second ass, and sought her return with him. The Hebrew phrase that is rendered "speak kindly" is always used in contexts of reassurance or persuasion. It is perhaps best known in Isaiah 40:2:

Speak tenderly to Jerusalem,
  and cry to her

that her warfare is ended,
    that her iniquity is pardoned,
that she has received from the Lord's hand
    double for all her sins.

Hosea similarly pictures the divine lover seeking the return of his former bride:

Therefore, behold, I will allure her,
    and bring her into the wilderness,
    and speak tenderly to her.
And there I will give her her vineyards,
    and make the Valley of Achor a door of hope.
And there she shall answer as in the days of her youth,
    as at the time when she came out of the land of Egypt.

(2:14–15)

The woman's father gives him a rich welcome; and we should not simply suppose that the man was keen to see the back of his daughter! The Levite made a first move to return north after three days (a suitable period for a visit to the in-laws?), but was detained again and again by pressing hospitality, and only achieved a departure on the fifth day much later than he would have chosen. Either the Levite was a bit feckless, or he was concerned not to upset his wife again; or perhaps his father-in-law was the sort of man whose hospitality indulges himself, rather than his guests. Like so many scandals the following scene was avoidable, but none-the-less shameless.

The servant was keen to stop for the night before they were well on their way. The old city of Jerusalem lies only about five miles north of Bethlehem. But that was not deemed a suitable place: "We will not turn aside into the city of foreigners, who do not belong to the people of Israel; but we will pass on to Gibeah" (v. 12). But the poor man's faith in Israelite security and hospitality was quite misplaced. They could as well have been in a foreign city, for only an elderly alien like themselves was prepared to take them off Gibeah's streets. His hospitality too was rich and generous.

(iii)

Gibeah was not simply inhospitable; there were elements in it that were downright vile. As the strangers were enjoying the company of the resident alien, the house was surrounded like Lot's before in Sodom (Gen. 19:4), and the same request made: "Bring out the man who came into your house, that we may know him." Carnal knowledge is not specified. However, those inside the house normally do suspect the worst of a hostile mob outside in the evening, even if they *say* they only want to take a look. Modern translations have quite accurately deprived us of one of the more colourful names of the Authorised Version to describe the mob—"men of Belial" (v. 22). In fact this colourful "demon" is simply a noun meaning "no use" or "worthlessness". Isaiah uses a related phrase to warn his people of the uselessness of Egypt as an ally (30:5–6); while Jeremiah makes a mocking pun on the name Baal (2:8, 11).

The dilemma of the host is acute. Concern for the sanctity of one's family and the virginity of one's daughters may be common to most men. But he was even more concerned over his responsibility for a stranger whom he had welcomed under his roof, whose feet had been washed, and who had eaten and drunk. For someone—but not for *all* the strangers under his roof. Why is the man's concubine offered to the rabble along with his virgin daughter?

It would be good to know for sure what is intended by the phrase (*ha-nebalah ha-zot*) the RSV translates as "this vile thing" (vv. 23 and 24). The Hebrew word is sometimes rendered "folly"; and it more often refers to speech than action. It is brilliantly personified in the Nabal episode in 1 Samuel 25: Nabal whose very name means that he blurts out churlish folly before he thinks (v. 25; see vv. 10–11). "This *vile* thing" fits the context well, but it may be more than the actual words say.

Is the host referring to the abuse of hospitality, or to their assumed homosexual proposition? Why is the man's concubine offered? Was she not a protected guest? Was she of lesser concern to him because she would have eaten and socialized with the women and not with himself? Was she in any case, as a second wife, of lesser social standing? Or did the offer of the two women, instead of his guest, imply an attempt to divert the rabble into regular rather than irregular sexual practice? To my mind, simply to state the issue is to answer it. It takes remarkable self-possession, under pressure, and especially when an alien, to be concerned for the moral well-being of one's intruders. Violation of hospitality is surely the problem. Maybe the offer of the moment is but a token of their secondary social situation. Perhaps the *offer* of his own virgin daughter was intended to shock the mob to their senses. His suggestion at least seems to have scandalized his guest; for at the mention of the daughter, he grabs his own concubine and thrusts her out the door.

However the writer intends us to judge that action, it seems to me that the reputation of the Levite does not emerge unscathed from the chapter. There is surely bitter comment between the lines of the scene next morning as he asks the lifeless lump on the threshold if she is ready to go, then puts her quietly on the ass and leaves. Has he no conception of what must have transpired? Does he not realize what she must have suffered over many hours? Or is it a grim charade, played by a man who now knows he can expect no justice in Gibeah, and who refuses to give the citizens of Gibeah the satisfaction of seeing him admit she is dead and he is unable to prosecute?

So he goes home, dismembers her, and sends her round Israel. "Have you ever seen such a thing?" Even the popular response is ambiguous. Do they mean the scandal at Gibeah? Do they mean the mute challenge to all Israel? Do they mean both together? No wonder they conclude: "consider it, take counsel, and speak."

"THEY MURDER ON THE WAY TO SHECHEM"

Judges 20:1–17

[1]Then all the people of Israel came out, from Dan to Beersheba, including the land of Gilead, and the congregation assembled as one man to the Lord at Mizpah. [2]And the chiefs of all the people, of all the tribes of Israel, presented themselves in the assembly of the people of God, four hundred thousand men on foot that drew the sword. [3](Now

the Benjaminites heard that the people of Israel had gone up to Mizpah.) And the people of Israel said, "Tell us, how was this wickedness brought to pass?" ⁴And the Levite, the husband of the woman who was murdered, answered and said, "I came to Gibe-ah that belongs to Benjamin, I and my concubine, to spend the night. ⁵And the men of Gibe-ah rose against me, and beset the house round about me by night; they meant to kill me, and they ravished my concubine, and she is dead. ⁶And I took my concubine and cut her in pieces, and sent her throughout all the country of the inheritance of Israel; for they have committed abomination and wantonness in Israel. ⁷Behold, you people of Israel, all of you, give your advice and counsel here."

⁸And all the people arose as one man, saying, "We will not any of us go to his tent, and none of us will return to his house. ⁹But now this is what we will do to Gibe-ah: we will go up against it by lot, ¹⁰and we will take ten men of a hundred throughout all the tribes of Israel, and a hundred of a thousand, and a thousand of ten thousand, to bring provisions for the people, that when they come they may requite Gibe-ah of Benjamin, for all the wanton crime which they have committed in Israel." ¹¹So all the men of Israel gathered against the city, united as one man.

¹²And the tribes of Israel sent men through all the tribe of Benjamin, saying, "What wickedness is this that has taken place among you? ¹³Now therefore give up the men, the base fellows in Gibe-ah, that we may put them to death, and put away evil from Israel." But the Benjaminites would not listen to the voice of their brethren, the people of Israel. ¹⁴And the Benjaminites came together out of the cities of Gibe-ah, to go out to battle against the people of Israel. ¹⁵And the Benjaminites mustered out of their cities on that day twenty-six thousand men that drew the sword, besides the inhabitants of Gibe-ah, who mustered seven hundred picked men. ¹⁶Among all these were seven hundred picked men who were left-handed; every one could sling a stone at a hair, and not miss. ¹⁷And the men of Israel, apart from Benjamin, mustered four hundred thousand men that drew sword; all these were men of war.

(i)

One significant element of the similar story about Lot in Gen. 19 is lacking from this narrative in Judg. 19–20. The scoundrels in Sodom rebuke immigrant Lot for daring to *judge* their behaviour. Their counterparts in Gibeah do not make the same charge against the old Ephraimite in their midst. Yet the theme is not lost from this narrative. The Levite's butchered concubine in her bloody journey round the whole country challenges all Israel to be judge. His challenge (19:29–30) results in a solemn assembly; and when he has testified before it, he repeats his challenge (20:4–7).

(ii)

There are echoes of many other Biblical passages too in these few verses. Some parts of it read like a string of quotations. This does help us to interpret the text; but it is an occasional hindrance as well: too much significance should not be attached to some words within Judg. 20, for they may only be there as part of an allusion elsewhere.

At first sight it appears that all Israel has prepared for a military operation before hearing the detailed evidence. When all Israel "come out", it usually means *for war*. This impression seems underscored by the end of verse 2 with its muster of men that "drew the sword", although that might just mean able-bodied men, and not that they actually had sword in hand. This military muster reminds us of King Saul's anger at Ammon's threat of brutality against Jabesh:

> He took a yoke of oxen, and cut them in pieces and sent them throughout all the territory of Israel by the hand of messengers, saying, "Whoever does not *come out* after Saul and Samuel, so shall it be done to his oxen!" Then the dread of the Lord fell upon the people, and they came out as one man. (1 Sam. 11:7)

On the other hand the solemn assembly of the congregation reminds us of the two gatherings at Shiloh reported in the Book of Joshua: one to solve the problem of land not yet taken up (18:1), and the other in response to the outrageous Transjordanian altar (22:12)—there too a military response is uppermost.

Again it is probably significant that the gathering is to Mizpah, which is also associated with the Samuel traditions. From there a victory was organized against the Philistines (1 Sam. 7:5–14). And there too Saul was chosen as king (1 Sam. 10:17–24).

When we recall that Saul himself came from Gibeah in Benjamin, that Samuel was less than enthusiastic about his becoming king, and that the kingship finally passed to David from Judah, we have all the clues necessary to deduce what at least one function of this story is. It is a piece of anti-Saul propaganda. It throws scorn on his birthplace. It charges Gibeah with an outrage worthy of Sodom, that proverbially wicked city. And it caps the story of Saul's dismembering a heifer to muster Israel against an odious threat from Ammon, by reproaching his ancestors with equal vileness in their midst. And all this was rehearsed at Mizpah, from which Philistines were worsted, and where Saul was chosen king. The associations are many, and they are laid on with a thick brush.

(iii)

Although the bias against Benjamin and Saul's birthplace cannot be denied, there is much more to this story than mere propaganda. It is a well-told tale as well. Repeated from Ehud in Judg. 3 is the delightful idea of left-handed Benjaminites (people of the right)—only now there are seven hundred of them (v. 16)! And as with Abimelech and his rabble drinking in the "saloon" (ch. 9), we find another touch of the Wild West in the idea that all of them could aim at a hair and not miss!

The Levite too makes the best possible case to the gathered assembly. He tells them he had feared first for his own life; and, while he does not press a charge of murder, he does note that his concubine is dead. His words are open to the construction that death was the accidental result and not the purpose of their mistreatment. However, the story-teller shows less restraint, and introduces the Levite as "the husband of the woman who was murdered" (v. 4). However, playing down one element in a story is often just a compensation for maximizing another. One nice touch in the Hebrew, passed over by the RSV as in chapter 9, is that the Levite points his finger not at the riff-raff of Gibeah but at the town's "lords" or "notables" or "property-owners" (v. 5)—not simply its "men". If a rabble is mentioned (19:22; 20:13), it is because the *whole* of Gibeah are "base fellows".

I wonder if this charge lost the case, at least as far as Benjamin's leaders were concerned. The other communities of that tribe might just have been content to string up a few young rowdies, to consent in the prosecution of the local hell-raisers, for a bad case of gang rape. But when it came to pointing a finger at all those good men and true, all those good fellow-citizens, kith and kin became more important than justice. There are too many shameless episodes of this sort in our own history for any enumeration to be required.

(iv)

Three further echoes, and we are finished. The first is in Deut. 13. Three sorts of apostasy are linked in that chapter, and we find familiar language in verses 5 and 14–16. Murder and mistreatment of an alien in the midst are no less wicked.

The next is in Isa. 32:1–8. This is the only other passage in the Bible which links the words translated "abomination and wantonness" here in v. 6. There they are rendered "folly" and "wicked devices" (vv. 5–7). What is even more interesting about this link is that Isaiah's words enshrine a rich ideal of monarchy: when a good king reigns then all is well in the world! And that hints at the recurring formula in Judges 17–21.

My final echo is the powerful appeal for vindication in Psalm 94. I quote just the first seven verses:

O Lord, thou God of vengeance,
  thou God of vengeance, shine forth!
Rise up, O judge of the earth;
  render to the proud their deserts!
O Lord, how long shall the wicked,
  how long shall the wicked exult?

They pour out their arrogant words,
  they boast, all the evildoers.
They crush thy people, O Lord,
  and afflict thy heritage.
They slay the widow and the sojourner,
  and murder the fatherless;

and they say, "The Lord does not see;
the God of Jacob does not perceive."

BENJAMIN BROUGHT TO BOOK

Judges 20:18–48

[18]The people of Israel arose and went up to Bethel, and inquired of God, "Which of us shall go up first to battle against the Benjaminites?" And the Lord said, "Judah shall go up first."

[19]Then the people of Israel rose in the morning, and encamped against Gibe-ah. [20]And the men of Israel went out to battle against Benjamin; and the men of Israel drew up the battle line against them at Gibe-ah. [21]The Benjaminites came out of Gibe-ah, and felled to the ground on that day twenty-two thousand men of the Israelites. [22]But the people, the men of Israel, took courage, and again formed the battle line in the same place where they had formed it on the first day. [23]And the people of Israel went up and wept before the Lord until the evening; and they inquired of the Lord, "Shall we again draw near to battle against our brethren the Benjaminites?" And the Lord said, "Go up against them."

[24]So the people of Israel came near against the Benjaminites the second day. [25]And Benjamin went against them out of Gibe-ah the second day, and felled to the ground eighteen thousand men of the people of Israel; all these were men who drew the sword. [26]Then all the people of Israel, the whole army, went up and came to Bethel and wept; they sat there before the Lord, and fasted that day until evening, and offered burnt offerings and peace offerings before the Lord. [27]And the people of Israel inquired of the Lord (for the ark of the covenant of God was there in those days, [28]and Phinehas the son of Eleazar, son of Aaron, ministered before it in those days), saying, "Shall we yet again go out to battle against our brethren the Benjaminites, or shall we cease?" And the Lord said, "Go up; for tomorrow I will give them into your hand."

[29]So Israel set men in ambush round about Gibe-ah. [30]And the people of Israel went up against the Benjaminites on the third day, and set themselves in array against Gibe-ah, as at other times. [31]And the Benjaminites went out against the people, and were drawn away from the city; and as at other times they began to smite and kill some of the people, in the highways, one of which goes up to Bethel and the other

to Gibe-ah, and in the open country, about thirty men of Israel. [32]And the Benjaminites said, "They are routed before us, as at the first." But the men of Israel said, "Let us flee, and draw them away from the city to the highways." [33]And all the men of Israel rose up out of their place, and set themselves in array at Baal-tamar; and the men of Israel who were in ambush rushed out of their place west of Geba. [34]And there came against Gibe-ah ten thousand picked men out of all Israel, and the battle was hard; but the Benjaminites did not know that disaster was close upon them. [35]And the Lord defeated Benjamin before Israel; and the men of Israel destroyed twenty-five thousand one hundred men of Benjamin that day; all these were men who drew the sword. [36]So the Benjaminites saw that they were defeated.

The men of Israel gave ground to Benjamin, because they trusted to the men in ambush whom they had set against Gibe-ah. [37]And the men in ambush made haste and rushed upon Gibe-ah; the men in ambush moved out and smote all the city with the edge of the sword. [38]Now the appointed signal between the men of Israel and the men in ambush was that when they made a great cloud of smoke rise up out of the city [39]the men of Israel should turn in battle. Now Benjamin had begun to smite and kill about thirty men of Israel; they said, "Surely they are smitten down before us, as in the first battle." [40]But when the signal began to rise out of the city in a column of smoke, the Benjaminites looked behind them; and behold, the whole of the city went up in smoke to heaven. [41]Then the men of Israel turned, and the men of Benjamin were dismayed, for they saw that disaster was close upon them. [42]Therefore they turned their backs before the men of Israel in the direction of the wilderness; but the battle overtook them, and those who came out of the cities destroyed them in the midst of them. [43]Cutting down the Benjaminites, they pursued them and trod them down from Nohah as far as opposite Gibe-ah on the east. [44]Eighteen thousand men of Benjamin fell, all of them men of valour. [45]And they turned and fled toward the wilderness to the rock of Rimmon; five thousand men of them were cut down in the highways, and they were pursued hard to Gidom, and two thousand men of them were slain. [46]So all who fell that day of Benjamin were twenty-five thousand men that drew the sword, all of them men of valour. [47]But six hundred men turned and fled toward the wilderness to the rock of Rimmon, and abode at the rock of Rimmon four months. [48]And the men of Israel turned back against the Benjaminites, and smote them with the edge of the sword, men and beasts and all that they found. And all the towns which they found they set on fire.

As the narrative of the assembly at Mizpah moves from speech to action, it becomes much harder to interpret. It is with greater than usual hesitation that I suggest the following comments over the next two portions.

(i)

There is a noticeable change (for the worse) in the quality of the narrative. It has lost the crisp terseness typical of so much of the Book of Judges, and has become complicated and turgid. This is particularly true of the account of the main campaign beginning in verse 29. After consultation to elicit the will of God, Judah leads the Israelite attack against Benjamin. The battles in the first two days are however a disaster for the avenging confederates; and Benjamin twice repulses the attack. Each day there is oracular consultation; and finally, on the third day, an unambiguously clear promise is given of success (vv. 27–28). And this is what happens.

It is the long report of the final element in the campaign that is hard to deal with. To an extent we feel we have seen all this before; for we are reminded forcibly of the tactics in Josh. 8 and Judg. 9. But that is not the whole problem. It is hard to escape the conclusion that two alternative accounts of the campaign have been fused together. It is rather as if in the given text of verses 29–48 we are looking at a screen on which two similar transparencies are being projected at the same time. The main subject is clear enough; but the details are fuzzy and unsatisfactory.

Some commentators argue for a simpler solution, supposing that the two sources of this chapter are quoted one after the other. Precise details vary from scholar to scholar; but there is fair agreement over the first version being vv. 29–36 and the second vv. 37–43. I rather prefer Professor Soggin's proposal to reconstruct the accounts as follows:

Version A
(29) Then Israel set ambushes around Gibeah, (36*b*) and then gave ground in front of the Benjaminites, trusting in the ambush which they

had set at Gibeah. (37a) And the men in ambush made haste to rush in the direction of Gibeah. (38) There had been an arrangement between the Israelites and those set in the main ambush: these last were to send up a smoke signal from the city, (39) and then the Israelites would turn in battle. Benjamin began to kill some of the Israelites in retreat, striking about thirty men, and they said among themselves, "Look, they are routed before us, as in the earlier battles." (40) But the signal, a column of smoke, began to rise from the city. Benjamin turned and saw the city in smoke like a burnt offering! (41) Then the men of Israel turned about, and the men of Benjamin were confounded, seeing that disaster was imminent. (42a) So they turned before the men of Israel in the direction of the desert, but the battle overtook them. (43) The Israelites cut Benjamin in pieces and pursued the survivors without respite, reassembling in front of Gibeah, on the side where the sun rises. (44) Eighteen thousand men of Benjamin fell, all picked warriors. (45) The survivors turned their backs and fled towards the desert, towards the "Rock of Rimmon". Israel cut down five thousand of them along the route and continued to pursue the others as far as Gidom, killing two thousand of them. (46) All those of Benjamin who fell on that day were twenty-five thousand, men experienced in war, all chosen warriors.

Version B

(30) Then the Israelites marched against the Benjaminites on the third day. They drew up against Gibeah as on the other occasions. (31) The Benjaminites made a sortie from the city to confront the army, and were drawn away from the city. As on previous occasions they began to smite and to kill people from the army along the roads, one of which goes up to Bethel and the other to Gibeon: about thirty of the Israelites in the open country. (32) The Benjaminites said, "They are routed by us as on the other occasions." But the Israelites said, "Let us flee and draw them away from the city, towards the road." (33) Then all the Israelites arose from their position and drew up at Baal-tamar, while the men in ambush broke out from their positions in the vicinity of Geba. (34) And there came against Gibeah eight thousand chosen men from all Israel, and the battle became more violent. The Benjaminites did not know that disaster was imminent. (35) And Yahweh smote Benjamin before Israel: the Israelites routed in that day twenty-five thousand and one hundred men, all skilled in the use of arms. (36a) And the Benjaminites saw that they were defeated. (37b) Then those who had been in ambush took up position and smote the city, putting it

to the sword. (42*b*) Those who came out of the city they routed, catching them between two fires. (47) They turned their backs and fled towards the desert, to the "Rock of Rimmon": six hundred men, and they stayed at the "Rock of Rimmon" for four months. (48) Then the Israelites again turned against the Benjaminites and put the population to the edge of the sword, men and animals, as many as they found. And they set fire to all the towns on their route.

(See his commentary on *Judges* in the Old Testament Library, pp. 294–6.)

Readers are invited to make up their own minds between these solutions, or to propose their own!

(ii)

We have more than once already had occasion in this volume to say a few words about the sacred "lot". It was by this process that the wretched Achan was detected in Josh. 7; and it was by this method that the seven wavering tribes were married up with the territorial demarcations produced by the sacred boundary college in Josh. 18:1–10.

The actual language used three times in this passage, "inquired of God/the Lord" (vv. 18, 23, 27), has been used already twice in Judges. We noted it in the very first verse of the book; and it occurs again in 18:5, where the Danites ask Micah's Levite whether they should proceed on their journey. This language is rather more often used in the stories of Saul and David: 1 Sam. 10:22; 14:37; 22:10,13,15; 23:2,4; 28:6; 30:8; 2 Sam. 2:1; 5:19, 23. Taking each passage on its own, we might suppose that an appropriate intermediary was being asked to find out by prayer what God thought. However, taken together, it seems probable that something more mechanical was in mind.

One clue is to be found in 1 Sam. 30:7–8:

And David said to Abiathar the priest, the son of Ahimelech, "Bring me the ephod." So Abiathar brought the ephod to David. And David inquired of the Lord, "Shall I pursue after this band? Shall I overtake them?" He answered him, "Pursue; for you shall surely overtake and shall surely rescue."

The ephod was a suitable accompaniment, if not a physical aid, for divination. In some of the other passages the issue is presented to God either in the form of a clear alternative or in stages. To each question, or to each stage in a question, the answer "Yes" or "No" could be given—or "This one, not that one". These were issues that could be settled by straws of different length, or dice, or sticks falling in a particular direction.

It seems that questions put to God were structured according to the same binary mathematics as is necessary now for consulting the computer!

"SPEAK A WORD, BUT IT WILL NOT STAND"

Judges 20:18–48 (*cont'd*)

(i)

We have reviewed *how* God's will was sought. Much less clear is just what the story-teller would have us make of this consultation of God. Why is it that the ultimately successful Israelites fail on the first two days? They have after all been told to proceed at the first two consultations.

In the very similar campaign against neighbouring Ai (Josh. 7–8), the first failure was explained as due to Achan's malpractice with the "devoted" booty after the capture of Jericho. No corresponding reason is given here. Similarly, it is only when Saul fails to elicit a response from oracular consultation of God that he finds out (also by lot!) that Jonathan has accidentally fallen foul of his curse (1 Sam. 14:36–46). Are we to search for a similar structural difficulty here?

Perhaps the approach was wrong. God is first asked a *double* question (v. 18): "Which of us shall go up first to battle against the Benjaminites?" He is not asked separately the prior question, whether there *should* be a battle against Benjamin. It is only to the subsidiary tactical question that God responds: Judah first.

Another possibility is this: Perhaps there was a certain appropriateness that there should be blood-letting all round. Remember that on the fateful evening on the road north, the Levite's objection to lodging with the Jebusites was that they were "foreigners who do not belong to the people of Israel". Gibeah was preferred, not as a *Benjaminite* town, but as an *Israelite* one. The dismembered victim is sent round all Israel, not so that they see what has happened *in Gibeah*, but what has been done *in their midst*. There should of course be action against Benjamin: not least because the perpetrators of the foul deed were not handed over to judgment. But *all Israel* is impaled on the hook of responsibility.

A third approach is hinted at in my title for this section. It may be but a variant of the first. It takes its starting point from a quite formal observation. Two Hebrew words which are paired in both Judg. 19:30 and 20:7 are similarly twinned only once more in the whole Bible. Those around Israel who see the woman in twelve pieces conclude, " . . . take counsel and speak." Their words are picked up at the end of the Levite's short address to the assembly: "Give your speech [RSV advice] and counsel here."

Isaiah 8:10 is a puzzling fragment of an equally puzzling short proclamation:

> Take counsel together, but it will come to naught;
>   speak a word, but it will not stand . . .

The same word-pair is there. And it may be significant that these words are part of a challenge, or even a threat, that the thought and discussion in question will be frustrated.

These words have become a political tag in modern Israel. In the determinedly conservative and ultra-orthodox quarter of Jerusalem known as Mea Shearim, these words are often repeated on handbills and hoardings, protesting against many of the policies of what is seen by that quarter's residents to be a secular and irreligious state whose very right to exist they question. This text is used as a blanket denunciation of what is not seen as explicitly ordained by God. We should remember that its original context is as part of a whole section of Isaiah devoted to criticism of the kingdom of Judah and its contemporary Davidic leadership (Isa. 7:1–8:18).

Perhaps the problem which led to the Israelite blood-letting over two anxious days was too much speech and counsel *before* there had been any consultation of God.

(ii)

Involved in this approach to Judg. 20 is the suggestion that to understand the narrative properly you have to spot and appreciate the allusions it contains to other Biblical texts. This makes the story resemble the riddle Samson posed to his wedding party, which could only be solved by special knowledge of a different situation. We have drawn attention to similar allusions to other Biblical—and often prophetic—texts within Judg. 17–21. And so this seems to be a feature of this appendix to the Book of Judges, and worthy of some further comment.

But first a distinction should be drawn. Earlier in our study of Judges, we noted several links with the Jacob traditions in Genesis (cf. on Judg. 9:23–57). There we could see no evidence that Judges was quoting Genesis. Perhaps rather we should suppose that originally free-floating stories and motifs became attached in time to different figures of the past—to both Jacob and Gideon/Jerubbaal.

By contrast, in the closing chapters of Judges, the story-tellers choose certain key words and pairs of words deliberately, to alert the attentive reader who knows the rest of the Biblical tradition that a significant link is being made. It is rather like advice on hanging a painting: that it will be viewed to greater effect if seen from *this* angle, and illuminated by *that* sort of light. Indeed, on the basis of some of our observations, we might wonder whether even more can be learned from such inner-scriptural connections. If geographical settings, religious problems and theological attitudes are all deliberate allusions elsewhere, are these tales of a time when there was no king in Israel *entirely* late-Biblical creations?

It seems to me that that would go too far, although we now have ample confirmation of our earlier suggestion that these two cycles of stories (Judg. 17–18 and 19–21) are far from being *early* records of Israel's pre-monarchical history. Yet not all is fiction, even sacred fiction!

We have noted links with Genesis, Deuteronomy, Samuel, Isaiah, and Nahum. Yet the largest concentration of significant links appears to be with the prophecy of Hosea. And it is precisely Hosea that alludes to Gibeah as a place with shameful associations:

> The prophet is the watchman of Ephraim,
>   the people of my God,
> yet a fowler's snare is on all his ways,
>   and hatred in the house of his God.
> They have deeply corrupted themselves
>   as in the days of Gibeah:
> he will remember their iniquity,
>   he will punish their sins.   (9:8–9)

Then Gibeah is seen as a suitable spot for the war of retribution to begin:

> From the days of Gibeah, you have sinned, O Israel;
>   there they have continued.
>   Shall not war overtake them in Gibeah?
> I will come against the wayward people to chastise them;
>   and nations shall be gathered against them
>   when they are chastised for their double iniquity.   (10:9–10)

There is no suggestion that Hosea is blaming Israel for their choice of Saul at Gibeah; it is for more general evildoing that they are censured throughout his prophecy. A flavour of this is provided in Hos. 6:9—

> As robbers lie in wait for a man,
>   so the priests are banded together;
> they murder on the way to Shechem,
>   yea, they commit villainy.

Murder on the route north—and villainy: another link with our Levite before the assembly at Mizpah, for "villainy" is yet another rendering of the word translated "abomination" in Judg. 20:6.

Hosea knew of ancient scandal at Gibeah. Our story-teller has reconstructed the tale, and decorated its texture with many rich threads from other Biblical materials, each to be separately identified and enjoyed. It is a task of more than one wedding week to solve all the attendant riddles!

BENJAMIN RESTORED

Judges 21:1–25

[1]Now the men of Israel had sworn at Mizpah, "No one of us shall give his daughter in marriage to Benjamin." [2]And the people came to Bethel, and sat there till evening before God, and they lifted up their voices and wept bitterly. [3]And they said, "O Lord, the God of Israel, why has this come to pass in Israel, that there should be today one tribe lacking in Israel?" [4]And on the morrow the people rose early, and built there an altar, and offered burnt offerings and peace offerings. [5]And the people of Israel said, "Which of all the tribes of Israel did not come up in the assembly to the Lord?" For they had taken a great oath concerning him who did not come up to the Lord to Mizpah, saying, "He shall be put to death." [6]And the people of Israel had compassion for Benjamin their brother, and said, "One tribe is cut off from Israel this day. [7]What shall we do for wives for those who are left, since we have sworn by the Lord that we will not give them any of our daughters for wives?"

[8]And they said, "What one is there of the tribes of Israel that did not come up to the Lord to Mizpah?" And behold, no one had come to the camp from Jabesh-gilead, to the assembly. [9]For when the people were mustered, behold, not one of the inhabitants of Jabesh-gilead was there. [10]So the congregation sent thither twelve thousand of their bravest men, and commanded them, "Go and smite the inhabitants of Jabesh-gilead with the edge of the sword; also the women and the little ones. [11]This is what you shall do; every male and every woman that has lain with a male you shall utterly destroy." [12]And they found among the inhabitants of Jabesh-gilead four hundred young virgins who had not known man by lying with him; and they brought them to the camp at Shiloh, which is in the land of Canaan.

[13]Then the whole congregation sent word to the Benjaminites who were at the rock of Rimmon, and proclaimed peace to them. [14]And

Benjamin returned at that time; and they gave them the women whom they had saved alive of the women of Jabesh-gilead; but they did not suffice for them. [15]And the people had compassion on Benjamin because the Lord had made a breach in the tribes of Israel.

[16]Then the elders of the congregation said, "What shall we do for wives for those who are left, since the women are destroyed out of Benjamin?" [17]And they said, "There must be an inheritance for the survivors of Benjamin, that a tribe be not blotted out from Israel. [18]Yet we cannot give them wives of our daughters." For the people of Israel had sworn, "Cursed be he who gives a wife to Benjamin." [19]So they said, "Behold, there is the yearly feast of the Lord at Shiloh, which is north of Bethel, on the east of the highway that goes up from Bethel to Shechem, and south of Lebonah." [20]And they commanded the Benjaminites, saying, "Go and lie in wait in the vineyards, [21]and watch; if the daughters of Shiloh come out to dance in the dances, then come out of the vineyards and seize each man his wife from the daughters of Shiloh, and go to the land of Benjamin. [22]And when their fathers or their brothers come to complain to us, we will say to them, 'Grant them graciously to us; because we did not take for each man of them his wife in battle, neither did you give them to them, else you would now be guilty.'" [23]And the Benjaminites did so, and took their wives, according to their number, from the dancers whom they carried off; then they went and returned to their inheritance, and rebuilt the towns, and dwelt in them. [24]And the people of Israel departed from there at that time, every man to his tribe and family, and they went out from there every man to his inheritance.

[25]In those days there was no king in Israel; every man did what was right in his own eyes.

This odd narrative is in many respects a fitting conclusion to the closing chapters of Judges. As in some of the preceding sections, the commentator must walk a difficult path between making too little and too much of striking features in the text. Certainly there is nothing else quite like it in the Bible.

(i)

For a third time this book returns to the theme of weeping at Bethel. We commented on it at 2:1–5, but passed it over in 20:26. In each passage there is talk of sacrifice (and burnt offering), seemingly in order for a legitimate sanctuary of Yahweh. Yet our knowledge that for the Deuteronomists at least this temple's status was questionable makes us suspect that these outer parts of the Book of Judges were doing more than simply explaining why a sacred oak was called the Oak of Weeping. All this unhappiness at a sanctuary hints at a basic instability.

However, the weeping plays a further role in the structure of this chapter. As in the battle sequences of chapter 20, the story-telling is rather repetitive. It may be that here too different sources have been combined. That is a likely enough explanation for the presence of two quite different stratagems for providing womenfolk for Benjamin. But other aspects like the repeated query (vv. 5 and 8) about absentees from Mizpah find a ready explanation in the context of the people's great lamentation. That brings with it a certain indecisiveness and lack of direction.

(ii)

Of all the characters in this strange story, it is for the people in Jabesh in Gilead that our sympathy is most appropriate. Having diminished the totality of Israel by their action against one of its members, the tribes go further down the same road—repairing the breach to Benjamin at the cost of extinction for some Trans-jordanians. It seems very much like robbing Peter to pay Paul. We are reminded too of our political leaders, who often appear so wedded to their own ideology that, when satisfactory results do not emerge, they tell us we need more of their policies, and not less.

But why the people of Jabesh? The story states that they had been absent from the tragic proceedings in chapter 20, although if anything that chapter hinted the reverse, claiming a complete muster including Gilead (20:1). Yet why does the *story* make this claim? I assume, if I may rather quixotically disregard the proper sequence of events, that they are paying the price of their future good relations with Saul. The town appears just four times in the Bible. We observed when discussing the dismembered concubine that Saul's similar action in 1 Sam. 11 was a response to a cruel threat against Jabesh from Nahash of Ammon. 1 Sam. 31:11–13 tells of the city's return kindness in stealing Saul's corpse from the

Philistines and giving it decent burial. It seems that when David heard of the piety (2 Sam. 2:4) he was not quite sure of their loyalty (to him):

> David sent messengers to the men of Jabesh-gilead, and said to them, "May you be blessed by the Lord, because you showed this loyalty to Saul your lord, and buried him! Now may the Lord show steadfast love and faithfulness to you! And I will do good to you because you have done this thing. Now therefore let your hands be strong, and be valiant; for Saul your lord is dead, and the house of Judah has anointed me king over them."
>
> (vv. 5–7)

I suspect that most of the speech is simply a polite prelude to the last news—I am king now, and don't you forget it! Finally 2 Sam. 21, which depicts David acquiescing in further mistreatment of Saul's family worthy of enemy Philistines, talks simply (v. 12) of the men of Jabesh stealing Saul's bones for the Philistines. To have been closer to Saul than David was not a good thing for any city's reputation!

(iii)

It is likely that something much more substantial than vindictive memory lies behind the rape of the Shiloh dancers. There are similar tales from other Mediterranean peoples. Best known is the fabled Roman rape of the nearby Sabine women organized by old Romulus himself. Perhaps more relevant is a Greek story about the men of Messene snatching virgins during a feast to the goddess Artemis. The fact that the victims in vv. 16–24 are dancing at a major festival at the great sanctuary of Shiloh at the time of the vintage makes it probable that our narrative is based on memory of ancient practices. Wine festivals are often associated with behaviour more exotic than the norm, including a degree of sexual licence. If at some stage in Israelite tradition such doings became questionable, the memory of the past could be made less scandalous by claiming that it happened just once—and in controlled circumstances.

(iv)

There is quite a deal of controversy among scholars over how to evaluate the assembly's "solutions" to these problems Israel faced in Judg. 19–21. Some I feel are blinded by their idealistic vision of an Israelite confederacy of twelve tribes. God was able to rule through its councils, and with the aid of judge/deliverers, quite adequately, while the later king and all the trappings of his court provided an unwelcome counterweight. Now it is true that some Old Testament traditions are hostile to the monarchy, and others no more than neutral about it. But we have met no traditions in the Book of Judges before these last two chapters which have pictured *all* Israel acting in concert.

I am clear that the narrator wants us to be appalled at the result of the assembly's deliberations. He reminds us, in the very last verse of the chapter and of the book, that all this happened when "there was no king in Israel; every man did what was right in his own eyes." That *could* just mean that people without a king were able to follow successfully their own lights. But that is not what it *does* mean. The "right" they did was wrong in God's sight. However, the anti-Saul propaganda and hints like the mention of Bethlehem in Judah suggest to me that these chapters do not look for salvation from *any* king, but look forward beyond Saul to a *proper* king.

(v)

In general the Old Testament does not talk about the past just for its own sake. If there is such emphasis on a time when there *were* no kings, it is likely the material is addressed to a time when there *are* no kings. A date in post-exilic times, after the collapse of Jerusalem in 586 B.C. and the Davidic monarchy with it, is therefore likely. That would square well with our earlier observation that these outer chapters of the book are supplementary to the Deuteronomic material on the judges (chapters 2–16), itself from the exilic period. Such a context encourages us to see one further layer of meaning in chapter 21.

After the general blood-letting of the recent campaign, blundered into with blame on all sides, there was need for restoration.

Benjamin might simply represent the broken community in need of rebuilding. But more likely it stands for something more precise. The problem stated is a refusal of marriage relations. Benjamin may represent a community, whether in Palestine or in the Diaspora, whose ostracism had to be overcome, who had to be brought back into fellowship. It may be that the royal, "messianic" ideal of the end of Judges is an ecumenical ideal as well.

RUTH

The Book of Ruth does not easily fit the conventions of this volume and series. It is a very carefully structured short story. In a manner typical of ancient Hebrew narrative not a single word is spare—and almost every sentence is worth pondering. Yet it is a single whole and the most useful task for the first day of study would be to ignore the various commentary sections and read the whole text of Ruth in a sitting. The four chapter divisions have their point and we will find it useful to consider smaller sections. However, each of these is only one element in the total artistic conception and it is well to start by reminding ourselves of this.

A SORRY SITUATION

Ruth 1:1–5

> In the days when the judges ruled there was a famine in the land, and a certain man of Bethlehem in Judah went to sojourn in the country of Moab, he and his wife and his two sons. ²The name of the man was Elimelech and the name of his wife Naomi, and the names of his two sons were Mahlon and Chilion; they were Ephrathites from Bethlehem in Judah. They went into the country of Moab and remained there. ³But Elimelech, the husband of Naomi, died, and she was left with her two sons. ⁴These took Moabite wives; the name of one was Orpah and the name of the other Ruth. They lived there about ten years; ⁵and both Mahlon and Chilion died, so that the woman was bereft of her two sons and her husband.

Ruth has been read in many different ways. This is partly because readers and students over the ages have brought their own very different attitudes and questions to their reading of the book. Another part of the reason is the very craft of the story-teller. Part of the skill shown in telling the tale consists in letting it address different readers in different situations.

It has been seen as a period piece—a tract for the times. In fact this approach has led to quite different datings for the story. Many have seen it as an artful protest against the exclusive nationalism encouraged in the period after Judah's exile in Babylon in the Books of Ezra and Nehemiah. An important feature of this policy was the repudiation of marriages between Jews and foreign women. The story of Ruth is told to argue for a more open policy and quotes the example of great King David's grandparents in its support. If this approach is valid the book must belong to around 400 B.C.

Another approach is to see Ruth as an attempt to defuse a much earlier situation. The Biblical traditions make plain that kingship in Judah and Israel was a contentious institution from its beginnings. Despite a military prowess many times greater than Saul's, despite the personal charm evident in many of the stories told about him, David confirmed, by his very ruthlessness and by his dealings with women who were not always of his own stock, some of the fears of those who were suspicious of monarchy in any case. His detractors may well have noted wryly that no better could be expected of someone with *Moabite* blood in his veins. Was the story of Ruth first told in the time of David to demonstrate that his ancestress was no ordinary Moabite but a woman who could hold her own in any company?

The book has been read and ransacked by historians. What may it tell us about relations between Judah and Moab? How rich are the seams of information we can mine for our store of knowledge about customary law—about women and property rights; about the responsibilities for a childless widow; about the recovery of alienated land? Just two points about these legal and historical interests before we pass on: (1) The earlier we feel able to date the *telling* of the story, the more reliable we may expect the information in that story to be. Yet (2), part of the humour and excitement of a good story may result from the *unaccustomed* and out-of-the-ordinary way its characters behave. That may make it a bad guide for the student of ordinary behaviour and normal custom.

I should like to mention one further perspective before turning to the opening verses. There is an increasing recognition amongst students of the Bible that there may be many examples within the Bible itself of a particular type of story telling which became prominent in Judaism after the Biblical period and which is known by its later Hebrew name *midrash*. Such stories often have an entertaining function but are of a much more serious purpose as well. And the purpose is often to seek to explain a difficult Biblical text and even to "tame" a Biblical command or explanation or situation which came to seem difficult or out of place or even improper in a later situation. Ruth itself reminds us just before its conclusion of the rather more risqué story of how Judah's daughter-in-law Tamar secured her widow's rights (Gen. 38). Perhaps Ruth is in part a "midrashic" re-presentation of the Tamar story.

Much more comment could be hung on these opening verses. However, I make only a few specific comments briefly.

1. The Judean hill country, like much of Palestine, is not rich farmland. Families must quite often have had to go for food elsewhere, like the caravan of Jacob's sons trekking to Egypt for food which forms the backdrop to the Joseph story. David himself chose Moab as a secure place to leave some of his family when he was in danger (1 Sam. 22:3–4).

2. Just as we have seen a number of times in the Book of Judges, so in Ruth some at least of the names are chosen to illustrate the characteristics of the actors in the drama. The end of chapter 1 sees Naomi herself deploring the meaning of her name. It is no great surprise to the Hebrew reader that Mahlon and Chilion come to an early death in Moab—the one reminds us of the Hebrew word for "illness" and the other of the verb "to come to an end". What more could be expected of a sickly, feeble pair?

3. We should note how quickly and subtly Naomi becomes one of the book's central characters. In verse 2 the lads are introduced as Elimelech's sons—and by verse 3 they are already hers. Despite the fact that the book bears Ruth's name, Naomi herself will never be far from the action.

4. The gaping wound which the opening five verses portray is of this woman left bereft of any man (v. 5)—husband or sons. It is to this situation that the closing verses of the story speak (4:14–17). Her neighbours in Bethlehem know that the baby is—after all else is said and done—most importantly *her* child. And many a long-suffering granny knows what that means.

RETURN TO BETHLEHEM

Ruth 1:6–22

⁶Then she started with her daughters-in-law to return from the country of Moab, for she had heard in the country of Moab that the Lord had visited his people and given them food. ⁷So she set out from the place where she was, with her two daughters-in-law, and they went on the way to return to the land of Judah. ⁸But Naomi said to her two daughters-in-law, "Go, return each of you to her mother's house. May the Lord deal kindly with you, as you have dealt with the dead and with me. ⁹The Lord grant that you may find a home, each of you in the house of her husband!" Then she kissed them, and they lifted up their voices and wept. ¹⁰And they said to her, "No, we will return with you to your people." ¹¹But Naomi said, "Turn back, my daughters, why will you go with me? Have I yet sons in my womb that they may become your husbands? ¹²Turn back, my daughters, go your way, for I am too old to have a husband. If I should say I have hope, even if I should have a husband this night and should bear sons, ¹³would you therefore wait till they were grown? Would you therefore refrain from marrying? No, my daughters, for it is exceedingly bitter to me for your sake that the hand of the Lord has gone forth against me." ¹⁴Then they lifted up their voices and wept again; and Orpah kissed her mother-in-law, but Ruth clung to her.

¹⁵And she said, "See, your sister-in-law has gone back to her people and to her gods; return after your sister-in-law." ¹⁶But Ruth said, "Entreat me not to leave you or to return from following you; for where you go I will go, and where you lodge I will lodge; your people shall be my people, and your God my God; ¹⁷where you die I will die, and there will I be buried. May the Lord do so to me and more also if even death parts me from you." ¹⁸And when Naomi saw that she was determined to go with her, she said no more.

¹⁹So the two of them went on until they came to Bethlehem. And when they came to Bethlehem, the whole town was stirred because of them; and the women said, "Is this Naomi?" ²⁰She said to them, "Do not call me Naomi, call me Mara, for the Almighty has dealt very bitterly with me. ²¹I went away full, and the Lord has brought me back empty. Why call me Naomi, when the Lord has afflicted me and the Almighty has brought calamity upon me?"

²²So Naomi returned, and Ruth the Moabitess her daughter-in-law with her, who returned from the country of Moab. And they came to Bethlehem at the beginning of barley harvest.

The complexities and conflicts in the Book of Ruth mirror those of life itself and certainly those of life before God. It is becoming commonplace in this age of psychological awareness to recognize that all of us are many characters at the same time with competing perceptions and aspirations. A report has reached Moab that there is food again in Judah. This the story sees as the Lord's doing (v. 6) and Naomi immediately sets off back home. Hunger (for which God is *not* blamed) had driven the family away from Bethlehem. God's good provision allows them back.

Yet Naomi's experience has taught her that the Lord is not just the author of good. When the women of Bethlehem are "in a stir", as at least one of the two strangers is recognized, Naomi snaps at them with an angry pun on her own name: How can they call her "Naomi", the pleasant one? They must understand that "Mara", bitter, would be more appropriate. And that too was the Lord's doing. She had left Bethlehem "full": and that is a striking way for a refugee from a famine-torn country to remember the circumstances of her leaving! But at least she had had a husband and two sons and time heals some wounds, while others get forgotten when new ones strike. The hungry refugee now remembers she was full when she left and that she deserved the name Naomi at that time. On her return to a place of plenty she is empty and embittered.

We have already noted how economically the story is told. In just a few words our narrator hints at a situation which other story-tellers would have lingered over in loving detail. Dialogue is important here but it is very restrained. It is the business of the critic or commentator to note this but not to supply what the story-teller has deliberately not offered. In fact, if we care to, any of us can supply the details from our own imagination and experience. Naomi seems to have started back to Bethlehem on a first impulse. Only when the three widows were under way did she suggest a return to their own homes to her two daughters-in-law. But what did she want? Did she know what she wanted? All of us know family life well enough, whether from good experience of it or bad, to be aware that proposals are not always what they seem. She kisses the young women farewell—perhaps the formal salute familiar in many cultures of a perfunctory kiss on each cheek accompanied by a light embrace. This Orpah reciprocates but Ruth clings to her, will not be fobbed off, and her poignant protestation (vv. 16 and 17) is all the more eloquent and effective against the background of a narrative which is so restrained as a whole.

Though I realize the danger of marring such fine words by pedestrian comment there are two points I would like to make.

The first is that the climax of Ruth's protestation comes not with her taking Naomi's God to be her God—that seems to follow naturally after taking Naomi's people as her people—but with her declaration that this is forever. Ruth's words go beyond the familiar "till you are parted by death" of the marriage service. She and Naomi will not be parted *even in death*. It is these words that mark her irrevocable break with Moab. The Old Testament is replete with references to the family grave. Death is followed by burial with your fathers. Being gathered to your fathers is a regular euphemism for dying. We are all familiar with those who loyally relinquish career opportunities, marriage prospects, privacy at home or on holiday, to support relatives or others in need and mostly these situations are temporary, "till death us do part". Ruth's commitment is total, not just in intensity but also in duration.

Secondly, this makes her pledge eminently suitable as a vow of Christian pilgrimage to a master from whom we shall not be separated even in death—to a master who calls us to leave family in his service. And when we are thinking of Jesus' words we should remember that in their original meaning the "mansions", of which there are many in his Father's house, are "stopping places" where we may "lodge" on our journey.

But we have gone too far too fast. Before we leave chapter 1 we should note, secondly, that the words with which Naomi attempts to dispatch her daughters-in-law also introduce a main theme of the book (vv. 11–13). Naomi ideally has first responsibility for the girls. Both the story of Tamar in Gen. 38 and the statement of the Law in Deut. 25:5–10 show that the first expectation of a young widow was to be married to another brother in her husband's family. But Naomi herself is widowed, she has not been left pregnant, and she is too old to find another husband, and so she says that she cannot provide. We will soon learn that in so saying "she is selling herself short".

"AMID ALIEN CORN" I

Ruth 2:1–23

1Now Naomi had a kinsman of her husband's, a man of wealth, of the family of Elimelech, whose name was Boaz. 2And Ruth the Moabitess said to Naomi, "Let me go to the field, and glean among the ears of grain after him in whose sight I shall find favour." And she said to her, "Go, my daughter." 3So she set forth and went and gleaned in the field after the reapers; and she happened to come to the part of the field belonging to Boaz, who was of the family of Elimelech. 4And behold, Boaz came from Bethlehem; and he said to the reapers, "The Lord be with you!" And they answered, "The Lord bless you." 5Then Boaz said to his servant who was in charge of the reapers, "Whose maiden is this?" 6And the servant who was in charge of the reapers answered, "It is the Moabite maiden, who came back with Naomi from the country of Moab. 7She said, 'Pray, let me glean and gather among the sheaves after the reapers.' So she came, and she has continued from early morning until now, without resting even for a moment."

8Then Boaz said to Ruth, "Now, listen, my daughter, do not go to glean in another field or leave this one, but keep close to my maidens. 9Let your eyes be upon the field which they are reaping, and go after them. Have I not charged the young men not to molest you? And when you are thirsty, go to the vessels and drink what the young men have drawn." ¹⁰Then she fell on her face, bowing to the ground, and said to him, "Why have I found favour in your eyes, that you should take notice of me, when I am a foreigner?" ¹¹But Boaz answered her, "All that you have done for your mother-in-law since the death of your husband has been fully told me, and how you left your father and mother and your native land and came to a people that you did not know before. ¹²The Lord recompense you for what you have done, and a full reward be given you by the Lord, the God of Israel, under whose wings you have come to take refuge!" ¹³Then she said, "You are most gracious to me, my lord, for you have comforted me and spoken kindly to your maidservant, though I am not one of your maidservants."

¹⁴And at mealtime Boaz said to her, "Come here, and eat some bread, and dip your morsel in the wine." So she sat beside the reapers, and he passed to her parched grain; and she ate until she was satisfied, and she had some left over. ¹⁵When she rose to glean, Boaz instructed his young men, saying, "Let her glean even among the sheaves, and do not reproach her. ¹⁶And also pull out some from the bundles for her, and leave it for her to glean, and do not rebuke her."

¹⁷So she gleaned in the field until evening; then she beat out what she had gleaned, and it was about an ephah of barley. ¹⁸And she took it up and went into the city; she showed her mother-in-law what she had gleaned, and she also brought out and gave her what food she had left over after being satisfied. ¹⁹And her mother-in-law said to her, "Where did you glean today? And where have you worked? Blessed be the man who took notice of you." So she told her mother-in-law with whom she had worked, and said, "The man's name with whom I worked today is Boaz." ²⁰And Naomi said to her daughter-in-law, "Blessed be he by the Lord, whose kindness has not forsaken the living or the dead!" Naomi also said to her, "The man is a relative of ours, one of our nearest kin." ²¹And Ruth the Moabitess said, "Besides, he said to me, 'You shall keep close by my servants, till they have finished all my harvest.'" ²²And Naomi said to Ruth, her daughter-in-law, "It is well, my daughter, that you go out with his maidens, lest in another field you be molested." ²³So she kept close to the maidens of Boaz, gleaning until the end of the barley and wheat harvests; and she lived with her mother-in-law.

The opening verse is not so much the beginning of the story told in chapter 2—that begins in verse 2—as a comment on it all. Ruth sets out to look for any opening. Naomi only finds out when she comes home (vv. 19–20) that it was with Boaz that Ruth had worked. But we the readers are let into the secret early. Verse 1 can be read like chapter headings in rather older novels which run like this: *How Justin ran away and Amelia consoled herself in his absence.* It was a convenient device and in its absence modern readers have to resort to cheating—they must skip to the end of the chapter or even the end of the story so that they know *what* will happen; and, with that excitement removed, read *how* it happens in a relaxed and attentive way. Boaz has an advantage over the two women. He knows just who is who when he asks his staff about the stranger in their midst in verses 5–6. But we the readers know about Boaz from the outset.

This Boaz belonged to Elimelech's *family*—and of course that means his clan, his extended family. He was also a man of substance—that seems to me closer to the original idea than "a man of wealth". The Hebrew word used (*hayil*) reminds us of the best of traditional feudal values. We are thinking of a man with some land and so of independent means. At his best he is supportive of his staff. When war comes he is a knight because he can afford a horse and ideally there he will evidence courage. In short *hayil* has overtones of both (modest) wealth and virtue. Hence the translation "man of substance", substantial person—or "man of worth". Then, of vital importance to Naomi, she knew that he knew her husband. That is all the Hebrew text says and the ancient Greek translation. Although at least as old as the King James Version it is a modern import into the translation to turn acquaintance into kinship. And it is an import that spoils the logic of the verse. That Boaz is of her late husband's kith and kin is made clear in a later phrase (v. 20).

We have been reading this opening verse backwards and have not yet stressed its beginning. Young Ruth goes out to take her chance but old Naomi knows someone. This is yet another example of something we have already discussed in chapter 1. We saw there, in connection with full and empty, bitter and pleasant, how the Book of Ruth invites us to see things from different perspectives; and another such double perspective runs through chapter 2 as a whole.

People often ask, "Is it fate or is it providence?" or "Is it luck or is it God?" It seems that Ruth prefers not to make such a distinction. Verse 3 tells us that Ruth "happened to come to the part of the field belonging to Boaz". However, when she tells her mother-in-law the news of the day, Naomi calls down a blessing on Boaz from the Lord "whose kindness has not forsaken the living or the dead" (v. 20).

Some of the subtleties of this chapter as indeed of the whole book are not readily translatable from Hebrew into English. However, they may be enjoyed by English readers once their attention has been drawn to them. "Servant" in verses 5 and 6, and "maiden" in the same verses, are just the masculine and feminine forms of the same noun in Hebrew—*na'ar*. The word refers to a junior, whether in age or in status. More or less equivalent English terms vary from area to area and from group to group. The male and female equivalents of *na'ar* might be "lad" and "lass"; "boy" and "girl" work all right for juniors in age—and "boy" certainly operates in colonial English for a (coloured) servant. Such a "boy" can even have a responsible position over the other reapers. Masculine and feminine plural forms of the noun are used frequently between verses 8 and 23 and are variously translated by the RSV as "young men", "servants", "maidens". There is even some subtle mischief between older and younger generations concerning Ruth's relations with Boaz's "lads" and "lasses". Boaz instructs Ruth to "keep close to my *maid*-servants". Ruth retails this to her mother-in-law as "You shall keep close by my servants" (v. 21), who remarks to her, "It is well my daughter that you go out with his *maid*-servants" (v. 22). Ruth is quite clear that she can look after herself in mixed company.

"AMID ALIEN CORN" II

Ruth 2:1–23 (*cont'd*)

Many visitors to the Middle East are still delighted to find old

world politeness as a living tradition. Apparently effortless
choice of the right word is almost an art form. It is still regarded as
very casual to return someone's greetings in his own words; and
so when Boaz enters his field with "the Lord be with you", his
reapers vary the phrase and answer "the Lord bless you". Then,
when he spots the stranger, he neither addresses her directly nor
does he infringe the rights of any man in her life. His question
(v. 5) seeks information about her husband or her father or her
master—for a girl would never be independent. Only when he
finds there is no man responsible for her, only Naomi, whom he
presumably knows to be a kinswoman, does he address Ruth
directly.

Ruth's responses to Boaz in verses 10 and 13 are a very model
of tact, although we have to rescue verse 13 a little from the
translators of the RSV. The very phrase the story uses—"find
favour in someone's eyes"—sums up the delicacy of the situation
beautifully. It recognizes on the one side how much we say,
especially with our eyes, before we even begin to speak. But it is
also aware on the other that such non-verbal communication
requires to be interpreted, discerned or "found". Between
strangers it is both more important and more fragile. To be paid
attention to, taken notice of, especially when you are a stranger,
can often be unwelcome. It depends on the *sort* of attention. Ruth
discerns favour in the overture but delicately questions the favour
with her "why" and then disarmingly provides Boaz with a way of
retreat should she have gone too far. She herself supplies a
matter-of-fact reason for notice taken—that she is a foreigner.

Following Boaz's enthusiastic response, which shows that he
knows Naomi's story, and believes that Ruth deserves well of his
God, Ruth again advances her case with some tact (v. 13). The
RSV's translation of her opening words conceals the fact that
they use the same phrase as she opened with in verse 10 but this
time without a question and so more positively. Then she was
exploring what had lain behind a simple invitation. When she
now opens, "I am finding favour in your eyes", she is no longer

exploring a simple past action but is describing the present and even seeking to discern the future. The other lapse of the translators in this verse is at the end where the Hebrew is much more subtle: it ends "... though I am not *as* one of your maid-servants." She has termed herself his "maid-servant" and then discreetly notes that this may not be so. The words cover two meanings and doubtless both are intended! She could be covering possible presumption and she could already be open to higher preferment—not *even* a servant, or not *just* a servant.

There is certainly a corresponding progression in Boaz's treatment of Ruth. Learning who she is he is immediately protective towards her. He calls her "my daughter". He not only permits her to work in his field but suggests she need not look elsewhere at all; and promises that there will be no unwelcome attention from his lads. An unprotected young widow would be "fair game". As we saw in connection with Rahab (Josh. 2), it was often the lot of a widow to become a prostitute. After her first response he notes that her service to Naomi deserves full recompense on the Lord's account and his own actions are commensurate with his words. He makes a fuss of her at the lunchtime picnic when we read that she ate and was satisfied and had some left over. "Satisfied" here does not mean that her needs were met but rather that she was "sated". The substantial snack over, Boaz is quite as generous in his instructions. Widows and orphans might reasonably expect the pickings after the harvesters had finished. Ruth was to glean among the *sheaves* without obstruction. The harvesters were even to untie some of their bundles to allow her to get more. The result of this profuse generosity was a take-home amount of an *ephah* of barley. Modern estimates of this ancient measure vary widely between some thirteen and some twenty-five kilograms. Even the smaller amount is an absurdly large "gleaning".

We turn briefly to Naomi waiting at home. It is difficult to decide whether emotion is revealed or concealed in her first remarks to Ruth: "Where did you glean today? And where have you worked? Blessed be the man who took notice of you." Was all this said in wide-eyed amazement at the amount of barley brought home and the left-overs from the picnic; or is the excitement suppressed under everyday questions? Does "Blessed be the man..." imply something special; or does it give away no more than we might if we said "Thank God somebody gave you a job". Naomi seems to show more excitement once Boaz has been mentioned but the excitement is channelled into a doxology—another kind of set formula. Then, when Ruth reports that she is welcome in the field until the very end of harvest, Naomi makes a typically safe parental response: "It's a good thing you are to be there, you might get into trouble elsewhere."

When the story-teller has Naomi address Ruth as "my daughter" in verse 22, he deftly puts a bracket round Ruth's conversations both with Boaz and Naomi, because that is how Boaz first addresses her in verse 8. This is just a first example of something that holds throughout the rest of the book. Boaz and Naomi never meet, but they think and speak the same way. They share the same attitudes and seem to know what to expect of each other. They communicate through Ruth and each understands the other's signals.

Naomi has remained at home throughout chapter 2. In a sense she has been more passive than we find her in either chapter 1 or chapter 3. Yet in a sense she is still the dominating figure. We already noticed that her name begins the chapter and mention of her ends the chapter too. Boaz's hospitality in the field stretches from barley harvest into wheat harvest (from Passover time to Pentecost)—and all the time Ruth is resident with Naomi.

AT MIDNIGHT ON THE THRESHING FLOOR

Ruth 3:1–18

¹Then Naomi her mother-in-law said to her, "My daughter, should I not seek a home for you, that it may be well with you? ²Now is not Boaz our kinsman, with whose maidens you were? See, he is winnowing barley tonight at the threshing floor. ³Wash therefore and anoint yourself, and put on your best clothes and go down to the threshing floor; but do not make yourself known to the man until he has finished eating and drinking. ⁴But when he lies down, observe the place where

he lies; then, go and uncover his feet and lie down; and he will tell you what to do." ⁵And she replied, "All that you say I will do."

⁶So she went down to the threshing floor and did just as her mother-in-law had told her. ⁷And when Boaz had eaten and drunk, and his heart was merry, he went to lie down at the end of the heap of grain. Then she came softly, and uncovered his feet, and lay down. ⁸At midnight the man was startled, and turned over, and behold, a woman lay at his feet! ⁹He said, "Who are you?" And she answered, "I am Ruth, your maidservant; spread your skirt over your maidservant, for you are next of kin." ¹⁰And he said, "May you be blessed by the Lord, my daughter; you have made this last kindness greater than the first, in that you have not gone after young men, whether poor or rich. ¹¹And now, my daughter, do not fear, I will do for you all that you ask, for all my fellow townsmen know that you are a woman of worth. ¹²And now it is true that I am a near kinsman, yet there is a kinsman nearer than I. ¹³Remain this night, and in the morning, if he will do the part of the next of kin for you, well; let him do it; but if he is not willing to do the part of the next of kin for you, then, as the Lord lives, I will do the part of the next of kin for you. Lie down until the morning."

¹⁴So she lay at his feet until the morning, but arose before one could recognise another; and he said, "Let it not be known that the woman came to the threshing floor." ¹⁵And he said, "Bring the mantle you are wearing and hold it out." So she held it, and he measured out six measures of barley, and laid it upon her; then she went into the city. ¹⁶And when she came to her mother-in-law, she said, "How did you fare, my daughter?" Then she told her all that the man had done for her, ¹⁷saying, "These six measures of barley he gave to me, for he said, 'You must not go back empty-handed to your mother-in-law.'" ¹⁸She replied, "Wait, my daughter, until you learn how the matter turns out, for the man will not rest, but will settle the matter today."

Many readers of the Bible are surprised when they turn to this vital episode in the story of Ruth. How can Naomi encourage Ruth to be such a forward young lady? Before we say any more we note yet again that this chapter too begins and ends with Naomi.

The two women have been back in Bethlehem for some few weeks. Ruth has fared well over the period of the grain harvest. Naomi now returns to the concern she expressed in 1:9—that her daughter-in-law should have her "home", a place of rest and security; and so she takes steps!

Students of the religion of ancient Israel are familiar with the fact that the main religious festivals each year were linked to the agricultural calendar. Passover and Unleavened Bread came first at the time of barley harvest. Then about seven weeks later followed the Feast of Weeks or Pentecost at the end of the wheat harvest. Then the Feast of In-gathering or the Feast of Booths (*Succoth* in Hebrew) came at the end of the summer when the harvest of the various fruits was complete. The other more local aspect of the matter is illustrated here. Each of these occasions was the opportunity for a good party. Naomi instructs Ruth to make her move when Boaz will be content, at least a little tipsy, and at his most receptive. Yet nothing should be left to chance—she should both smell and look her best.

Yet just what does take place between Boaz and Ruth after the party in the middle of the night? Typically little is stated explicitly and much is only suggested. Readers are left to judge for themselves whether they are dealing with delicacy of feeling or deliberate innuendo. There are certainly some significant cases of double meaning. Ruth is instructed not to make herself known to the man until after the party. Is this a matter of wearing a veil and not allowing him to recognize her, or should we remember the frequent use of "know" in Hebrew, and in English too, in the sense of *sexual* knowledge? What is meant by uncovering his feet and lying down at them? Should we remember that the Hebrew word *regel* refers to the whole limb from the thigh to the toes? If we translate "uncover his 'legs'", we would get a different and perhaps more accurate picture of what the text intends. At least we learn from verse 8 that Ruth is positioned where Boaz will notice her when he rolls over. How far is this more suggestive reading of the episode more appropriate? At least it must be clear that it does not stand alone in the Old Testament. We should remember the steps taken by Tamar to secure a child by Judah when he would not make due arrangement for his son (see Gen. 38:13–19) and the stratagem of Lot's daughters (Gen. 19:30–38) when they feared they would die without issue.

Ruth's night-time initiative was certainly open to misinterpretation—Boaz's unwillingness (v. 14) to let it become public knowledge makes that clear. But we have two different indications that it was neither unwelcome nor improper. Boaz, after he recovers from his first surprise, certainly does not take her visit amiss. He blesses her, he describes her approach in terms of *hesed*: a rich word that is always hard to translate—but it may involve even more of "loyalty" than "kindness". And he talks of her high reputation in Bethlehem. Clearly he does not believe her reputation is impaired. Of course one could scoff, suggest that the middle-aged man's head has been "turned" by young Ruth seeking him out rather than a younger man (v. 10). However, I do not feel that that is what the text intends.

The other indication that her approach to Boaz should be applauded I find in the language used in the Hebrew text in verse 9 when Ruth claims Boaz as "her next of kin". The Hebrew word is *go'el*. That word is often and properly translated "redeemer". We shall leave a fuller discussion of the term until we consider the beginning of chapter 4. All I want to insist on here is that she is making a claim on Boaz which has important social, legal and religious overtones. The second point which has to be spelled out—and it may seem rather strange at first sight—is that the Hebrew word *kanaph*, translated "skirt" in our verse, is the same word as we met in 2:12 where its plural form was rendered "wings". Ruth returns to Boaz an expression very similar to one he has used to her. Then he hoped God would repay her for her loyalty—that God under the cover of whose spreading wings she had come to take refuge. Ruth now challenges Boaz to become an agent of that repayment and to spread his cover over her.

Before we leave this scene we should notice that Boaz sends Ruth away not just with a promise that he will try to square the legal problems involved in her proposition, but also with a practical pledge of grain—a token of fertility and fruitfulness—telling her that she should not return to her mother-in-law "empty" (v. 17). This is exactly the word Naomi had used herself bitterly as she described how the Lord had brought her back to Bethlehem. Naomi had left Bethlehem full and been brought back empty. However Ruth was not returning to her empty.

REDEMPTION

Ruth 4:1–6

¹And Boaz went up to the gate and sat down there; and behold, the next of kin, of whom Boaz had spoken, came by. So Boaz said, "Turn aside, friend; sit down here"; and he turned aside and sat down. ²And he took ten men of the elders of the city, and said, "Sit down here"; so they sat down. ³Then he said to the next of kin, "Naomi, who has come back from the country of Moab, is selling the parcel of land which belonged to our kinsman Elimelech. ⁴So I thought I would tell you of it, and say, Buy it in the presence of those sitting here, and in the presence of the elders of my people. If you will redeem it, redeem it; but if you will not, tell me, that I may know, for there is no one besides you to redeem it, and I come after you." And he said, "I will redeem it." ⁵Then Boaz said, "The day you buy the field from the hand of Naomi, you are also buying Ruth the Moabitess, the widow of the dead, in order to restore the name of the dead to his inheritance." ⁶Then the next of kin said, "I cannot redeem it for myself, lest I impair my own inheritance. Take my right of redemption yourself, for I cannot redeem it."

Most of us know the word "redemption" in one or other of two contexts. We use it in back-street economic terms as the word to describe the buying back of some item of value left as a pledge or deposit with a pawnbroker or money-lender. And we know it also in Christian theological terms as one of the words which describes the deliverance achieved by Jesus Christ.

The situation described here is rather different. The essence of "redemption" in the story of Ruth is family solidarity and responsibility. We sketched the main features when discussing Joshua 20—that special case of family responsibility where family blood has been shed.

(i)

In a relatively poor agricultural environment people and land are mutually dependent. If the area of land is diminished in some way there is a danger that its people will not be fed. If, on the other hand, the people are reduced there is a danger that the land will not be fully worked, and so will be less than fully productive. The people of the Old Testament had customary law to deal with both of these dangerous situations. (a) A free-born independent land-working citizen might be forced by circumstances to sell himself into slavery to his economic creditor. Alternatively a man might die without fathering a family to succeed him. (b) Death in the family through disease or war, accident, or exile because of famine, could result in family land lapsing into unproductivity. Both together are the presenting problem in the Book of Ruth. Elimelech is forced off his land because of famine; and while *he* does provide a family, both of his sons die without achieving this.

(ii)

It seems that taking the initiative towards "redemption" was more of a responsibility than a right. There was clearly an ideal order of priority within any family when it had to find a "re-deemer"—and this priority was probably simply closeness in blood relationship. Boaz was perfectly willing to undertake responsibility for Ruth but he knew that another member of his clan was closer to Elimelech than he himself. Naomi may have suspected as much: when Ruth first mentioned his name to her she responded, "The man is a relative of ours, one of our nearest kin" (2:20). He was a potential redeemer but not the only possible one.

It appears from the opening of Ruth 4 that Boaz played a trick on the closer relative. If we knew the law better we might be more confident in our reading of the story. (Yet we have to remind ourselves that good stories often concentrate on exceptional as-pects of the law rather than its normal workings.) Throughout the first three chapters of the book, security for Ruth has been a recurring theme—and this she would find in the home of a hus-band (1:9). Boaz has been receptive to her midnight overture. However, he surprises most modern readers by immediately taking a public initiative over the plot of land Elimelech had deserted for exile many years before. Securing a quorum of ten citizens at the proper place of business—the wide space at the city gate—he tells his unnamed relative that Naomi has put the plot of land up for sale. The relative is willing to buy and keep the land within the wider family. Apparently this closer relative knows nothing of widow Ruth. Elimelech had lost both land and family but he did have a daughter-in-law who was willing to secure family for him. When confronted with this "intelligence" the "redeemer" renounces his rights to acquire the land. If Elimelech had had no heir the land would have passed into the "redeemer's" section of the wider family. However, if widow Ruth passed to the "redeemer" along with the land then her child whom he would father would be legally deemed Elimelech's heir. Then in time the money and effort he and his own family put into the redeemed land would be lost to them as Ruth's son came to take responsibility for his own land. And so his response: "I cannot redeem it for myself, lest I impair my own inheritance" (4:6).

(iii)

The story gives us no clue as to whether this mysterious unnamed character acted responsibly or irresponsibly. He certainly pleased Boaz and Ruth—their marriage could go forward and their love prosper. But equally he was certainly in a situation which many of us face again and again. Service beckons—and we do not know whether it is an opportunity or an obligation. Our excuses are often expressed in terms of solemn undertakings already given such as our family commitments. "I cannot . . . lest I impair my own inheritance."

Those who seek to shape their lives by the gospel tradition must remember the several sayings which warn against giving the family an ultimate veto. Jesus talks of those who have left house or brothers or sisters or mother or father or children or land for his sake and for the gospel (Mark 10:29); and he also notes that "Whoever does the will of God is my brother, and sister, and mother" (Mark 3:35).

Christians may not readily think of *themselves* as sharing in the responsibility of *redemption*. Yet solidarity with brother and neighbour is precisely our calling—with brothers who are not of our own family, and with neighbours who are far from our own doors.

A HAPPY ENDING

Ruth 4:7–22

[7]Now this was the custom in former times in Israel concerning redeeming and exchanging: to confirm a transaction, the one drew off his sandal and gave it to the other, and this was the manner of attesting in Israel. [8]So when the next of kin said to Boaz, "Buy it for yourself," he drew off his sandal. [9]Then Boaz said to the elders and all the people, "You are witnesses this day that I have bought from the hand of Naomi all that belonged to Elimelech and all that belonged to Chilion and to Mahlon. [10]Also Ruth the Moabitess, the widow of Mahlon, I have bought to be my wife, to perpetuate the name of the dead in his inheritance, that the name of the dead may not be cut off from among his brethren and from the gate of his native place; you are witnesses this day." [11]Then all the people who were at the gate, and the elders, said, "We are witnesses. May the Lord make the woman, who is coming into your house, like Rachel and Leah, who together built up the house of Israel. May you prosper in Ephrathah and be renowned in Bethlehem; [12]and may your house be like the house of Perez, whom Tamar bore to Judah, because of the children that the Lord will give you by this young woman."

[13]So Boaz took Ruth and she became his wife; and he went in to her, and the Lord gave her conception, and she bore a son. [14]Then the women said to Naomi, "Blessed be the Lord, who has not left you this day without next of kin; and may his name be renowned in Israel! [15]He shall be to you a restorer of life and a nourisher of your old age; for your daughter-in-law who loves you, who is more to you than seven sons, has borne him." [16]Then Naomi took the child and laid him in her bosom, and became his nurse. [17]And the women of the neighbourhood gave him a name, saying, "A son has been born to Naomi." They named him Obed; he was the father of Jesse, the father of David.

[18]Now these are the descendants of Perez: Perez was the father of Hezron, [19]Hezron of Ram, Ram of Amminadab, [20]Amminadab of Nahshon, Nahshon of Salmon, [21]Salmon of Boaz, Boaz of Obed, [22]Obed of Jesse, and Jesse of David.

In this delightful tale all the main characters are winners—there are no losers at all. Naomi, Ruth and Boaz all get what they want and even the unnamed relative is glad not to acquire the extra piece of land when he finds out that Ruth and a son that will not be reckoned his own go with it. The tale has romantic interest: there is an obstacle to the union of Boaz and Ruth. But it is not the competition of another suitor; and if there is a "triangle" of forces in this story, it is Naomi and not the potential "redeemer" that is the third force!

(i) The end of the story is rich in detail, and springs some more surprises to savour. We start with a learned note about a custom from ancient times which symbolized the exchange of responsibility involved in redemption. The unnamed party who had prior responsibility took off his shoe and gave it to Boaz. The related law in Deut. 25:5–10 presents another aspect of this custom when a brother persisted in his refusal to do the right thing by the widow of his deceased brother:

> "... then his brother's wife shall go up to him in the presence of the elders, and pull his sandal off his foot, and spit in his face; and she shall answer and say, 'So shall it be done to the man who does not build up his brother's house.' And the name of his house shall be called in Israel, The house of him that had his sandal pulled off."
>
> (vv. 9–10)

We cannot be certain what is involved in this custom; but there is some evidence that the fit of a foot in a shoe was a symbol of sexual union.

(ii) Boaz makes it publicly plain (v. 9) that he is acting in respect of the whole heritage of Elimelech and his sons. And the very structure of his words in verses 9 and 10 underscores the point made in our general discussion of redemption in the last section—ongoing ownership of land and ongoing family seed were intimately related. Boaz has acquired Elimelech's land; yet in acquiring Ruth also, he is acting for Elimelech and not for himself—and ten Bethlehem worthies are witness to this.

The ten good men and true at the gate, however, are not mere witnesses but enthusiastic well-wishers in addition. They draw deep from the patriarchal traditions in Genesis for their toasts. An all-Israel flavour is chosen first: Ruth should be like Jacob's wives, Rachel and Leah, who together built the House of Israel—

may Boaz be father of twelve. Then more local Judean colouring is provided in the reference to Perez—that child of Tamar whom she tricked out of her father-in-law Judah.

(iii) Appropriately Ruth conceives, and a son is born. But whose son is he? Verses 13–17 end up by noting that the lad Obed was to be the father of Jesse, David's father. This in turn prompts the whole family tree from Perez to David. There *Boaz* is reckoned as Obed's father. Of course this is physically true, yet the customary law which this story illustrates seems to demand that Ruth's first son be deemed Mahlon's; and is that not what Boaz had just publicly proclaimed (v. 10)? Of course the genealogy in the closing five verses (18–22) may have been added by someone later than the main story-teller.

Yet the artful narrator brings us back to Naomi. The women of the neighbourhood are quite as profuse to her as the official witnesses had been to Boaz. Ruth too is praised by the matrons as better than seven sons! One can only hope she was with Naomi when the neighbours said it. The womenfolk insist that Obed is *Naomi's* child. She holds him to her breast, she is a proud and attentive granny; and her neighbours are quite clear that her old age is now provided for. It is not just land that needs to be looked after; old people need that too.

Obed was the boy's official name, while another way of translating the beginning of verse 17 would be that the matrons *nicknamed* him "Naomi's boy-child". If the story-teller makes some play over whose the child is, he also makes us think once more about the word "redeemer". For it reappears in a stricter translation of the blessing in verse 14: "Blessed be the Lord, who has not left you this day without *redeemer*; and may his name be renowned in Israel! He shall be to you a restorer of life..." Of course it could just be that the women are talking about Boaz here: he had acted as the responsible "next-of-kin" and undertaken the duty of "redemption". But surely they are already beginning to talk of what Obed will do for Naomi in her old age. He will be her "redeemer"; and that will mean "a restorer of life and a nourisher of your old age" (v. 15).

(iv) We may never be certain whether the Book of Ruth was intended to serve a wider political purpose; but it certainly entertains, and is a touching tribute to an attractive social mechanism for overcoming widowhood and alienation. It sees God's blessing in loyal and gracious attention to proven customs. And that may be enough said!

FURTHER READING

COMMENTARIES

R. G. Boling, *Judges: A New Translation with Introduction and Commentary* (Anchor Bible) (Doubleday, 1975)

E. F. Campbell, *Ruth: A New Translation with Introduction and Commentary* (Anchor Bible) (Doubleday, 1975)

J. Gray, *Joshua, Judges and Ruth* (New Century Bible) (Marshall, Morgan & Scott and Wm. B. Eerdmans, 1967)

J. D. Martin, *The Book of Judges* (The Cambridge Bible Commentary on the New English Bible) (Cambridge University Press, 1975)

J. M. Miller and G. M. Tucker, *The Book of Joshua* (The Cambridge Bible Commentary on the New English Bible) (Cambridge University Press, 1974)

J. A. Soggin, *Joshua: A Commentary* (Old Testament Library) (SCM and Westminster, 1972)

J. A. Soggin, *Judges: A Commentary* (Old Testament Library) (SCM and Westminster, 1981)

OTHER STUDIES

Y. Aharoni and M. Avi-Yonah, *The Macmillan Bible Atlas* (The Macmillan Company, 1968)

S. Herrmann, *A History of Israel in Old Testament Times (SCM, 1975)*

H. G. May, *Oxford Bible Atlas* (Oxford University Press, 1974)

A. D. H. Mayes, *The Story of Israel between Settlement and Exile* (SCM, 1983)

J. M. Miller, *The Old Testament and the Historian* (SPCK and Fortress, 1976)

R. Moorey, *Excavation in Palestine* (Cities of the Biblical World) (Lutterworth, 1982)

M. Noth, *The Deuteronomistic History* (Journal for the Study of the Old Testament Supplement Series, 15) (JSOT, 1981)

S. Sandmel, *The Enjoyment of Scripture: The Law, the Prophets, and the Writings* (OUP, 1972)